Anarchism and
Animal Liberation

Anarchism and Animal Liberation
Essays on Complementary Elements of Total Liberation

Edited by ANTHONY J. NOCELLA II,
RICHARD J. WHITE *and*
ERIKA CUDWORTH

Forewords by David N. Pellow
and John C. Alessio

McFarland & Company, Inc., Publishers
Jefferson, North Carolina

LIBRARY OF CONGRESS CATALOGUING-IN-PUBLICATION DATA

Anarchism and animal liberation : essays on complementary elements of total liberation / edited by Anthony J. Nocella II, Richard J. White and Erika Cudworth ; forewords by David N. Pellow and John C. Alessio.
  p. cm.
Includes bibliographical references and index.

ISBN 978-0-7864-9457-6 (softcover : acid free paper) ∞
ISBN 978-1-4766-2132-6 (ebook)

1. Anarchism. 2. Animal welfare. I. Nocella, Anthony J., editor. II. White, Richard J., 1978– editor. III. Cudworth, Erika, 1966– editor.

HX833.A5684 2015
179'.3—dc23   2015020705

BRITISH LIBRARY CATALOGUING DATA ARE AVAILABLE

© 2015 Anthony J. Nocella II, Richard J. White and Erika Cudworth. All rights reserved

No part of this book may be reproduced or transmitted in any form or by any means, electronic or mechanical, including photocopying or recording, or by any information storage and retrieval system, without permission in writing from the publisher.

Cover image: George Tsartsianidis/Thinkstock

Printed in the United States of America

McFarland & Company, Inc., Publishers
  Box 611, Jefferson, North Carolina 28640
  www.mcfarlandpub.com

To all those who continue to struggle against
supremacy, oppression and domination.

Acknowledgments

Anthony, Richard and Erika would like to thank everyone who assisted in the production and publishing of this book. Special mention must go to David N. Pellow and John C. Alessio for each writing a foreword for the book and, of course, to the contributors of the book—Brian Dominick, Drew Robert Winter, Will Boisseau, Jim Donaghey, Nekeisha Alayna Alexis, Mara J. Pfeffer, Sean Parson, Lara Drew, Kim Socha, John Lupinacci and Aragorn Eloff. Our thanks to Sarat Colling, Reyna Crow, Carrie Freeman, Ruth Kinna, Joel Helfrich, Peter McLaren, Nick Ryan, John Sorenson and Tanya Loughead for their first reviews of the book. We would also like to thank the Institute for Critical Animal Studies for supporting this book. More generally, we are indebted to all those who—through their work and their activism—continue to expand the horizons of the field of Critical Animal Studies. Finally we would also like to thank our interspecies families and friends for their love and support. We hope that this book helps to bring a more socially just and peaceable future into being for them, for all.

Table of Contents

Acknowledgments   vi

Foreword
    David N. Pellow   1

Foreword
    John C. Alessio   4

Introduction: The Intersections of Critical Animal Studies and Anarchist Studies for Total Liberation
    Anthony J. Nocella II, Richard J. White *and* Erika Cudworth   7

Part I. Histories/Futures   21

Anarcho-Veganism Revisited
    Brian Dominick   23

Anarchist Criminology Against Racism and Ableism and for Animal Liberation
    Anthony J. Nocella II   40

Doing Liberation: The Story and Strategy of Food Not Bombs
    Drew Robert Winter   59

"Nailing Descartes to the wall": Animal Rights, Veganism and Punk Culture
    Will Boisseau *and* Jim Donaghey   71

Part II. Intersections   91

Intersectionality, Species and Social Domination
    Erika Cudworth   93

Beyond Suffering: Resisting Patriarchy and Reproductive Control
    Nekeisha Alayna Alexis   108

Industrial Society Is Both the Fabrication Department and the Kill Floor: Total Liberation, Green Anarchism and the Violence of Industrialism
    Mara J. Pfeffer *and* Sean Parson   126

"A wider vision": Coercion, Solidarity and Animal Liberation
    Will Boisseau   141

Part III. Strategies   161

Anarchy for Educational Praxis in the Animal Liberation Movement in an Era of Capitalist Triumphalism
    Lara Drew *and* Kim Socha   163

Recognizing Human Supremacy: Interrupt, Inspire and Expose
    John Lupinacci   179

Do Anarchists Dream of Emancipated Sheep? Contemporary Anarchism, Animal Liberation and the Implications of New Philosophy
    Aragorn Eloff   194

Following in the Footsteps of Élisée Reclus: Disturbing Places of Inter-Species Violence That Are Hidden in Plain Sight
    Richard J. White   212

About the Contributors   231

Index   233

Foreword

David N. Pellow

Ashanti Alston, a former Black Panther and Black Liberation Army activist and one-time political prisoner, once told me, "I really feel like of all the groups, the anarchist mindset is open to understanding all the different oppressions." I concur and I share Alston's perspective because, like him, I also identify as an anarchist person of color and I see evidence every day of my life that anarchism's core principles and promises make a lot of sense to those of us who are committed to total liberation—ideas, scholarship, artistic expression, and action aimed at challenging all forms of oppression. To my knowledge *Anarchism and Animal Liberation* is the first book to place anarchist studies and Critical Animal Studies in conversation with one another, and for that reason alone, this is a path-breaking work.

In so many ways, the essays in this book focus on expanding our understanding of hierarchy and inequality by making sense of the often tense and violent relationships among humans and nonhuman animal species. In so doing, the editors and contributors facilitate the goal of achieving a better grasp of inequality's ramifications while also deepening our understanding of the nature of inequality itself. Only then can we truly grasp the depths of our socioecological crises and address them effectively.

As a sociologist I must confront the most basic yet profound questions raised in this book: what is inequality and why does it matter? At its most basic level, inequality means that if you are "on top" of a social system, or higher on a social status ladder when compared with another being, then you possess or have access to more resources, wealth, and privileges. But more importantly—and from the standpoint of anarchist studies and Critical Animal Studies—your elevated position above others also means that your *life* is of greater value than others living within that social system. You likely own or control and affect more of the planet and its constituent residents and life support systems than others, you likely own or control and affect more living beings (and, therefore, likely produce more death) than others, and you control and benefit from the ideational systems that give meaning and legitimacy to such dynamics. Inequality is a means of ordering the human and nonhuman worlds for the relative benefit of some and to the detriment of others. Anarchist studies and Critical Animal Studies explore the origins and consequences of varied forms of inequality and hierarchy, and resolve to oppose them at every level.

Public health scholarship reveals that human life expectancy, morbidity, mortality, and wellbeing are highly correlated with key measures of inequality. In the case of environmental inequality and environmental racism, working class people, people of color, women, immigrants, and Indigenous persons are more likely to face health risks as a result of the uneven exposure to environmental harm that social and institutional forces routinely perpetrate (practices that are rooted in multiple forms of social inequality and hierarchy). Thus social or human inequalities derive their existence through inequalities that also divide, rank, and exert control over nonhumans and ecosystems. Inequality is, above all, *unnatural* in the sense that it does not "just happen"—it requires a great deal of energy, labor, and institutional effort to produce and maintain unequal societies. This point is crucial because there is often a great deal of energy invested into making inequalities appear to be a natural state of affairs. As ecofeminist Greta Gaard writes, "Appeals to nature have often been used to justify social norms, to the detriment of women, nature, queers, and persons of color." Inequality is not just an imbalance of resources or power, but is frequently experienced as unearned privileges made possible by domination and injustice. Those who suffer its consequences also routinely resist inequality. This book is a clarion call to solidarity and a call to join those who are leading these resistance efforts.

Anarchism and Animal Liberation embraces the idea, vision, and practice of total liberation, which views inequality as a threat to life itself—for oppressed peoples, species, and ecosystems—and is organized around the struggle for justice for all life forms. Individuals, collectives, organizations, networks, and movements seeking total liberation organize and mobilize in favor of symbols, metaphors, language, signs, representations, practices, and structures of equality and justice to do what social movements have always done: to imagine and create a better world. Only this world would be based on the idea that inequality and unfreedom in all their known manifestations should be eradicated.

The editors and contributors to this invaluable collection contend that one cannot fully grasp the foundations of racism, classism, sexism, patriarchy, ageism, and ableism without also understanding speciesism and dominionism because they are all ideologies and practices rooted in hierarchy and the creation of oppositional superior and inferior subjects. This total liberation framework links oppression and privileges across species, ecosystems, and human populations, suggesting a theory and path toward justice and freedom—something missing in traditional models of intersectionality. Thus the concept of total liberation reveals both the complexity of various systems of hierarchy while also suggesting points of intervention, transformative change, solidarity and coalition building across myriad boundaries. Total liberation is, above all, a *cultural* force because its greatest power lies in the strength and audacity of its vision. And while it may never gain widespread appeal, it is socially significant because the ideas embodied in the concept of total liberation constitute a threat to the core operating principles and assumptions behind the current social order. Read this book with great care because you will never be the same again.

REFERENCE

Gaard, G. (2004). "Toward a queer ecofeminism." In Rachel Stein (Ed.). *New perspectives on environmental justice: Gender, sexuality, and activism.* New Brunswick: Rutgers University Press. Pp. 21–44.

David N. Pellow is the Don Martindale Professor of Sociology at the University of Minnesota. He is the author of three books on animal rights and environmental topics. He has served on the boards of directors for Global Response, the Global Action Research Center, the Center for Urban Transformation, Greenpeace USA, and International Rivers.

Foreword

John C. Alessio

Twenty-five years ago I was looking for a good book about anarchism to use in one of my classes. At the time there was little discussion about the integration of oppression issues among anarchists. In fact, I would have been happy to find a decent book that served my classroom needs that wasn't notably sexist. I was unsuccessful. I am pleased to write a foreword for a book that brings anarchism into the twenty-first century by pulling together the various threads of oppression around an anarchist framework. I thus begin by giving high praise to the editors and the authors. When I mention an author by name please assume I am referring to one of the authors of an essay within the present work, *Anarchism and Animal Liberation*.

This book inspired me to review my own thinking and writing related to anarchism and animal rights, so I apologize in advance for referring to my own works. Issues related to the relationship between the state and capitalism were nicely covered by Nocella et al., something I discuss in a slightly different way within my 2011 book, *Social Problems and Inequality*. The state (typically nation-state) is not only controlled by wealthy capitalists; it was designed and constructed by and for wealthy capitalists. Of course this construction took place over a long period of time, but it greatly accelerated and took its contemporary form during the industrial revolution and was reshaped through various imperial wars. It is difficult to determine causal order. While the state was necessary for the industrial revolution to take place, the evolving cultural instruments of the industrial revolution greatly inspired and solidified the importance of the state for capitalist interests. Hence, Boisseau and Donaghey's focus on the violence of industrialism and Pfeffer and Parson's critique of "industrial civilization" are important contributions toward understanding the relationship between the state and capitalism.

There is often confusion about the general concepts of "government" and "state." They are sometimes treated by anarchists and right wing conservatives alike as if they are the same concept. Anarchist thinking that grew out of the Kropotkin-Marx/Engels debates was clearly about the oppressive nature of the state and what should be done with it. Government, on the other hand, is something that can take place by mutual agreement among individuals. Such agreements don't have to be called government, since that concept carries some baggage. But the point is that people can decide how they want to live together by consensus and this can only take place in a reasonable manner among local populations. Local populations can also form agreements with other local populations, and so on.

Can we expect a perfectly balanced system? Touched by Dominick's realism one might ask if anyone knows of any perfectly balanced system that involves human interaction, even among friends or intimate partners? Not likely. But that is the goal toward which all anarchists might strive to create a more just and sustainable world. Perfection, or some sort of utopian life, is not expected. But freedom from an oppressive capitalist state and the various forms of oppression fostered therein is a reasonable expectation. This book does an excellent job of moving the reader toward that understanding. Intersectionality, interconnectedness, holistic thinking, critical thinking, and integrative activism, teaching, and scholarship are well addressed by many in this important volume, but see Drew & Socha for a particularly cogent statement on integration.

As we look specifically toward the often neglected issue of nonhuman animal oppression we must recognize, as do the authors of this book, that no being is free until all beings are free. I am impressed with Lupinacci's plea to make friends with all forms of life, including trees and other non-animal forms of life and parts of nature. The impending disaster of dramatic climate change that most independent scientists are predicting (sixth mass extinction) will continue to seize the futures of many species, including humans. When reproduction and growth are completely controlled, living organisms are denied their own forms of biological and social organization—forms of organization that can only develop slowly through a gradual process of complex mutual adaptation with other forms of life. This is just as true for plants as it is for animals.

The most serious questions for all forms of life, particularly humans, are what shall we eat to survive and then what shall we *not* eat to survive as a species? The answer to the latter question, I discussed in my 2008 paper, "Being Sentient and Sentient Being," drives part of the answer to the first question, but more importantly contextualizes speciesism within a very broad framework: the world isn't just for human and nonhuman animals, and animals cannot survive without plants. As Alexis points out, there are reasons for objecting to animal mistreatment that are beyond the arguments related to suffering. Patriarchy, gendering and other forms of oppression are among those reasons, as Alexis emphasizes. I would extend Alexis' argument to include why people might choose to be vegan. It isn't just that animals in agribusiness suffer, although that is very important. Animal production denigrates all life in multiple ways, including the plants fed to the agribusiness animals. Generally an organic vegan diet is the healthiest for most humans in the short run and the healthiest for all species of Earth in the long run.

Perhaps stretching Lupinacci's comment further than intended, we must, indeed, make friends with all life forms. Those of us who are vegan might at least suspect that the plants we are eating are no less sentient in their own way, and certainly no less important, than ourselves. All life requires sustenance that comes from consuming other forms of life. Can consumption take place with respect, gratitude, and wisdom about what is healthiest for us and the environment? Complete elimination of suffering is not possible as long as living beings must consume other forms of living beings, but we still might ask how much suffering could be eliminated now and into the future if everyone adopted a vegan diet. Of course it is not possible to know, but it would certainly be an extremely high percentage of all the suffering that currently takes place and that will take place into the future based on current food production and consumption patterns.

Contemporary anarchists know that actualizing the answers to the above two questions requires dramatically altering human social life from its current form, and creating a form of human social life free of hierarchies and oppression, as promoted by all the authors of this book. While we can look forward to the eventual absence of the capitalist state, clever people around the globe are finding ways of living locally now despite the continuing existence of nation-states. The wealthy benefactors of the state know this well and are spending a lot of money (with frightening success in some areas) to take over local community life (for example, the Koch Brothers in the United States). The imperative of decentralized horizontal decision-making becomes obvious, and such decision-making is sorely missing in most communities. Awareness is critical and people are sometimes easily confused by propaganda. The various social movements we have witnessed in recent years; Occupy, community gardens, organic farming, local farmer's markets, local exchange economies, etc., are all signs of hope on what can otherwise seem a dark landscape. Contemporary anarchists don't have to fit into an anarchist mold, but nor do they have to be disorganized and lost. We might not agree on what the final picture should look like, but we have considerable agreement about what it should not look like. This book is a powerful testament to that claim.

John C. Alessio is a professor emeritus of sociology and a former academic dean at two universities. He has been an activist for social justice and social responsibility within and outside of his various employment roles. He is the author of a book and numerous articles published in sociology journals and in cross-disciplinary venues.

Introduction
The Intersections of Critical Animal Studies and Anarchist Studies for Total Liberation

ANTHONY J. NOCELLA II,
RICHARD J. WHITE *and*
ERIKA CUDWORTH

Anarchism and animal liberation have advanced in many intersectional ways for the goal of fostering peace and justice. For example, Kimberly Socha (2014) has opened the door even more widely by writing a book on anarchism, animal liberation, and atheism. Socha emphasizes the importance of a political and economic analysis of speciesism that will enable us to address systems of oppression that exploit, torture, murder, and dominate nonhuman animals. Some animal liberationists have been drawn in to various intersected struggles: opposing organizations which promote capitalism and encouraging radical political struggles to address various kinds of social oppression including sexism, racism, and ableism. Critical Animal Studies is providing space and place for scholar-activists to go beyond the limits of connecting marginalized oppressed groups together for total liberation (Pellow 2014) and can be seen to build bridges between anarchist theory and practice and animal liberation. Anarchism is a socio-political theory which opposes all systems of domination and oppression such as racism, ableism, sexism, anti–LGBTTQIA, ageism, sizeism, government, competition, capitalism, colonialism, imperialism and punitive justice, and promotes direct democracy, collaboration, interdependency, mutual aid, diversity, peace, transformative justice and equity (Amster, DeLeon, Fernandez, Nocella, and Shannon 2009). Critical Animal Studies grounded in anarchism is intersectional and radical. It stands against all systems of oppression and domination, and promotes activism and community organizing. This does not mean simply writing articles and books and building a career within the academy, or seeking reward for writing about popular topics (Nocella, Sorenson, Socha, and Matsuoka 2014). Critical Animal Studies, therefore, is about liberation, total liberation (Pellow 2014).

It is no exaggeration to observe that, at a time of deep and prolonged crises which threatens the very existence of the world as we know it, anarchist thought and practice has enjoyed a resurgence of popularity and influence across (radical) academic and activist circles. Anarchism, with its explicit intent of challenging and ending *all* forms of domination, is seen to bring something of real value, hope and possibility. Those who study this theory and action are situated in anarchist studies, a field dedicated to not only promoting the theory and action, but studying and conducting research on anarchists and anarchist movements throughout world history (Amster, DeLeon, Fernandez, Nocella, and Shannon 2009). This collection, written by anarcho-vegans, re-visits influential streams of thought evident within the anarchist canon, and shows that this can be a fruitful endeavor, not least in understanding the barren impotency of both "state-" and "market-" based solutions to the entrenched problems we face. Indeed, the anarchist critique—unlike other radical approaches—has seen the market and the state as being absolutely central to creating and perpetuating the violent geographies that we see (Shannon, Nocella, and Asimakopoulos 2012). However, while looking backward—like the two-headed dog of Janus—anarchists have also looked forward for inspiration and guidance in the here and now. What does our contemporary world offer in terms of providing appropriate resources with which to create new visions, and with an on-going commitment to practice and realize new futures?

This challenge—to create something of substance and import at a time of crisis—burns brightly at the heart of this book. Violence and domination know few boundaries; nowhere is this truer than in our relationship(s) with other sentient beings, be they human or other animals. In agitating for a (new) anarchist consciousness in the reader, one claim rings out: we concede too much power to others to "make the right choice" on our behalf. Acknowledging this, and recognizing the importance of engaging one's body and mind to create and maintain meaningful forms of direct action, a pre-figurative praxis needs to be taken to heart. To be encouraged to make new connections and to be open to learning from the experiences of others are always important. In this context, for many authors in the book, inspiration has been found in the critical space which a Critical Animal Studies approach creates, to which we now turn our attention.

Critical Animal Studies should be both a field of study and a movement focused on telling and fighting for the truth about the treatment of other animals by many humans, and this truth clearly threatens the powers that be.

Critical Animal Studies stands with the oppressed and against the establishment. Critical Animal Studies will always experience a range of problems in its relations with institutions such as the academy and government which many of its adherents—certainly many of those contributing to this collection—see as oppressive institutions. Therefore it is not surprising that Critical Animal Studies scholar-activists often have a difficult time finding academic full-time careers in higher education. Many Critical Animal Studies scholars are not waiting to get tenure or a safe position to challenge oppression and domination, but are organizing now, conducting hunt sabotage, civil disobedience, street blockades, sit-ins, banner drops, and store occupations. Critical Animal Studies has not been preoccupied with establishing an academic field that can secure academic jobs for its adherents, but is focused on liberation of those that are oppressed. Many Critical Animal Studies scholars write on academic repression (Nocella, Best, and McLaren 2010), and argue that those seeking tenured positions may be better advised to align themselves with non-contestationary scholarship in mainstream animal studies. Critical Animal Studies does not seek reform, but transformative revolution and total liberation. Our scholarship in Critical Animal Studies therefore, is by definition, emancipatory. As such, CAS scholars are critical of existing social arrangements and established institutions which are understood to be unjust (see Best 2009). Rather, the agenda of CAS is one of transformation, and such transformation implies a confrontational stance.

Critical Animal Studies (or CAS), founded in 2006–07, arose out the work of the Institute for Critical Animal Studies. Both today are international and supported by the efforts of volunteer activist-scholars. CAS has been growing rapidly with the greatest effort coming from students rather than professors. While there are some professors doing great work, academia tends to restrict individuals and encourage conformity not radicalism, for which they are certainly unlikely to be rewarded. As Richard Khan (2010) notes, the labelling of some high profile U.S. scholar-activists in CAS as domestic or international "terrorists" operates as a warning, and suggests that engaging with CAS may be more likely to be a strategy for "getting fired" rather than ensuring tenure or promotion. CAS, while scholarly, is opposed to much of what passes for scholarship and teaching in academia. It does not feign neutrality or disinterest, but rather an engaged scholarship that seeks to promote radical change. In addition to its politicization, it deals with the nonhuman, and for mainstream academic scholarship in the humanities and social sciences (and elsewhere) this is not to be taken seriously. As Rhoda Wilkie (2013) has recently suggested, on both grounds (that of politics and of subject matter), the labor we engage in as CAS scholars is "tainted labor" or "dirty work" at disciplinary borderlands.

Critical Animal Studies sets itself against "nonemancipatory" scholarship (Peggs 2012, p. 149). Rather, it is demanding everyone to think critically about their own positions and their own privileges, and to resist and fight the forms of domination we criticize as though we are fighting for our lives. Yet if we did just that, we would be living our lives a great deal differently. Currently we say radical things, while doing very little for animals, as long as it is not too much of an inconvenience. We must destroy colonialism and civilization, but how? As a number of contributions to this collection emphasize, change cannot come from a politics based on ethical veganism exclusively, and certainly not by simply eating fake meats, wearing faux leather, and shopping in ethical stores. Rather, emancipatory scholarship and activism demands a broader view, a politics of coalition and solidarity around multifaceted oppression. And in thinking about what this means, the concept and praxis of intersectionality is a useful way forwards.

Intersectionality

Intersectionality is important for two strategic reasons. First, it brings movements together so that there is more support and room for collaboration. Second, intersectionality allows activists to educate themselves about the goals, purpose, tactics, history, and campaigns of movements with which they have has less involvement. Many activists who begin to study and analyze social movements for their own social causes and identity have often joined those other struggles after finding out about their own experiences of oppression. It is through this process that people become aware of multiple experiences of oppression and that no one has a single identity. Out of this process of exchange arose conceptual and theoretical intersectionality, first associated with black feminist scholarship in the United States (see Crenshaw 1989). This stresses that groups, movements, and people often have multiple experiences of oppression related to their different axes of identity, such as ability, gender, sexuality, race, class, age, nationality, and religion. Therefore, intersectionality highlights the need to understand feelings of oppression as a phenomenon rooted in people's diverse, overlapping socio-political economic identities and locations in relation to social power and cultural hegemony. Intersectionality is both a methodology and theory that speaks to "the relationships among multiple dimensions and modalities of social relationships and subject formations" (McCall 2005). The development within social movements embracing intersectionality aided in the initiative of multi-movement alliance politics.

Intersectionality emphasizes that oppression is related by systems of domination (hooks 1994). This concept was made well-known by feminists of color (Collins 1998; Collins 2000a), who emphasized that while being a woman is difficult in society because of patriarchy, it is even harder to be a Black women, and harder for those Black women who are poor and may also be lesbians and/or have disabilities. In addition, the developing field of intersectionality studies in feminism over the last twenty years has also shown that intersections are complex. Within what Collins (2000b) calls the matrix of oppression and domination, there are situations on multiple axes so that it is not simply a case of listing forms of oppression and assuming that inhabiting multiple categories makes for a greater degree of oppression. Rather we need to examine how the intersections of various forms of oppression work for various groups in specific locations, especially in the context of globalization (Walby 2009). Examining oppression and relating experiences of oppression together is a strategy of organizing people together in order to increase resistance, deconstruct, and challenge multiple systems of domination. Many intersectional social justice activist-scholars (some who also identify themselves as total liberationists, see later) argue that only when everyone in the world understands and respects they are not one dimension (Marcuse 1964) and are related through identity and experience, can we end domination of one another through massive social transformation (Lederach 2003). Intersectional social justice activist-scholars believe people are inherently capable of good and will be more unlikely to harm and dominate others if they understand that forms of injustice are related. This mass social transformation will lead to transforming individual acts and perspectives as well, influenced by an oppressive society that promotes sexism, homophobia, ableism, racism, ageism, and classism (Morris 2000).

Intersectionality, a theory that examines subjects from a multi-standpoint perspective, arose greatly out of the efforts of interdisciplinary studies. A great deal of interdisciplinary fields of study emerged out of successful social movements, for example, the civil rights movement in the United States fostered Africana studies and the women's rights movement fostered women's studies. Often, intersectional scholarship will be found within interdisciplinary fields, and certainly attempts to consider various kinds of social/political/cultural/economic exclusion, oppression and domination within varied overlapping fields of gender, race, age, ability, class and others, lends itself to interdisciplinary scholarship and multi-movement politics. While there has been concerted resistance to this in traditional disciplines, the increased popularity and use of intersectionality as a framework has helped mitigate this resistance. Intersectionality and multi-movement politics within the animal liberation movement most notably emerged with the work of eco-feminists such as Carol Adams, whose book *The Sexual Politics of Meat* (1990) was influential. Today the intersections have grown more diverse and complex such as between race and nonhuman animals (Harper 2010) and between disability, environment, and animal justice (Bentley, Duncan and Nocella

2010), for example. In thinking critically about human relations with non-human animals, CAS draws in scholars from a wide range of disciplinary backgrounds and furthers interdisciplinary studies and multi-movement politics, for total liberation.

Total Liberation

Total liberation is intersectionality in action. Intersectionality can be found in moments when multiple identities cross and the same moment because of an experience an individual, group or community has. Ideas about total liberation were voiced in the 1960s by many radical political organizations, and was used to describe an uncompromising multifaceted approach to complete freedom and justice for all suffering from oppression and domination. Total liberation as practice does not mean that each rally, protest, conference and forum, must address every injustice in the world. If this was the case we would not be able to ever discuss specific strategies, tactics, and experiences. Moreover, total liberation is not academics writing about radical ideas or advocating revolutionary change. Rather, it is about individuals organizing together in collaborative transformative ways in their community and globally against systems of oppression and domination (Del Gandio and Nocella 2014). Consequently it is not, for example, about vegan activists going to a LGBGTTIQ parade and promoting veganism; it involves being at other social movement's events in order to fully to support them and to be in solidarity with them. In light of this, the following are organizing strategies we suggest might be helpful for supporting other movements.

- Be invited to the movement and community, thus don't go where you are not invited
- Listen before speaking or suggesting ideas and make sure you are asked to speak and for your suggestions
- Make sure to articulate one's commitment so everyone knows your limitations
- Explain to others in the movement your skills so others can utilize you to your fullest capability
- Explain to others in the movement your motivation and personal goals on why you want to help and join the movement
- Be willing to follow and never lead
- Be willing to not get credit, but give credit to non-dominate voices
- Be willing to take accountability and own one's supremacy and domination
- Be willing to be challenged personally and be called out publicly

- Be willing to learn new processes and cultural practices
- Be willing to take more risks than others that are more oppressed
- Be willing to do more labor
- Be willing to not take money or other benefits from organizations
- Challenge acts that tokenize, patronize, commodity, appropriate, and coopt
- Be willing to leave when asked and not blame others for being asked to leave

These suggestions on coalition and solidarity building are unlikely to be a solution to the emergence of tensions and conflicts. However, conflict should not necessarily be viewed as a problem, but rather as an opportunity to learn and address challenges.

Total liberation is greatly influenced by anarchism in that it is opposed to all forms of oppression and domination and is also not reformist. Therefore total liberation, Critical Animal Studies, and anarchism supports the Animal Liberation Front, Earth Liberation Front, and other revolutionary and resistance organizations (Colling & Nocella 2011, Best & Nocella 2006; Best & Nocella 2004). To change the enormous and intertwined problems that we face, we must think creatively and in community, rather than thinking that the answer will be by using oppressive strategies, cultural traditions, and established systems. Audre Lorde's well-known phrase captures this best: "The master's tools will never dismantle the master's house." Thus total liberationists must develop alternative ways of transforming social, political and economic relationships and systemic structures.

Overview of Book

At the heart of this collection, and opening the book, is Brian Dominick's "Anarcho-Veganism Revisited." This is a critical reflection of the highly influential concept *veganarchist*, which was introduced by Dominick in the mid–1990s. Rejecting a fundamentalist culture that has, on many levels—sought to appropriate the term *veganarchy* over the last twenty years, the essay critically addresses the limits of a militant or dogmatic interpretation of veganarchy. In this context, the essay makes an excellent and persuasive case for developing a more nuanced understanding of veganism and anarchism, one composed of constellations of values and principles. To this end Dominick outlines a powerful, important and brave new animal ethic, one which seeks to agitate for and create new spaces of resistance and liberation.

"Anarchist Criminology Against Racism and Ableism and for Animal Liberation" by Anthony J. Nocella II draws some important connections and implications between a diverse range of social justice causes. Nocella encourages the reader to think critically about the nuances and complexity that define each of these concepts, beginning with the very idea of anarchism itself. The powerful connections between both oppression and liberation of humans and other animals are convincingly made. In this context, Nocella demonstrates how some of the most important and well known forms of direct action, undertaken in the name of the Animal Liberation Front, embody the principles of anarchism, both in organization and in targeting the sources of domination and economic exploitation. An important discussion of the various strategies of resistance employed, particularly those which focus on property and economic sabotage in the name of liberation is forthcoming. The relative success of these tactics, Nocella argues, can be seen in how this organization has attracted such powerful propaganda (especially the association with terrorism) that the ALF has attracted from the economic and political elite. A more detailed critique of (private) property—including animals as property—is then developed before the essay then goes on to problematize the uncritical call for incarceration (of animal abusers) that many in the animal rights movement make. Critiquing the criminal justice system as a necessary part of critiquing the oppressive State apparatus needs to be engaged at all times. This is crucial if we are to take a significant step nearer to the truly free and liberated society—for all—that we hope is possible.

In "Doing Liberation: The Story and Strategy of Food Not Bombs," Drew Robert Winter provides a timely and important critique of an organization that has done, and continues to, engage in some incredibly important forms of intervention and action. As Winter notes, the success of the Food Not Bombs movement has come in the face of great adversity and the dedication, commitment, and resilience that has allowed it to thrive (not merely survive) pays testimony to the individuals and groups involved. Drawing on personal experience with FNB, and undertaking interviews with Keith McHenry (FNB co-founder) Winter develops a range of powerful insights, themes, arguments and conclusions which demonstrate how many of the principles of FNB are animated by anarchist praxis, and the significance of this. Also the practice of giving food—we all need food—as Winter reminds us, can be fun, and the basis of conversation and expressions of solidity and support. We should do well not to forget this.

In "'Nailing Descartes to the wall': Animal Rights, Veganism and Punk Culture," Will Boisseau and Jim Donaghey explore the considerable (but rarely discussed) overlaps between punk culture and animal rights activism/vegan consumption habits and anarchism. Drawing on first-hand interviews with key individuals and influential bands associated with contemporary UK punk scene, the authors present a range of valuable—and contested—insights concerning the influence of anarchism and intersectional opposition to all forms of domination. The deeper links between punk music, animal rights, and anarchy against broader forms of domination and exploitation, particularly capitalism, are confidently explored. The essay is rich in detail and significance on many levels. It contains many new and important insights and connections of great relevance to a wide audience.

"Intersectionality, Species and Social Domination" makes the case that anarchism is highly open to, if not already characterized by, intersectionality. Erika Cudworth considers the history of anarchist thought and practical political engagement to demonstrate concern with an eclectic range of dominations—around "race," ethnicity and nation; caste, class and wealth; formations of sex, sexuality and gender; colonialism, imperialism and warfare amongst others. This openness of anarchism to considering multiple forms of domination, she suggests, means that it is well-suited to develop powerful critiques of the human domination of other animals. The essay begins with a consideration of two important anarchist contributions to debates on human relations with other animals: those of Kropotkin and Bookchin, both of whom see humanity as co-constituted in "federations" of life with nonhumans, despite Bookchin's inability to move decisively away from the dichotomy between humans and other animals. The essay proceeds to examine anarchist work which foregrounds the intersectionalized oppression of humans and other animals, arguing that while intersectionality and social domination are increasingly engaged with by both anarchism and animal liberation discourse, there is a significant way to go. Nevertheless, anarchist theory and politics—opposed as they are, to a range of dominations that are understood to be interlinked and interdependent—are highly compatible with a politics which contests the human oppression and exploitation of nonhuman animals.

"Beyond Suffering: Resisting Patriarchy and Reproductive Control" pushes these intersectionalized understandings of the world further with a detailed and compelling account of ways in which the control of the reproductive capacity of farmed animals constitutes a form of gendered oppression. Nekeisha Alayna Alexis wants to take animal liberation "beyond suffering." She shows how a focus on suffering has been key to resistance against factory farms, with activists recording and disclosing undercover footage of creatures languishing in appalling conditions; of humans beating, electrocuting, kicking and using other forms of extreme force against animals; and of animals enduring bloody and excruciating deaths in slaughterhouses. The essay begins by outlining the possibilities and inherent limitations of using the suffering narrative to make changes on behalf of farmed animals and identifies some he external pressures challenging this narrative. The essay proceeds to explore the ways patriarchy manifests itself in animal agriculture, particularly in the area of reproductive control, and highlight the connections between animal liberation and gendered oppression. Alexis makes a provocative and convincing case that building an argument for animal liberation that does not rely on narrative of suffering is currently an urgent task facing animal advocates. Rather, she argues that expanding the farmed animal advocacy narrative to include concerns of resisting patriarchy and reproductive tyranny can undergird a currently beleaguered suffering agenda.

In "Industrial Society Is Both the Fabrication Department and the Kill Floor: Total Liberation, Green Anarchism and the Violence of Industrialism," Mara J. Pfeffer and Sean Parson make a powerful and provocative argument through an examination of the linkage between ideas of total liberation, green anarchism and a critique of the inevitable large-scale violence embedded in industrial practices and lifeways. Through a series of cases and vignettes, they argue that if we are to be concerned with animal liberation and ending unneeded suffering, then our politics must go further than attacking the state and capitalism. The key contention of this essay is that there can be no "total liberation" without addressing the problem of industrial civilization. Further, Pasons and Pfeffer suggest that there is only one alternative—the demise of industrial society. They begin by documenting the violence of industrial society. Millions of human animal deaths and countless billions of nonhuman animal deaths are a direct result of the industrial system in which increasingly, we all live. Significant levels of mass destruction of living creatures (both human and nonhuman) and ecosystems is an inevitable product of resource extraction. Parson and Pfeffer proceed to argue for a politics beyond veganism and centered around solidarity with various oppressed groups. A key element of this is not just a thorough critique of capitalism and colonialism, but a profound questioning of industrial civilization as a form of systemic oppression itself. While this is an argument for a primitivist anarchism, it is a nuanced one, for the authors are clear that primitivist politics needs to be much more critical in understanding animality and in calling for "rewilding." Rather we need a critical politics of "becoming animal" where we avoid reproducing patterns of colonialism, classism, racism, and sexism and promote a postindustrialist politics for total liberation.

In "'A wider vision': Coercion, Solidarity and Animal Liberation," Will Boisseau considers the relationship between animal rights groups and the contemporary anarchist movement in Britain, concentrating in particular on tensions around coercive or violent tactics. As such, this essay begins by mapping the range of ways in which anarchist and animal liberation tactics might coincide, for instance discussing how both forms of radical politics may be organized as affinity groups or under wider "banners." Drawing on primary interview data with animal advocates, including former political prisoners, and activist publications, Boisseau proceeds with a more detailed examination of the use of allegedly coercive or violent tactics by some animal rights groups and considers how this may or may not coincide with contemporary anarchist conceptions of legitimate tactics. The focus on tactics in this essay is important because it acknowledges that animal liberation has often acted as the site of interchanges (both co-operative and conflictual) between anarchist groups and the wider British left. Illustrating this is a discussion of relations between the class struggle anarchist group Class War (perhaps the most recognizable anarchist presence in Britain after their formation in 1983), and the Animal Liberation Front. The essay concludes with some examples of ways in which anarchist animal liberationists have either succeeded or failed to combine their efforts for animals with other social justice issues.

Lara Drew and Kim Socha provide an interesting and heartfelt case, in "Anarchy for Educational Praxis in the Animal Liberation Movement in an Era of Capitalist Triumphalism," for intersectional approaches to activism through engaging in radical education to reveal new ways of seeing the world. They begin with the claim that animal liberation activists are *de facto* educators as they overtly or covertly attempt to effect change by using a range of techniques which teach others about human (mis)use of other species. The need for radical learning and education through activist communities is more urgent now than ever, Drew and Socha argue, given the various crises faced by human animals, nonhuman animals, and the Earth. Bringing together anarchist studies, Critical Animal Studies, and adult education literature, they offer engaging ideas for how such theories generated by these different yet compatible fields of study can inform activists to resist oppressive practices. Drawing on diverse literatures from these fields, and on personal accounts they demonstrate how educator-activism is effective in revealing new ways of seeing the world. They further suggest that informal learning spaces, which implement liberatory pedagogies can both be an effective strategy for change for animal activism and one which encourages better practices grounded in the politics of intersectionality.

In "Recognizing Human Supremacy: Interrupt, Inspire and Expose," John Lupinacci draws attention to the importance of anarchist praxis through the presence of direct action organizations, networks and groups including the Animal Liberation Front (ALF) and the Earth Liberation Front (ELF). Lupinacci argues that such commitment to action, in order to challenge and confront animal abuse, social suffering and environmental degradation, should never be overlooked or taken for granted. Among other arguments of great merit, this essay makes an excellent case for scholar-activists to explicitly address anthropocentrism among social justice activists, and to better recognize and tackle the interconnected natures of violence and oppression. To stand the best chance of success the essay argues that activists of all persuasions should strive to be building bridges across old divides, express new forms of solidarity, and form new identities—and friendship—with both humans and more-than-human animals.

Aragorn Eloff's "Do Anarchists Dream of Emancipated Sheep? Contemporary Anarchism, Animal Liberation and the Implications of New Philosophy" focuses on the relations between contemporary anarchism and animal right/liberation through the lens of Deleuze/Guattari–inflected complex systems theory. The content is rich and thought-provoking. Indeed there is much to be gained from focusing on the interesting research findings that Eloff highlights concerning the number of vegans in the broader anarchist milieu. The insights into the rationales behind the responses are particularly illuminating. The essay also includes an engaging historical discussion of anarchism and animal liberation, which will be of general interest to many readers. The essay then focuses intently, and critically, on the abstract machine of hierarchy and domination, which leads to an important consideration of the implications that this has for the everyday practices as anarchists and/or animal liberationists.

Finally, Richard J. White, in "Following in the Footsteps of Élisée Reclus: Disturbing Places of Inter-Species Violence That Are Hidden in Plain Sight," begins by taking us with him on his walk from home to the station for his morning commute. In doing so, he pushes us to think about the extreme levels of violence against nonhuman animals entangled in the urban fabric which is so commonplace and pervasive that most do not see it. White contends that intersectional politics challenges us to see violence in everyday spaces that we move through, and argues for the importance of taking place seriously when understanding how violence toward nonhuman animals is normalized and made invisible. In doing so, the essay concentrates not on spatially marginal, "exceptional" places of violence (such as slaughterhouses), but apparently "civilized" public places that we regularly encounter, such as a high street. The essay begins by exploring the contested geographical definitions of space and place, proceeding with more detailed discussion of an emerging critical animal geography, and then anarchism and anarchist geography. This field of study actively acknowledges the presence/absence of more-than-human violence, and the essay revisits White's walk to the station with these insights, before briefly discussing forms of street-based activism that are able to unsettle and disturb these everyday spaces of speciesist violence. Ultimately, the essay argues that strategies focused on total liberation, which are sensitive to the interconnected oppression and violence affecting human and other animals, need also to pay attention to the imperative to liberate "the spatial" landscapes, and disturb the normalization of violence-toward nonhuman animals.

This is the first book bringing anarchist studies and Critical Animal Studies together, which means that it cannot represent all voices and does not cover every topic on the intersection of multiple dominations. There are many animal liberationists and anarchists not present here (including those who are currently held as political prisoners), and the book, despite the efforts of the editors, is dominated by white voices. This book, therefore, is just one of many efforts to discuss the intersection between animal liberation and anarchism. This book moreover, is more rooted in scholarship and academia, than experiences and narratives from the activist trenches, hence this book is more rooted in anarchist studies and Critical Animal Studies, than anarchism and animal liberation. Consequently, these fields and scholars are not detached from radical organizing, but rather their scholarship and activism inform one another. In conclusion, this book is a critical reflection of our theories, perspectives, and actions from scholar-activists and activist-scholars. It is not a defining statement, but rather a contribution to an emerging conversation which we very much hope will flourish.

REFERENCES

Adams, C. J. (1990). *The sexual politics of meat.* New York: Continuum.
Amster, R., DeLeon, A., Fernandez, L., Nocella, A. J., II, & Shannon, D. (2009). *Contemporary anarchist studies: An introductory anthology to anarchy in the academy.* New York: Routledge.
Best, S. (2009). "The rise of critical animal studies: Putting theory into action and animal liberation into higher education." *Journal for Critical Animal Studies* VII, no. I: 9–52.
Best, S., & Nocella, A. J., II (2004). *Terrorists or freedom fighters? Reflections on the liberation of animals.* New York: Lantern Books.
Best, S., and Nocella, A. J., II (2006). *Igniting a revolution: Voices in defense of the Earth.* Oakland: AK Press.
Best, S., Nocella, A. J., II, Kahn, R., Gigliotti, C., & Kemmerer, L. (2007). "Introducing critical animal studies." *Journal of Critical Animal Studies* 5(1), 4–5.
Colling, S., & Nocella, A. J., II (2011). *Love and liberation: An animal liberation front story.* Temple: Arissa Media Group.
Collins, P. H. (1998). "It's all in the family: Intersections of gender, race and nation." *Hypatia Special Issue Border Crossings: Multiculturalism and Postcolonial Challenges* 13(3): 62–82.
Collins, P. H. (2000a). "Gender, black feminism, and black political economy." *Annals of the American Academy of Political and Social Science* 568: 41–53.
Collins, P. H. (2000b). *Black Feminist Thought,* 2d ed. London: Routledge.
Crenshaw, K. (1989). "Demarginalizing the intersection of race and sex: A black feminist critique of antidiscrimination doctrine, feminist theory and antiracist politics." *University of Chicago Legal Forum,* 139–67.
Del Gandio, J., & Nocella, A. J., II (2014). *Educating for action: Strategies to ignite social justice.* Gabriola Island, BC: New Society Press.
Harper, A. B., ed. *Sistah vegan: Black female vegans speak on food, identity, health and society.* New York: Lantern Books.
hooks, b. (1994). *Teaching to transgress: Education as the practice of freedom.* New York: Routledge.
Lederach, J. P. (2003). *The little book of conflict transformation.* Intercourse, PA: Good Books.

Marcuse, H. (1964). *One-dimensional man: Studies in the ideology of advanced industrial society.* Boston: Beacon Press.
McCall, L. (2005). "The complexity of intersectionality." *Journal of Women in Culture and Society* 30(3): 1771–1800.
Morris, R. (2000). *Stories of transformative justice.* Toronto: Canadian Scholar's Press.
Nocella, A. J., II, Bentley, J. K. C., & Duncan, J. (2012). *Earth, animal, and disability liberation: The rise of the eco-ability movement.* New York: Peter Lang.
Nocella, A. J., II, Best, S., & McLaren, P. (2010). *Academic repression: Reflections from the academic industrial complex.* Oakland: AK Press.
Nocella, A. J., II, Sorenson, J., Socha, K., & Matsuoka, A. (2013). *Defining critical animal studies: An intersectional social justice approach for liberation.* New York: Peter Lang Publishing.
Pellow, D. (2014). *Total liberation: The power and promise of animal rights and the radical Earth liberation movement.* Minneapolis: University of Minnesota Press.
Shannon, D., Nocella, A. J., II, & Asimakopoulos, J. (2012). *The accumulation of freedom: Writings on Anarchist Economics.* Oakland: AK Press.
Walby, S. (2009). *Globalization and inequalities: Complexity and contested modernities.* London: Sage.

Part I
Histories/Futures

"No theory, no ready-made system, no book that
has ever been written will save the world.
I cleave to no system. I am a true seeker."
—Mikhail Bakunin

"I die, as I have lived, a free spirit, an Anarchist,
owing no allegiance to rulers, heavenly or earthly."
—Voltairine de Cleyre

"Above all we should not forget that government
is an evil, a usurpation upon the private judgment
and individual conscience of mankind."
—William Godwin

Anarcho-Veganism Revisited

BRIAN DOMINICK

Twenty Years of "Veganarchy"

In 1994, at age 20, I wholeheartedly adopted two new labels for myself: *anarchist* and *vegan*. So fully did I identify with the concepts behind these terms, as I understood them, that I created a symbol to represent their combination and had it tattooed on my right arm. Two decades later, while I don't regret the ink or my past, I am far less comfortable with the labels I once embraced with pride—so much so that I now barely and rarely identify as either. Yet I believe my current views are as radical as ever; possibly more so, since *radicalism* is a self-critical approach to social change rather than a measure of ideological extremeness.

A year after I went vegan and came out as an anarchist, some friends and I published a pamphlet featuring an essay I wrote that introduced the term *veganarchist*. As we saw it, a critique of human rights and social oppressions was missing from the vegan mindset, which also lacked a sophisticated understanding of social institutions and systems. Likewise, a truly humble, empathic, animal-respecting stance was conspicuously lacking in anarchism—even the "green" varieties, namely social ecology, anarcho-primitivism, and deep ecology. Despite the fact that these intellectual tendencies focus on the environment, they were fundamentally humanistic or mystic in orientation. Although I never really used the label veganarchism or its variants outside of that piece, I have maintained the belief that an animal-freedom outlook is a requisite component of a truly holistic liberation theory.

My little collective was by no means alone in this view, but our contemporaries were an unorganized lot, young and without an audience or means to reach one. At the time, adherents of the minuscule movements behind anarchism and animal rights were casually co-infiltrating each other's milieus.

Still, the football-shaped overlap in the Venn diagram representing the anarchist and vegan scenes never got very big. Once in a while, you could sense that someone was a vegan who had come to sympathize with anarchism and adopt its organizing tendencies, often inspired by the underground, reputedly autonomist Animal Liberation Front. With other folks, you might glean that adopting a vegan lifestyle had been deemed consistent with a longer-standing identification with anarchism, against *all* oppression and domination. But more and more, people were arriving at the two big conclusions around the same time: We were coming to believe that human oppression had its roots in social systems of state, capital, white supremacy, patriarchy, and so forth, just as we discovered that animals suffered unnecessarily at human hands due to structures remarkably similar to the economic and other juggernauts of human social exploitation.

That 1995 pamphlet, *Animal Liberation and Social Revolution*, expressed (and in places overstated) the case connecting these two identities. We argued that both human liberation and animal freedom were integral aspects of anti-oppression perspective, and we went after both "camps" for ignoring the other. The one thing I do not recall questioning in those days, despite countless hours spent arguing the finer points of fighting oppression, was the notion that veganism is the most basic form of animal rights activism. Indeed, we often took it for granted that to be a true animal advocate was to be vegan, so these concepts of serious animal advocacy and the vegan lifestyle are intentionally conflated in much of this current essay, until I address the matter head on in the final section.

In both anarchism and veganism, many find that accepting a fundamentalist interpretation of a very simplistic definition is the most comfortable way to come to terms with a newly adopted worldview. In my observation, strident extremism is rarely the product of a long-standing affiliation with either animal rights or anarchism. Most devout vegans and anarchists who tend toward orthodoxy do so more during early exposure, often growing more sophisticated and nuanced with both experience and age. Oversimplification of complex social and political problems is highly tempting when we lack experience, wisdom, and sophistication. It makes more sense to blame problems on simple causes and pursue equally reductionist negations of those causes as a way forward.

But both anarchism and the beliefs upholding veganism suffer from *reductio ad absurdum* when nuance is eschewed in favor of orthodoxy. The Vegan Society of the UK defines veganism as "a way of living which seeks to exclude, as far as is possible and practicable, all forms of exploitation of, and cruelty to, animals for food, clothing or any other purpose." But you will almost never hear this nuanced definition from hardcore vegans, who are far more likely to drop "seeks to" and "as far as is possible and practicable" from their versions. Gary L. Francione, arguably the most influential "abolitionist" vegan activist, treats the practice in much more absolutist terms: "In my view, a 'vegan' is someone who does not eat, use, or wear any animal products" (Francione 2009). Of course, at its base veganism is just a lifestyle not necessarily accompanied by a philosophical analysis, let alone a strategic program for improving the lot of nonhuman animals, and adherence to veganism always requires somewhat arbitrary demarcations of what actions violate the rules.

Anarchism, meanwhile, from the Greek meaning "without rule," can be neatly defined as opposition to authority and domination, having long since outgrown the more basic legacy definition, "opposition to the state," now widely considered an archaic 19th Century formulation. "Unlike most other political movements," wrote L. Susan Brown in *Reinventing Anarchy, Again*, "anarchism understands that all oppressions are mutually reinforcing; therefore it urges that libertarian struggle take place on many fronts at once.... Anarchism fights all oppression in all its forms" (Brown 1996, p. 154). And what a far-reaching statement is opposition to all oppression, so inviting to the hyperbolically inclined. Unlike the relatively passive vegan worldview, which at its essence preaches mere abstinence, anarchism typically envisions revolutionary change brought about by sweeping popular action; it is anything but passive, though the devil resides in the details of vision, strategy, and tactics.

In a sure sign of creeping fundamentalism, some activists see other worldviews and practices through dichotomist lenses. It isn't just that animal freedom activists or anarchists believe something extreme, but that they obtain a sense of superiority from this belief. Neither anarchism nor veganism requires attitudes rooted in disdain for non-adherents, but both are fertile ground for such strident, dogmatic fidelity. Lots of self-identified vegans are not harshly critical of others' personal behaviors, recognizing the importance of gradual influence. Plenty of anarchists are patient, thoughtful people who would prefer to insert subversive arguments here and there to make people think differently, rather than constantly leveling in-your-face demands for insurrection and total anarchy. Predictably, these are not the folks that stand out in either camp, nor the ones critics seize on to discredit broader ideas.

Animal Liberation and Social Revolution, I fear, may continue to contribute to the notion, dearly held among some acolytes, that veganism and anarchism are prescriptive, as opposed to aspirational. The pamphlet still turns up in translations all over the world. In the years after it came out, I wrote innumerable essays (e.g., Dominick 1998; Dominick 2000) and lectured every chance I got against fundamentalist interpretations of anarchism. I criticized black blocs and black flags as alienating and off-putting. I argued that fetishizing insurrection was beyond absurd. So many of the characteristics of anarchism that make it easy for extreme personalities to adopt were just not consistent with a sensible critique of oppression and its root causes; they had virtually nothing to do with a sound path forward.

My parallel concerns about vegan fundamentalism came up at least as often, usually in more personal settings. I don't recall writing or lecturing publicly on the matter, but when it became clear to me that vegan circles were rife with orthodoxy, I took every opportunity to challenge extreme interpretations. When fellow vegans expressed that not only were they unwilling to eat a single piece of cheese that was otherwise going to be thrown out, but they considered it an act of violence when I did so, I was dealing with more than a few people who prioritized their personal mission over the welfare of nonhuman animals. For them, veganism had ceased being a principled boycott, as it starts for most; it had become a quasi-religious ritual. One even described the consumption of salvaged dairy products as a "spiritual violation" of the vegan way.

None of this is easy or pleasing for me to write. Note that I have no intention of making a case against a vegan lifestyle; I merely criticize treating it as an imperative, and I caution against considering it a strategy for significantly reducing animal suffering. I very much want simple solutions to also be sensible and basic ideals effectively practicable. But my two decades of experience and observation don't bear this out. Who would have believed: struggle is hard.

Fundamental Disconnectedness

So what has changed in 20 years? It would be impossible to measure, but there has been a steady stream of anarchists and vegans who express orthodox interpretations of the labels, and at least a handful who stridently insist on a combined ideology. There has never been much documentation in professional or academic literature. In the 1990s, the ideas and presence of such folks was most consistently evident in the hundreds if not thousands of self-published zines produced by anarchists and animal rights activists at the time. Their contemporary parallel can be found in highly personalized blogs, especially on the Tumblr platform most popular with slogan- and image-oriented youth. There we find thousands of anarchist, vegan, and veganarchist bloggers, a great many engaged in orthodox thinking.

Both veganism and anarchism attract many, many reasonable people, whose varied practices of each make clear just how unnecessary fundamentalist interpretations really are. While some of the earliest proponents of each may have been strident or extremist, there is no holy book defining the way of the vegan or the outlook of the anarchist. This is a huge advantage over doctrinal belief systems. Unlike religions and proper-noun political ideologies like Marxism, worldviews that lack authorship can be reduced to principles instead of specific prescriptions and proscriptions. With no one true reference to interpret and fight over, we can instead debate which strategic and tactical options offer the best foundation for further advances, be they policy reforms, consumer attrition, or more radical steps. We can actually use rationality to determine how to build a movement, rather than fear, intimidation, conformism, or appeals to authority. What if we just did what was most sound, rather than what made us seem the most militant, committed, or saintly?

An acceptance of nuance is another key to developing potentially effective movements with true appeal. All-or-nothing approaches attract a certain type of character. They're most obvious on the fringes, but the key attributes are more quietly exhibited in a range of adherents. Stricter tendencies among both the anarchist and vegan milieus would be well served to recognize that while reformism is not the way to victory, reform plays a key role in the struggle for progress and public awareness. But fundamentalists are impatient; they insist on immediate revolutionary change, which is both unrealistic and off-putting.

Overbearing approaches don't just alienate the timid. People sensitive to nuance are hesitant to rally around an ideological flag. Anyone who intuits that lasting change is rarely effected by hurried purists will balk at loud voices crying out for insurrection at any cost or demands for absolute adherence to a diet or lifestyle. And it's not a good idea to drive off the sharpest and shrewdest activists and potential activists. These are folks we want to attract to our cause, even if at first glance it seems their deliberations might slow us down. (It isn't like we are getting anywhere quickly without them.)

What if veganism and anarchism weren't do-or-die, go-for-broke ideologies, but rather constellations of values and principles helping us plot our way to a better future? The labels might lose some of their cachet, thus suffering in terms of attractiveness to angst-addled youth and anyone seeking marginalization as a virtue in and of itself. Otherwise, it's not as if these movements' reputations have much to lose. Surely if we recognize veganist and anarchist lifestyles and tactics as an aspect of a way forward, rather than as the objective themselves, they would also lose much of their enforceability; that would not be a bad thing.

One key difference between veganism and anarchism is that veganism is a lifestyle with an associated, subordinated ideology, whereas anarchism is an ideology with an associated but not well-defined lifestyle that perhaps most anarchists do not particularly value, let alone subscribe to. Veganism is not a counter-power movement. It involves at most a hint of a strategy and lacks even the pretense of an institutional alternative to decrease human impact on nonhuman animals. For this reason I will focus mostly on animal advocacy and activism from this point on, as developing a strategic understanding of how change can occur is imperative for this nascent movement.

Those of us who would strongly prefer to live with only positive and neutral impacts on the rest of the world must face that we cannot. And those of us who actively make a point of limiting our negative impact must also acknowledge that we are not in this way special; most people—the truly vast majority of people in the world—would prefer not to cause harm. Indeed, nearly everyone actually puts this preference into practice to at least some degree, foregoing certain opportunities for self-advancement or pleasure.

Dispositions toward this principle of restricting one's negative impact on the rest of the world range broadly. Maybe someone eats meat regularly, with exceptions for veal and *foie gras*, which they consider too cruel. This person also would probably not steal the money from a blind panhandler's cup, no matter how full that cup appeared. A pure, vicious form of self-interest rarely underlies even severe personality disorders; pretty much all of us have at least some conscience.

Near the other extreme, millions of practitioners of Jainism make extraordinary efforts to reduce their negative impact on humans and animals, going so far as to filter their drinking water through a mesh to ensure they don't swallow complex animal life forms. Jaina monks even cover their mouths with cloths and gently sweep the ground they walk on. Such people are likely the only who could plausibly stake claim to being truly vegan, but crucially, they would also be the first to admit the limitations of devoutly practicing their beliefs. There are many secular and other religious examples of extreme asceticism, including people who engage in extraordinary self-sacrifice for a cause, such as hunger strikers or those who self-immolate to bring attention to injustice, potentially making a world-changing contribution for the better.

That leaves most of my presumed audience and me somewhere between these extremes—probably far closer to the first example of the casual self-sacrificer than the Jain or the martyr, upon honest review. It is uncontroversial that social context plays a big role in the relative purity of one's lifestyle. If you are a social activist who is kind to all those around you and abstains completely from directly consuming animal products, you almost certainly still buy or cause to be bought at least some products made with super-exploited labor. If you ride in cars as anything other than a hitchhiker or an abductee, you're complicit in a method of transportation that kills millions of vertebrates alone every year, just in the United States, not to mention the billions more displaced or mangled during construction of our 4 million miles of roadway. Even if you rely on public transportation, most of the above is true for you. Just stop to think about the rat poison used in your subway system, paid for by your transit fees.

Meanwhile, people living in the so-called "developing world," while equally kind and thoughtful of their neighbors, might never even be passengers in a car or consider the ethics of their impact on the rest of the world, striving as they are to survive on $2 a day. Their entire existence could have less negative impact on people and animals than a practicing vegan anarchist in the Global North has in a single year.

I realize these are all arguments used by opponents to undermine the practice of veganism, such as the case put forth by Lierre Keith in *The Vegetarian Myth* (2009). But we need to understand why that is, and why it has such wide appeal. Excepting for a moment that critics are often being overly defensive or just plain nasty, they also detect that veganism is based on a relatively arbitrary scope. Sure, a strict vegan won't buy or even eat anything that was tested on animals or that is made from animal parts or byproducts, perhaps falsely believing that has an actual impact on saving animals' lives. But they'll risk directly running over an animal with their car, destroying habitats indirectly with pollution, or having billions incidentally slaughtered by equipment used in modern large-scale vegetable farming.

The standard response, of course, is that we can nourish ourselves sufficiently without meat, eggs, dairy, etc., but we still have to get around, and we still have to eat *something*, and a plant-based diet is the *least* harmful. That's not an unreasonable retort, but it's also not really true. We're resourceful; we could find a way to live a life—however relatively unfulfilling, frustrating, and arduous—with far less impact on the animal kingdom than just abstaining from cheese and donning shoes made from synthetic materials. Instead, most vegans choose to only substitute their consumption habits, not drastically reduce them. They sell their gas-guzzler and get a Prius or use biodiesel or take the bus most places. But they don't cancel that overseas vacation, let alone move biking or walking distance from work, let alone subscribe to a severely ascetic lifestyle like the Jain, let alone self-sacrifice our very lives for a better world.

There are limitations and contradictions to any lifestyle that is modestly ascetic, rooted in those half-measures extreme practitioners are known for scoffing at. And the critic of animal rights, in their Socratic challenge to that lifestyle, may also sound a lot like those more ardent vegan practitioners, always pushing themselves and their friends toward living a more inclusive, farther-reaching vegan ideal. It should not be too surprising that critics pulling in each opposite direction point to the same logical vulnerabilities; it can be understood to highlight a very powerful weakness of conventional veganism as a prescriptive notion.

I am not an opponent of the vegan lifestyle nor an extremist nor even a consistent practitioner. In some ways, I have respect for the extremist more than for the moderate, because the former self-consciously pushes relatively arbitrary lines toward an ideal, while the typical vegan rests on laurels, asserting that they "don't consume animal products" but rarely if ever acknowledging the cluster of asterisks associated with that claim. Fundamentalist vegans are ironically more likely to recognize their lifestyle as striving toward an unattainable ideal than the typical vegan acknowledges the same of simply cutting off direct consumption of products derived from animal abuse. We would all do well to remember that progress toward a better way of life does not stop the day we quit eating cheese and eggs and start shopping for leather-free shoes. Unfortunately, actual progress doesn't begin there, either.

But here's the real point: If you are privileged yet choose not to alter your whole life drastically overnight, just to have minimal perceptible effect on the world, you may very well still be a reasonable, considerate person; you may opt to change (or re-engage with) the world in some other way. And if you do make drastic changes and engage in extremely ascetic choices in hopes of lessening your negative impact, you may just be more committed or better able to endure the sacrifices. Yet in both cases, you lack the prerogative to dictate your standards of righteous consumption to others, no matter how much relatively "better" yours seem, because there's always someone behaving relatively "better" than you.

The Bankruptcy of Vegan "Strategy"

The path to a radically more animal-friendly society will not be achieved by lifestyle choices alone, no matter how popularly implemented. To understand why this is, the animal-freedom fighter must have a decent grasp of radical social theory and get past the prevailing, willful naiveté about the difference between individual and even collective conduct within, and the aggregate impacts of, complex social systems.

If every American were to go vegan over the next five years but capitalism and our current system of governance remained intact, the animal agriculture industry would accommodate the change. The probable move would be shifting capital-intensive channels (such as marketing and industrial infrastructure) to growing overseas markets. This would be accompanied by lobbying state and federal governments for even more drastic subsidies and tax breaks to compensate for any losses in workforce or profits. And this would be in the service of continued torturing and killing of sentient nonhumans for the pleasure of consumers.

In my observation, vegans seem less likely to understand this than some people who rarely if ever think about the source of what they put in their stomachs. Cynicism about how difficult it is to make serious, lasting change in society is well founded. It is extremely hard; systems are in place to co-opt attempts at change if not destroy them outright. So personal actions, however momentous they may feel to the practitioner, often appear meaningless from the outside. And while one could make the same statement about, say, non-violent resistance in the early 1960s civil rights movement, there was an actual theory and strategy behind those tactics. Restricting one's diet and consumption are, in essence, a tactic divorced from theory and strategy, as well as being effectively invisible as a movement, quite unlike the masses actively resisting systemic segregation and disenfranchisement in the South.

Most vegans are not revolutionaries in the first place. They simply want to do their part. We see all sorts of factoids and infographics about how meat eating is more ecologically damaging than driving a Hummer, how many animals are slaughtered each year to feed humans, and so forth. The commonsense conclusion is that if you stop consuming animal products, you'll reduce your impact by that much, and you can just start tallying your contribution. A blog called Counting Animals published a piece that exemplifies the popular perception (even by many non-vegetarians) of the reputedly humane impact of a plant-based diet. "A vegetarian spares the lives of a certain number of animals each time he or she chooses to forgo meat for vegetables, fruits, grains, legumes and nuts," the post opens. It goes on to calculate conservatively that every lacto-ovo vegetarian saves 405 lives of sea, air, and land animals a year (Harish 2012).

Imagine that. More than 400 animals alive that would not have been, all because of your diet. A praiseworthy choice indeed, if only it bore a shred of truth. In fact, only in extremely specific circumstances is this self-congratulating notion even possibly true. Unless you were offered a feast of fish or fowl but told the fisher or hunter on their way out the door, "Don't kill any animals on my account," your round-the-clock choice not to put meat or dairy in your body actually saves exactly zero animals. Even refusing to eat freshly killed animals after the fact has no impact.

There are some exceptions to this cynically realistic view of the limitations of our behavior. For instance, opting to serve vegetarian food at a cookout instead of ordering a pig to roast could spare a pig from slaughter for a little while. But that pig will probably just continue a life of misery until the next order, and it won't necessarily affect the supplier's future inventory decisions. Nevertheless, eating salad at a pig roast makes no objective difference at all.

Even rudimentary analysis matters. To be precise, demand for meat is not the root cause of animal slaughter; *perceived demand* for meat is. Your act of abstinence has to be noticed by market analysts and wholesale product purchasers, or it counts for nothing on that front. In a painful paradox, people concerned about animal mistreatment who switch from factory farmed eggs or meats to local, "free-range" alternatives—even in cases where treatment is fundamentally better—may be in fact suddenly "coming online" in terms of being noticed as demanders of animal products. Purchasing or boycotting factory-farmed products (or not) likely made no difference due to the sheer scale. But showing up every week to buy eggs from a farmer with just a few hens experiencing relatively humane conditions actually makes a difference to that small operation, influencing their exploitative inventory.

Even if the above rings true for you, you might suggest that collectively, the small but significant percentage of us who boycott animal products must be having an impact. I am unconvinced, but in any case, don't forget how ready capital is to shift markets. It is not enough simply to not demand meat while new outlets for it emerge and grow. We can at most hope to hurt their margins and reduce the number of animals suffering for a short period. As long as consumers don't have to directly pay the environmental and health costs of animal-based diets, relatively few will turn completely away from meat, dairy, and eggs. We see lots of dietary changes when the costs are paid in chronic disease, but this change of heart comes far too late for our satisfaction. If we want to alter behavior before reckless diets cause health problems in old age, meat, dairy, and eggs need to cost more in the near term.

This has not stopped many radical animal-freedom activists from arguing that veganism is the quintessential act in pursuit of a world free of animal abuse. In his book *Making a Killing: The Political Economy of Animal Rights*, anarchist vegan Bob Torres argues that "veganism must be a baseline for the animal rights movement." Torres believes veganism is

> the daily, lived expression of abolition in one's life, and a rejection of the logic of speciesism. While we should do work to help animals through a variety of rescue and other programs, vegan education should form the basis of our outreach and activism; in our interactions with people outside the movement, we should discuss why veganism is a viable option.... If we want to eradicate exploitation, we must begin by ending it in our own lives, and encouraging others to do the same.

Even in a book that levels a masterful argument against exploitation of animals, naming capitalism as a lynchpin of oppression, Torres remarkably makes no case for the real-world effectiveness of the veganism he advocates, practiced on an individual or even a mass scale. Nor does he make a case that mass-scale veganism would be fundamentally better than far-more-mass-scale near-veganism. Yet it seems unlikely that the optimal overall approach is to insist that everybody interested in saving animals go vegan as their first and most important step, a prerequisite to being accepted as a legitimate fighter for animals or against the system that exploits them, as he essentially lays it out.

Make no mistake: Torres is positing veganism as a strategy in and of itself—just not by the efficacy of boycott, which he admits is insignificant. Instead, Torres's argument is that veganism is a symbolic protest:

> While a single vegan (or even a group of them) may not make much of a dent in animal agriculture today, living as a vegan is important—it is a real and potent objection to speciesism and the processes of domination that enslave animals to our wants. It shows that living life as an anti-speciesist is possible, and it reminds people of our needless exploitation of others.

No doubt the existence of vegans demonstrates that a life of reduced animal exploitation is possible and serves as a conversation piece about humans' relationship to nonhumans. But that truism doesn't establish why *every* anti-speciesist must adopt veganism, which is just one popular way to demonstrate opposition to human exploitation of animals. Surely an anti-speciesist should try to avoid directly harming animals, but that's not actually an argument against ever consuming a product derived from animal exploitation. In fact, it's a stronger argument against ever getting into an automobile than it is an argument against ever accepting a slice of pepperoni pizza at a party.

Torres posits veganism as "a great refusal of the system itself," but in truth it refuses no system, just one highly egregious element of the capitalist system and a speciesist culture. He further states change-oriented vegans are prefigurative in their practice, living "in ways that mirror the kind of world we think we would like to see, even if we are realistic about lasting and long-term change being difficult and requiring social struggle." But prefigurative activism can't magically spawn a new world; it has to either change institutions or foster new ones that can affect radical change. Veganism simply does not do this. Even to the extent it encourages capitalists to invent new products or agricultural methods to serve the emerging vegan market, the vegan movement in no way establishes institutions that could ever constitute a radically alternative system.

Moreover, the vegan movement is no hundredth-monkey scenario. It's not like veganism will spread at a steady or increasing rate until one day the world will have put animal abuses behind us. If this hasn't worked with racism and sexism after more than a century of concerted activism, why would we expect changing minds through argumentation to be the path to freedom for animals? What a long, slow, passive path to freedom that strategy consigns nonhumans to, even in the best scenario of deliberate progress.

Ironically, given the subtitle of his book about "political economy," even after demonstrating a keen grasp of structural economic matters fueling animal abuse on a modern scale, Torres at no point conveys an imperative for structural economic changes. He proposes cultural change but nothing in the institutional makeup of economy. Yet it remains true that person-at-a-time lifestyle adjustments are inherently limited, especially up against ingrained cultural beliefs and massive, powerful industries with strong political ties. Until we break that self-reinforcing web of cruelty-driven social institutions, our individual choices will be of pathetically limited consequence.

Advocates of veganism fetishize the power of personal consumption, seemingly without acknowledgment of the chain of relationships between one's palate and those who deal suffering and death to animals. That there are typically numerous institutions and multiple exchanges of money mediating the connection between mouth and farm is lost on the likes of Gary Francione when he urges audiences to "go vegan, today." But the imperative to alter one's life must be accompanied by a logical argument for how it will actually affect the world objectively. Very unfortunately, that logic is not forthcoming.

Toward an Actual Strategy

Despite all the above points, I do believe organized consumers in the U.S. and other industrialized countries can make a major contribution to significantly reducing long-term worldwide demand by establishing an example of environmental stewardship. The real threat of emerging consumer markets (the "growing middle class") is the extent to which the newly affluent demand material abundance, American style. That means not paying for the consequences of their actions. While animal-product consumption in the industrializing world increases, U.S. residents are suddenly eating less red meat for a range of reasons, health risks and rising prices chief among them, with concern for animal welfare and the environment cited by nearly a third of Americans who've reduced red meat intake (Barclay 2012).

Rather than using common sense or what feels right, both of which can be deceptive when applied to the real world of social change, it's imperative that we develop a strategic framework. A movement for animals needs objectives, but it also needs a way to leverage power beyond the direct capacities of the population that actively, explicitly supports and participates in the movement. The strategy is to raise the costs to the abusers until they exceed the perceived benefits of their actions. The tactics can be any nonviolent means that will increase those operating costs without causing a greater public backlash.

So a mass movement choosing to support businesses that explicitly avoid animal exploitation and an emerging culture of responsibility for ecological impact, can conceivably make a difference in setting the standard for taking these issues seriously as economies and cultures change. The real question is how a movement can have a deterrent effect on animal-product consumption beyond mere personal choices—even beyond an organized boycott dependent on conscience. Part of this arm of our strategy would involve exposing the brutality of the industry directly to consumers. But we'll also need to add more severe consumer deterrents over time, all while minimizing backlash.

In the near term, campaigns and tactics other than a diffuse vegan boycott could have far greater impacts. Heavy regulation of producers would increase the costs of meat, eggs, and dairy market-wide. As much as anarchists may dislike using government to solve problems, in our present society any headache we can give animal-harming capitalists is a move worth considering. For those disinclined to seek radical social change, serious reforms can be much better than business as usual, which means agitating for regulations might well be more impactful than simply going vegan. Such reforms would help build a foundation for further activism.

Animal rights activists will often balk at this notion, arguing not unreasonably that when consumers feel confident government is addressing a problem, they relax their consumer vigilance. In this case, that might take the form of eating even more "grass-fed" or "cage-free" or "free-range" or "antibiotics-free" meat, eggs, and dairy. Therefore, they say, the only option is to abolish the industry; mere animal welfare objectives are insufficient.

There is no question that if the goal is animal freedom, improving the treatment of exploited animals is not a sound end goal, as it condemns animals to unfathomable suffering and involves many other complications such as continued greenhouse gas emissions. But we know factory farming wasn't invented as a means of mass sadism; it was established because abusing animals on a large scale is generally more profitable than mistreating them less severely on a small scale. So raising the costs of such behavior would disincentivize massive operations and pass the cost along to the consumer. If all meat, dairy, and eggs had to be produced by the "more humane" methods some animal welfare advocates cheer today, there is no question this would drastically reduce the suffering and death of animals in ways the vegan movement has little hope of achieving through its strategy-free approach to converting true believers.

An early step toward this objective could be the enforcement of product labeling that highlights how animals and the environment were impacted by the process of making and delivering everything we consume. Animal freedom activists have long engaged in creative forms of direct-action product labeling: attaching expository messages to retail items or highlighting unseen costs of popular products in online consumer reviews. Further, a concerted movement of activists who don't find lobbying distasteful could pressure the government to establish and enforce a system that exposes information about how products come to be.

Direct action in the form of animal rescues and sabotage on a significant scale would have a strong, systemic influence over time, in ways potentially far more powerful than passive consumption changes. The industry operates in utter fear of nonviolent direct action, as proved by the steady rash of state and federal laws targeting peaceful animal-freedom activists. While raising costs to producers (and thus consumers), these actions may also decrease demand for products on a wide scale, where even subtle consumer attitude changes can be significant in the aggregate. Only serious social change will achieve these short- and mid-term results, subtly reorienting society to incline toward a plant-based diet and an animal-respecting culture.

A longer-term goal is a system of pricing that factors in the monumental health care and environmental impacts of raising for slaughter untold billions of animals each year. These are called "externalities"—costs of economic activity that are not taken account in the price of a product. For the meat and dairy industries, this of course means everything from chronic disease to pollution to global warming to soil depletion to antibiotic-resistant bacteria. There are also the opportunity costs of all that acreage diverted from growing crops for people to eat, not to mention deforestation and its compounding effects. (There is sadly little hope of "pricing in" the "cost" in anguish and death of sentient beings, but by the grace of reason—or physics— the truth is humanity pays a dear enough price for animal husbandry, especially its crueler, more industrialized versions.) And we *can* calculate what those who wish to consume the products of such systems "owe" society and our habitat. Factoring those costs in, which is the only rational way to operate a sustainable economy, would drastically reduce demand for animal exploitation.

The final objective is the abolition of capital, which would eliminate the most profoundly disproportionate incentive to establish mass-scale apparatuses of animal exploitation. Otherwise, even cultural changes and institutionalized reforms will always be at risk of rollback by innovative capitalists seeking new ways to generate perverse returns on the backs of defenseless animals and easily manipulated consumers. Eliminating the concentrated power to build and maintain animal-exploitative enterprises is also the only way to avoid market drift, where capital can be moved overseas. Expropriating land and money is the only way to ensure those who would privately control it have no way to repurpose it. An economic system structurally driven by principles over profit would value a different kind of efficiency, assessed by how well society's overall needs are serviced rather than what practices generate the most capital for the few in power.

Revolutionary economic change is no small order, but the inescapable need for it is the key reason I have spent 20 years advocating an infusion of anticapitalism into a radicalized animal freedom orientation. Purchasing power rises in parts of the world that were recently destitute, precisely at the moment agricultural resources are hitting significant limits and climate change wreaks havoc on crop capacities worldwide, but meat and dairy prices will not rise proportionately, and their true costs will never be reflected by market signals. The economies of the world lack the means to respond to these trends in a sane way. Demand by the affluent will still divert scarce land from growing crops for humans (or trees for Earth) to growing feed for animals so the wealthiest can obtain calories from gluttonously inefficient sources. This perpetuates the condition of contrived scarcity worldwide, condemning many to starvation and malnutrition while a relative few enjoy abundance. That system must end.

A New Animal Ethic

As long as the effect of practicing veganism is questionable and there are objectively superior ways to reduce animal suffering, personal abstinence from directly consuming animal products remains an option, not an imperative, for the sincere animal advocate. Vegans must understand that they cannot have it both ways. Veganism can be either (1) a must-do precondition of striving for animal freedom, or it can be (2) "strict" in practice and enforceability. If you want to argue that "going vegan" is a requisite part of standing for animal freedom, then the definition of vegan can only be that one will not generate *significant demand* for animal harm. This definition would excuse acts such as eating meat or dairy that would otherwise go to waste, and probably other occasional consumption including actual purchases not detected by producers. Yet even such a loose, practical definition is essentially unrealistic due to all the ways in which everyday life inevitably causes harm to animals, not to mention the dearth of ways one can actually impact perceived demand.

If you want to define veganism as a sort of spiritual practice by which one does not put the flesh or byproducts of animals into or onto one's body, by no rationale can you insist this is an integral part of working for animal rights or freedom. It is a subjective preference that you are absolutely welcome to have for your own life. Throwing away your leather belt when you go vegan and replacing it with one made from petroleum is *not* an act of kindness toward animals (though it's also not immoral just because it consumes a small amount of petroleum). Likewise, if veganism is purely prefigurative, then it cannot rationally be an imperative. If you insist the label *vegan* refers to this symbolic way of being, then by all means, have the label. Just understand it is profoundly disingenuous to contend it has anything to do with actually reducing animal suffering. It does not.

Still, part of the strategy for reducing animal suffering is to decrease overall demand for animal products. It is not at all clear this would better result from the small share of people who might actually practice strict veganism, as compared to the far greater number who might be convinced to significantly reduce their consumption of animal products were the option articulated to them, let alone if they were forced to simply pay the true costs of their preferences. What if we once and for all took the rug out from under the typical refrain, "I could never give up cheese," by encouraging progressive reduction rather than abstinence?

The greatest reticence to being vegan, in my observation, is rooted neither in an unwillingness to do the right thing, nor in a lack of concern over animal mistreatment. It seems more likely based on a realistic sense that one cannot make a difference up against a system like capitalism, combined for some with distaste for absolutism and pious-sounding ascetic lifestyles. Not seeing the point in an insignificant boycott does not necessarily indicate a lack of caring; in fact, it might be a sign of sophisticated analysis.

So after 20 years of living an anarchistic and veganistic lifestyle, to the best of my ability, my conclusion is that it has made staggeringly little objective difference in the world. I feel good about my choices viewed through a cultural lens, and I haven't drifted significantly from this lifestyle. It suits me. But I have relaxed my personal rules slightly and shed the *vegan* label, resigned as I am that I sadly cannot reduce perceived demand for animal products out of sheer force of my own will, and hopeful as I am that a slightly tempered practice will be deemed more inviting by more people I encounter.

An incredulous vegan recently asked me what "mostly vegan" could possibly mean, having seen I'd selected it to describe my "diet" on a social network profile. "You are either vegan, or you are not," she wrote. I have similarly seen disgusted reactions to the term *veganish*. This idea that one always abstains or one is unworthy of the label, is on its face utterly absurd. Nevertheless, I respect the definition and shed the label in part to separate myself from those who eagerly proclaim *vegan* and defend it through self-righteousness and disdain. As a defining characteristic of the label, this absolutism is ironically veganism's greatest inhibitor. The time has come to stop considering veganism a requisite for pursuing animal rights or else adjust its definition.

In place of veganism, people committed to massively reducing humans' impact on the natural world could develop an entirely new strategic system in between the tepid "animal welfare" cause and strictly consumption-oriented arch-veganism. This would include a personal mandate to engage in demonstrative behavioral changes that signal a willingness to lessen the harm we do to animals and the environment. It would also embrace a goal of systemic change to secure any such gains as well as encourage and facilitate preferred behaviors.

I don't know what to call this new ethos, but here's a proposed definition:

> *A practicable theory opposed to causing suffering to any sentient animals, favoring widespread personal behavioral changes and system-targeted social activism to curb and eventually eliminate abuses.*

This definition is simple enough to grasp easily and work toward, but open to wide interpretation and broad adoption. It does *not* imply just personal action. No more loopholes allowing vegans to think they are doing all they can for the cause without organizing against the forces of speciesism, statism, patriarchy, adultarchy, racism, and capitalism, all of which contribute to our society's mass exploitation of sentient animals. Most importantly for the animal advocate who wants to see an actual reduction in suffering, this activist worldview insists on institutional changes that can have serious impact. This is how an ethos of animal freedom can make a real difference, not just a symbolic statement about how we could live. It's not enough to behave as if the world were different; we have to make the world different.

It is hard to imagine an Earth on which absolutely nobody harms or kills animals for food, fashion, research, or entertainment. But it's harder still to expect anything close to a total moratorium will result from either the passive, personal activism of conventional veganism or the strident rhetoric of the fundamentalist. As opposed to falling back on labels and sweeping proscriptions, both social revolution and animal freedom would be better served by holistic movements promoting the understanding of, and a willingness to undermine, deep seated systems of oppression. Our tactics can include a different way of being, as well as social action to bring about a society that encourages and enables that better mode of existence. If our very behavior is part of the problem, how much more the nemesis is a system that renders altering our individual behavior impotent against the machinations of oppression?

References

Barclay, E. (2012). "Why there's less red meat on American plates." NPR.
Brown, L. S. (1996). *Reinventing Anarchy, Again*. H.J. Ehrlich (Ed.). San Francisco: AK Press.
Dominick, B. (1995). *Animal Liberation and Social Revolution: An Anarchist Perspective on Veganism or a Vegan Perspective on Anarchism*. Syracuse: Critical Mess Media.
Dominick, B. (1998). An Introduction to Dual Power Strategy. Retrieved from http://left-liberty.net/?p=265.
Dominick, B. (1999). Anarchy, Nonviolence, and the Seattle Actions. ZNet. Retrieved from http://smashfacism.itgo.com/news/anarchy.html.
Dominick, B. (2000). Anarchists in the Neighborhood. *Arsenal: A Magazine of Anarchist Strategy and Culture*, Fall.
Francione, G.L. (2009). Some Thoughts on the Meaning of "Vegan." Retrieved from http://www.abolitionistapproach.com/some-thoughts-on-the-meaning-of-vegan/.
Harish. (2012, February 6). How many animals does a vegetarian save? http://www.countinganimals.com/how-many-animals-does-a-vegetarian-save/.
Keith, L. (2009). *The Vegetarian Myth*. Oakland: PM Press.

Anarchist Criminology Against Racism and Ableism and for Animal Liberation

Anthony J. Nocella II

Anarchism is an ideology that has long been (deliberately) misrepresented by the government, the media, educators, and indeed by other "radical" activists. Claiming to be an anarchist or being labeled an "anarchist" carries with it serious stigmatization. Violent, reactionary, deviant, and unruly are some of the many labels used to describe anarchists (see Bowen, 2004; Chomsky, 2005; Day, 2004). For those who look beyond this dominant propaganda, to see what anarchism actually represents, it comes as no surprise that Critical Animal Studies (CAS), together with the animal liberation movement more broadly, are both greatly influenced by anarchist praxis. This influence can be demonstrated in many ways, not least through appreciating the commitment to animal liberation within key areas of the anarchist canon. For example, Torres, a social anarchist, argues that anarchists need to be vegan: "As a needless and unnecessary form of hierarchy, anarchists should reject the consumption, enslavement, and subjugation of [nonhuman] animals for human ends, and identify it as yet another oppressive aspect of the relations of capital and a needless form of domination" (2007, p. 130). Furthermore, Brian Dominick, who coined the term "veganarchist" in his pamphlet "Animal Liberation and Social Revolution: A Vegan Perspective on Anarchism or an Anarchist Perspective on Veganism" (1997), writes that

> [l]ikewise, many vegans and animal liberationists are being influenced by anarchist thought and its rich tradition. This is evidenced by growing hostility among some animal lib activists towards the statist, capitalist, sexist, racist and ageist Establishment which has been escalating the intensity of its war not only on nonhuman animals, but also on their human advocates.

...

Besides our far-reaching vision, anarchists and animal liberationists share strategical methodology. ... But unlike liberals and progressives, whose objectives are limited to reforms, we are willing to admit that real change will only be brought about if we add destructive force to our creative transformation of oppressive society [para. 2 and 3].

This essay, written from an anarchist criminology perspective, is dedicated to explaining what anarchism *is* and how it *should* be related to animal liberation. Having first established a working understanding of the grounds that anarchism is based on, the essay then draws attention to the most well-known anarchist-influenced organization within the animal liberation movement: the Animal Liberation Front (ALF). In particular, the discussion is concerned with examining how the actions of the ALF imply a critique of the concept of property. Following this, the essay suggests why the animal liberation movement, to be consistent with an anarchist perspective, must also oppose the current criminal justice system, which is punitive and fuels the prison industrial complex, and other forms of oppression such as racism and ableism. The essay concludes by proposing some alternative solutions to the current criminal justice system.

Anarchism: A Brief Overview

"Anarchism" is not easy to define because it is anti-dogmatic but defined by common principles. The theory of anarchism was first introduced and defined by William Godwin, who wrote *Political Justice* in 1793. Another influential theorist at that time was Johann Schmidt, also known as Max Stirner. Stirner wrote *The Ego and His Own* (1845), which examined the complex relationship between the individual and society and which argued that individuals are responsible for being active members in their communities and that communities are made of individuals working together. A third key anarchist of the 19th century was Pierre-Joseph Proudhon who most notably examined the definition of property and participated in electoral politics and the French Revolution. While these individuals were important in laying the foundation of anarchism, Mikhail Bakunin (1814–1876), Peter Kropotkin (1842–1921), and Emma Goldman (1869–1940) are arguably the most influential of all anarchists in shaping how we understand anarchism today. Mikhail Bakunin (1970) writes about freedom in *God and the State*, "I cannot claim and feel myself free except in the presence of and with regard to other men. ... I am truly free only when all human beings around me, men and women alike are equally free" (Guerin, 2005, p. 151). This quote reinforces and reflects current intersectional multi-issued movements, including Black

Lives Matter, Occupy, and Idle No More; hence we can see how these theorists have aided in shaping today's movements. Oppression is systematic; therefore, it affects everyone in society, not just those who are directly targeted by a particular form of oppression.

While one must be cautious when discussing "anarchism" writ large, most anarchists have two important attributes in common. First, they believe that hierarchical structures of authority do not allow human beings to participate in social and political change via direct democracy. Second, notwithstanding the existence of anarcho-capitalists, anarchists are anti-capitalist because capitalism promotes divisions and hierarchies among peoples in terms of their identities, intellects, and abilities, as well as divides people into classes and class strata based on their relationship to the means of production (see Berkman, 2003; Chomsky, 2005; Guerin, 1970). Anarchists believe that hierarchies, such as the state, are structured to oppress and subvert individual and group rights.

It does not take much imagination to realize why anarchists oppose the existence of the state. States, often in the name of security, freedom, and economic development, have employed mass violence. Moreover, states control their citizens through a top-down hierarchical coercive and punitive justice system, and when citizens dissent, they are quickly repressed. Because of their inherently hierarchical nature, states also sustain traditional power structures, which do not allow their citizens to make decisions. Anarchists argue that all individuals need to have autonomy, freedom, the chance to participate in policy making, and, when necessary, the opportunity to build community through activism (Bowen, 2005; Purkis & Bowen, 2005; Guerin, 1970).

Power, the ability to create change, is a central concept with which anarchists engage (Rabinow, 1984). Power is not necessarily based on the strength or the size of one's military force, but the ability to influence individuals through information or government propaganda as well as to build collective experience that can build a social movement to resist government control. Roger N. Baldwin, editor of *Anarchism: A Collection of Revolutionary Writings* by Peter Kropotkin (2002), explains that control of morality by institutions is also a form of authority. He states, "This natural moral sense [mutual aid] was perverted, Kropotkin says, by the superstitions surrounding law, religion and authority, deliberately cultivated by conquerors, exploiters and priests for their own benefit. Morality has therefore become the instrument of ruling classes to protect their privileges" (Baldwin, 2002, p. 79).

Anarchism is against authoritarianism, domination and hierarchies, and anarchists such as Kropotkin promoted equality (Baldwin, 2002, p. 52). However, more recently, debates in anarchism have been more critical of the concept of equality because it is a socially constructed measurement which, in promoting sameness, often can be seen as promoting a restrictive idea of normalcy (Ben-Moshe, Hill, Nocella, & Templer, 2009). For example, disability anarchism, rooted in anarchism and disability studies, challenges the social construction of equality which promotes normalcy, arguing that respect for difference needs to be the basis on which we challenge hierarchy. People with disabilities have also been historically viewed as property and placed in mental wards where they have been tested and experimented on (Corrigan, 2006). Labels have been used to stigmatize those with disabilities for the purpose of controlling, dominating, oppressing, and repressing (Corrigan, 2006). When critiquing capitalism and promoting an alternative economic system, Pierre-Joseph Proudhon, as well as anarcho-communist Peter Kropotkin in *Mutual Aid: A Factor of Evolution* (1972), argued that cooperation within species promotes survival and security. This critiques individualism, competition and the understanding of evolution in terms of a competitive struggle in which only the fittest will survive. Kropotkin's research and studies of indigenous peoples in Siberia guided him to the conclusion that not all human societies are based on competition and individualism, but rather on supportive and voluntary cooperation. Kropotkin writes:

> ANARCHISM, the no-government system of socialism, has a double origin. It is an outgrowth of the two great movements of thought in the economic and the political fields which characterize the nineteenth century, and especially its second part. In common with all socialists, the anarchists hold that private ownership of land, capital, and machinery has had its time; that it is condemned to disappear; and that all requisites for production must, and will, become the common property of society, and be managed in common by the producers of wealth [2002, p. 46].

In kind, Proudhon's 1840 book *What Is Property? Or, an Inquiry into the Principle of Right and Government*, first coined the phrase "property is theft." Proudhon writes:

> Had I to answer the following question: What is slavery? And answer with a single word—Murder—my reasoning would be grasped immediately. I would not need any protracted discourse to demonstrate that the power to strip a man of his mind, his will, his personality, is a power over life and death, and that making a man a slave is tantamount to murder. So why cannot I answer the other query: What is property? In similar vein—Theft—without being assured that I would not be heeded, even though this second proposition is merely a re-casting of the first?

This argument of Proudhon has been put into action by many subsequent activists, including the famous Vietnam War protestors the Berrigan Brothers, who burned draft cards and military documents from a recruitment office (Lynd & Lynd, 1995). Anarchist-motivated property destruction, has, in my analysis, is motivated by the following: (1) symbolic protest (flag burning), (2) liberation (breaking a lock to remove an imprisoned animal), (3) economic sabotage (burning down a McDonalds, and (4) resistance (gluing locks, destroying computers, or burning documents). These four motivations can be sought simultaneously and are not incongruent (more on property destruction below).

Of course, mention of property destruction leads to consideration of what states have determined counts as crimes. Indeed, anarchists have long been interested in criminology, the study of crime, discipline, and punishment. Early anarchists such as Peter Kropotkin and Mikhail Bakunin have argued against state law and authority to control and discipline the people. Anarchist criminology emerged in the 1980s and 1990s through the work of Jeff Ferrell, Larry Tifft, Dennis Sullivan, and others who sought to challenge centralized state authority and the binary of criminal and victim. They advocated for community-based, inclusive direct democracy to determine discipline for harms done (Ferrell, 2002). Anarchist criminology was associated with the development of critical criminology that emerged in the 1970s, and which was influenced by critical and Marxist theory (DeKeseredy and Perry, 2006; Lynch, Michalowski, and Grove, 2006; Taylor, Walton, and Young 1974; Michalowski, 1996). The difference between anarchist criminology and critical criminology is similar to the primary difference between anarchism and Marxism: while anarchists do not want centralized authority and state, Marxism supports the idea of authority by suggesting that the means of production and the state should be controlled by the proletariat and collectively owned.

Anarchism, Animals and the Animal Liberation Front

Animal liberation anarchists argue that by seeing humans as the only beings with value to consider when determining how a community should carry out a task or develop rules is speciesist. Speciesism is the oppression of nonhuman animals by the human species, first coined by Richard D. Ryder in the early 1970s.

Animal liberation anarchists view power through authoritarianism and domination carried out by humans in testing poisonous substances on nonhuman animals, in killing nonhuman domesticated animals for food, and/or in exploiting nonhuman animals for human entertainment. David A. Nibert, in *Animal Rights Human Rights: Entanglements of Oppression and Liberation* (2002), writes that those who relate speciesism to racism, sexism, homophobia, ageism, ableism, and other oppressions "are correct when they assert that speciesism and other forms of oppression are comparable" (p. 8). However, the oppressions are related because of authoritarian institutions, individuals, and systems of domination, *not* because the experiences of oppression are completely parallel. It is for this reason that many argue against directly comparing human slavery, Native American genocide, and the Holocaust to animal (mis)treatment; they are all different experiences and should be treated as distinct and separate. Indeed, one of those components that differentiates human oppression from animal oppression is that the animal liberation movement is populated by those who fight for other species, such as the Animal Liberation Front.

Established in 1976 in Britain, the Animal Liberation Front (ALF) is an international, decentralized, underground, militant organization with open membership to all and no leaders; rather, the identities of those part of the ALF are purposely withheld from the public. The ALF is the most well-known anarchist influenced group in the animal rights movement. Its organizational structure, symbolism, support network, known arrested members, and communiques arise from the history of anarchist activism. And like many anarchists and anarchist organizations that are politically repressed, the ALF has been identified by the Federal Bureau of Investigation (FBI) as the top domestic terrorist organization in the U.S. despite its clearly defined rules. The Animal Liberation Front guidelines, which serve as the ALF's foundational doctrine, are as follows:

1. To liberate animals from places of abuse, i.e., laboratories, factory farms, fur farms, etc., and place them in good homes where they may live out their natural lives, free from suffering.
2. To inflict economic damage to those who profit from the misery and exploitation of animals.
3. To reveal the horror and atrocities committed against animals behind locked doors, by performing nonviolent direct actions and liberations.
4. To take all necessary precautions against harming any animal, human and nonhuman [Best & Nocella, 2004].

It is important to note here that since the ALF's establishment, the organization has engaged in many diverse forms of direct action, yet the group has not harmed one human being.

The ALF's Critique of Capitalism and Property

By destroying property and causing economic sabotage to help free animals in the name of liberation, the ALF provides a compelling critique of corporate capitalist society (Best & Nocella, 2004). The ALF's critique of capitalism is rooted in anarchist and politically-progressive literature and ideas, which is supported by the field of CAS (Best & Nocella, 2004; Best, Nocella, Kahn, Gigliotti, and Kemmerer, 2007; Best, 2009a; Best, 2009b). The ALF targets companies, corporations, universities, and other institutions that exploit, torture, and kill nonhuman animals (Best & Nocella, 2004). Why, then, is this group at the top of the domestic terror list? Property.

Property has a long and important history, especially if one is concerned with social justice, freedom, and economics. Property is defined as anything that a person or group of people owns. Throughout history, property included, but was not limited to, land, plants, bodies of water, air space, ideas, people in debt, People of Color, women, children, nonhuman animals, concepts, and physical entities such as phones, cars, and domiciles. Ownership is constituted by the legal claim of possession and the political and social acceptance of such a claim. Ownership also includes responsibility for one's property. For instance, if one's dog attacks a child, that person would be responsible for the actions of his or her "property." Politically, relations of ownership have been a way to dominate others by individuals, groups, and systems. The concept of private property has been strongly critiqued by anarchists, for the above reasons, but also because it provides an individual ownership, and thus domination, over something or someone, rather than the community having rights to it. In sum, private property ownership trumps the importance and needs of the community. As Bob Torres writes,

> Much as the private property involved in human labor represents the exploitation of humans, the private property involved in human labor represents the exploitation of humans, the private property involved in animal production represents the systematic exploitation of [nonhuman] animals over time [2007, p. 66].

Therefore, the labeling of human and nonhuman animals as private property allows for exploitation for economic, social, religious, and political reasons, including profit. Nonviolence scholar Gene Sharp of *The Politics of Nonviolent Action* (1973), along with the ALF and anarchists, do not see property destruction as violent. Steve Best argues that CAS "challenges not only the property status of animals, but the institution of (corporate controlled) private property itself. Therefore, it is crucial that we continue to develop alternative, broader, alliance-based, bridge-building, anti-capitalist, anti-hierarchical social movements" (2009b, p. 44).

CAS and the ALF argue that nonhuman animals are not property from a moral and socio-political perspective. Gary Francione (1995) argues that animals will be liberated when they are not seen as property in the legal sense:

> The normativity of the law as it concerns animals supports structures regulating animal use that focus our attention on notions like "humane" treatment and "unnecessary" suffering and away from the status of animals as property and the primary consequence of that status: that these terms have completely different legal meanings from the ones they have in ordinary language [p. 199].

In contrast, anarchists argue that social change should be based on morality, not law, which can write rights into effect and, more importantly, write them out.

The FBI identifies the animal rights movement as extremist due to its challenge to the numerous multi-billion dollar industrial complexes serving as the foundation of much of Western society, including the agricultural, medical (including universities and pharmaceutical companies), fashion, technological (including the test and use of animal by-products to develop many types of plastics and computer boards), and entertainment (such as theme parks, zoos, and circuses) industries (Best & Nocella 2004; Best & Nocella 2006a; Lovitz 2010). From the ALF's perspective, maintaining corporate power and the supremacy of capitalism is more important to the U.S. government and intelligence agencies than protecting the lives of nonhuman animals. The ALF resists and challenges these dominative and oppressive roles and systems, and it is for these reasons that they are considered a threat. Let us be very clear on this: their status is not due to directly threatening people, the government, or the democratic process. While they break the law and are criminals under the law, this should not warrant them being the number one top domestic threat in the U.S. (Del Gandio and Nocella 2014).

Animals as Property

Capitalism is rooted in competition and values all things as products and has become one of the most individualist and exploitive economic systems in history (Amster, DeLeon, Fernandez, Nocella, & Shannon, 2009; Harvey, 2007; Klein, 2007). Capitalism places emphasis on accumulating wealth, instead of on community interests, collaboration, group-building, team building, or win-win resolutions where no one loses or is exploited (Kriesberg, 2007). Capitalism promotes a win-lose competitive resolution, while anarchism, grounded in direct democracy and mutual aid, promotes, as noted above, a win-win dynamic if attended to with care (Harvey, 2006; Parenti, 1995; Yuen, Burton-Rose, & Katsiaficas, 2004). Supporters of the capitalist system—such as CEOs of banks and corporations—have become so competitive and interested in profit that the economic leaders within capitalism influence the system to put a value on everything, including birds, trees, water, air, people, and land (Best & Nocella, 2004; Best & Nocella, 2006; Bodley, 2005; Kahn, 2010; Kovel, 2002); we have seen this with the privatization of water in South American countries. In effect, if capitalism has its way, everyone and everything has the potential to become the property of someone else. The definition of property is important for the animal liberation movement, specifically because nonhuman animals are legally deemed property, a cultural norm that animal advocates vehemently argue is wrong. Further, as I have already noted, while anarchists view property as theft, proponents of capitalism and other monetized economic systems identify everything as property with economic value.

Liat Ben-Moshe, a scholar of disability anarchism, believes that "destroying property is a form of economic boycott" (personal communication, January 20, 2011). Michael Loadenthal has noted the following in defense of radical anarchist and underground activist movements: "even when these movements have used 'extreme' tactics such as use of explosives to destroy property, they've taken extreme efforts to not target people; to not injure people and to not instill fear in people" (personal communication, February 16, 2011).

The significant difference between anarchists and capitalists is that the former oppose the concept of property, while the latter view everything as property (Amster et al., 2009). Further, capitalism puts a higher value on material goods such as cars, houses, and clothes than it does on living creatures such as redwood trees, endangered owls, and seals. In a personal interview with Dara Lovitz about the tradition of anarchism, she stated, "If you're just destroying property and no persons are harmed, I don't think that's violent" (January 22, 2011). To defend this argument, Colin Salter, in a personal interview, provided the example of Nazi resisters destroying property such as fences, train tracks, and military equipment (January 30, 2011). Colin noted that factories used to support the German war machine were a target of Danish resistance. Sarat Colling gives the example of members of the Underground Railroad in the U.S. destroying property such as chains and living quarters in order to free the enslaved (personal communication, January 22, 2011).

To add to Loadenthal's comments about not instilling fear, Lovitz stresses, "I don't want to restrict violence to just when your actions result in physical harm [of a being], but threatening physical harm, I think also could be considered violent" (personal communication, January 22, 2011). She goes on to explain in more detail that

> harming could mean the body of a human or nonhuman, so if you're kicking a dog, you're causing physical harm to the body of the nonhuman, so that's violent. But as for the destruction of property—*other* property because technically your dogs are your property, and when I say property, I'm talking about non-living property—the destruction of non-living property I don't see as violent, again unless you do it in a way that causes the person to think that you're going to hurt them next. For example, throwing a vase at somebody's head and missing—just because you missed, it shouldn't be called a nonviolent act [personal communication, January 22, 2011].

While Lovitz is a lawyer, her philosophy of nonhuman animals and property is clearly rooted in anarchist ideas. Jenny Grubbs, an anarchist and animal liberationist, believes that the notion of property stems from legal systems and speciesism (personal communication, January 30, 2011). She argues that nonhuman animals should not be considered property, as slaves once were, for the purpose of economic exploitation or domination, such as in the case of "wives to their husbands" or "dogs to their human owners" (personal communication, January 30, 2011).

A contemporary example of a relationship in which one party is identified by the other as property is the prison system. In the U.S. and in other countries, prisoners are the property of corrections departments. Although the 13th Amendment to the Constitution abolished slavery as many think of it today, slavery is sanctioned in the U.S. if one has been "duly convicted of a crime." Consequently, inmates are used as free or cheap labor within prisons, making products for companies as varied as Victoria's Secret and Microsoft. Prisoners, identified in American history as the property of an owner, live that same dynamic today, but the owner is the state. Prisoners in the U.S., of which there are more than two million, are in the custody of the state (Davis, 2003). This is why the prison industrial complex is one of the largest growing domestic industries in the U.S. and contracts cheap labor to corporations (Davis, 2003; Gilmore, 2007).

Anarchists Are Prison Abolitionists

Anarchists are against all forms of unjust repression and punitive justice, which would, or should, certainly include prisons and the death penalty. This is important because although the animal rights movement does an excellent job of identifying injustices toward nonhuman animals, it does a poor job of promoting justice among humans. Like many social justice activists, animal rights activists perpetuate injustices by uncritically calling for the punishment and imprisonment of those found responsible for cruel and unlawful treatment of nonhuman animals. To use the current criminal justice system to punish those who abuse other species is to support a punitive system that has historically and currently exploited People of Color and people with disabilities.

With the rise of animal advocacy as an intersectional social justice cause, advocates need to address what should be done with those who illegally abuse nonhuman animals and adopt an anarchist analysis of crime and justice. This question of "punishment" must be critically asked by animal advocates who also fight for racial and disability justice because anyone who opposes racism, slavery, and ableism should also oppose prisons and the current criminal justice system. Why? Because injustice does not exist in a vacuum, and to truly understand how oppression works, one should analyze the many ways in which it is manifested. Therefore, anti-racist animal advocates should not support the conviction, sentencing, and incarceration of those who abuse nonhuman animals. While many individuals and organizations advocate for harsh prison sentences for animal abusers, this viewpoint, in effect, promotes slavery, a social injustice inherently connected to mainstream views of nonhuman animals as products and machinery. With so many organizations and individuals within animal rights supporting the current criminal justice system, it must be asked why they would support the same oppressive, repressive and violent institutional structure that labels animal advocates as "terrorists."

The answer is that many animal advocates fail to critique the criminal justice system because they do not understand that this system and the oppression of nonhuman animals are interconnected. Just as nonhuman animals are cheap labor and often property of the state, so too are human prisoners. Beyond just providing free labor to corporations, prisoners are also forced to work in slaughterhouses and on dairy farms. Finally, the criminal justice system protects the very corporations that animal advocates contest. Animal advocates' protests and boycotts, once protected under the 1st Amendment, are now considered illegal and a domestic terrorist threat under laws such as the Animal Enterprise Terrorism Act (AETA) (Del Gandio & Nocella, 2014). Those activists who adopt such once-legal tactics now frequently find themselves arrested, charged, and convicted as criminals and sometimes even as terrorists. As a result, many animal advocates have begun to educate themselves about political repression and unjust laws such as the AETA and ag-gag laws, but many still support the current U.S. justice system via their calls for the imprisonment of people who abuse nonhuman animals.

The Racism Behind Animal Entertainment

Michael Vick, an African American football player, has been vilified for running a dog fighting ring by PETA; Native Americans have been critiqued for hunting by the Sea Shepherd Society; and the Chinese are regularly castigated for eating dog meat by PETA. Animal rights campaigns against historically-oppressed racial groups have been launched by both radical grassroots organizations as well as by corporate international nonprofits. To be clear, Sea Shepherd and PETA did not actively develop campaigns targeting People of Color such as African Americans, Native Americans, and the Chinese. However, their subtle rhetoric against an African American accused of animal abuse, their vilification of native people's hunting traditions, and their emphasis on Chinese food culture is inarguably based on (perhaps unconscious) racist ideologies.

When Michael Vick's dog fighting ring first hit the news, social media was abuzz with commentary focusing on his wealth and status, as if those two facts remove race from the reason he was targeted. As one might expect, the law and race are inherently connected when considering this case. If we examine illegal animal entertainment in the United States, we find cock fighting culturally associated in popular media with Latino communities and dog fighting with African American communities. Compare these standards to *legal* animal entertainment such as bull riding, zoos, rodeos, and marine aquariums, which are seen by many as mere family fun and often advertised with the depiction of smiling white parents and their excited white children.

There are two reasons beyond animal protection here that explain the selection of these issues by advocacy groups. First, the animal rights movement is predominantly comprised of white people and emerged from colonial Western countries. (Of course, intersectional animal rights activists of the West should not be forgotten. For example, Frances Power Cobbe was a suffragist from the U.K. who also founded the British Union for the Abolition of Vivisection in 1898.) Second, targeting the oppressed leads to easily winnable campaigns (a.k.a. the low-hanging fruit). This emphasis on animal rights as Euro-American movement is not to erase the People of Color in the movement, as such a general focus on whiteness might lead one to conclude. In fact, within the last decade, more People of Color have joined the cause, and many of them are challenging racism within the movement from de-colonial perspectives. In this context, focusing on North and Latin America alone, some of these key scholar-activists include Sarat Colling, Breeze Harper, David Pellow, Alma Williams, Kevin Tillman, Lauren Ornelas, Riaz Sayani-Mulji, Nekeisha Alayna Alexis, Federico Alfredo Berghmans, Daniela Romero Waldhorn, Anastasia Yarbrough, Andrea Padilla Villarraga. Veronica Guevara-Lovgren, Rosie Little Thunder, Linda Fisher, and Reyna Crow.

White Privilege Within Political Repression

Another example of white domination of the animal rights movement is the treatment of activists arrested or imprisoned for their role in the modern "green scare," a term used to address the political repression of environmentalists and animal advocates. Not a single radical animal liberation activist has been assassinated, put on Death Row, shot by police, or given a life sentence. While activists have certainly been repressed, most of the animal and eco-activists who have been arrested are privileged, white, able-bodied males with college degrees who are in a position to employ lawyers and successfully use the media and family support to their advantage because they do not have to deal with the stigmas associated with particular racial identities. I suspect that if a group of Black youths bombed a McDonalds for political reasons in the name of the ALF, they would likely receive much harsher penalties than their white peers. Recent racial unrest in the U.S. resulting from police brutality against men of color leads me to this conclusion (for example, Mike Brown, Eric Garner, and Oscar Grant).

It is for this reason that many Black liberationists claim all Black individuals in prison are de facto political prisoners because prison is a modern form of slavery. As previously noted, we only need to read the 13th Amendment to prove that slavery in the U.S. exists in prisons (Davis, 2003). Along with the usual targets, these forms of oppression should be challenged by animal activists who acknowledge the interconnected nature of oppression. They should fight against all forms of oppression because they are interconnected; therefore, they should protest unjust laws, police-imposed curfews, surveillance cameras in predominantly poor communities of color, and the daily police sweeps traumatizing marginalized communities. No one should expect anyone to fight for others such as nonhuman animals if those in question are engaged in daily struggles for basic survival.

The "green scare," concerned as it is with a few select animal and eco-activists, is simply not comparable to the repression that People of Color and people who are poor face on a daily basis. Ida Hammer (2010) cogently explains the dilemma of comparing the oppression of vegans to that of oppressed racial or sexual groups:

> As such, I believe it is inappropriate when we use how other groups are the targets of oppression to describe being vegan or to use their struggles against oppression as a metaphor for the vegan movement. I say this for the simple reason that vegans as a group are not ourselves the targets of oppression [para. 1].

Animal advocates may be politically repressed, but we are not ourselves oppressed. Animal rights activists must remember that their activism is voluntary. People choose to join the animal advocacy movement. They are not forced to join to survive; hence, this is not a struggle for them, but a movement for other species. Their children will not grow up to be incarcerated, beaten, or given a second-rate education because their parents are animal advocates.

Ableism within the Movement

As anarchism is by nature not exclusionary, focus on the culturally marginalized should be a primary goal of anarchist animal advocates. This brings me to further review ableism in the animal rights and liberation movement. To begin, another reason prisons and punitive justice are not the solution to ending animal abuse is that many of those in prisons and jails have mental disabilities. Nicholas Kristof (2014) writes,

> Psychiatric disorders are the only kind of sickness that we as a society regularly respond to not with sympathy but with handcuffs and incarceration. And as more humane and cost-effective ways of treating mental illness have been cut back, we increasingly resort to the law-enforcement toolbox: jails and prisons [para. 3].

In fact, "there are 10 times more mentally ill Americans in prisons and jails than in state psychiatric hospitals" (Lewis, para. 1, 2014). Moreover, "those individuals' conditions often deteriorate while they are incarcerated" (Lewis para. 1, 2014). Consequently, when they are released from prison, they have more personal struggles and social conflicts, which often lead them in three directions: to homelessness, to suicide, or to re-incarceration. The National Alliance on Mental Illness reports that "in 2006, 1,623 children were incarcerated in Minnesota's juvenile justice system. Nationally, approximately 70 percent of youth in juvenile justice systems experience mental health disorders, with 20 percent experiencing a severe mental health condition" (p. 1, 2010). For example, James E. Gates (2014) writes:

> In Mississippi, the largest mental institution is not the State Hospital at Whitfield. It's the East Mississippi Correctional Facility near Meridian, a national study says. A prison or jail is now de facto the largest mental institution in Mississippi and almost every state, says the study released this week by the Arlington, Va.-based Treatment Advocacy Center and the National Sheriffs' Association. The survey found that, in 44 states, the largest institution housing people with severe psychiatric disease is a prison or jail. Nationwide, the study reports an estimated 356,000 mentally ill inmates compared with 35,000 public hospital patients [para. 1–3].

Throughout U.S. history, many mental hospitals and prison facilities were interconnected, periodically swapping institutional roles and populations of inmates between them. Both hospitals and prisons functioned as state mechanisms to institutionalize and control the marginalized, such as women, people with disabilities, People of Color, political dissenters, and the homeless.

In conclusion, Liat Ben-Moshe, a leading scholar on disability studies and prison abolition, writes, "I contend that the deinstitutionalization movements in mental health and developmental disabilities could be construed as historical models to guide us through the transition to decarceration and prison abolition" (2013p. 83). Ben-Moshe goes on to write,

> Closure of repressive institutions, such as mental hospitals and prisons, can be conceptualized as necessary, but not sufficient action on the road to abolition. The most important element in institutional closure is to ensure that people do not end up re-incarcerated in other formats such as groups homes or other institutional placements [Blatt, et al., 1997, p. 84].

Transformative Justice

Being a prison abolitionist is not enough, for the whole U.S. criminal justice system that employs punitive justice must be eliminated so that the death penalty, incarceration and other alternative punishments do not take the place of prisons. Social justice activists cannot on one hand demand the end of oppression and repression, while on the other hand demand violence and torture via the prison system. Alternatives to punitive justice do exist and are being embraced by anarchists such as mediation, transformative justice, and conflict transformation (Nocella, 2011). These alternatives are not possible if society does not end its oppressive relationship between ownership and property, which is the essence of capitalism and all forms of domination. Alternatives to punitive justice are possible if we take from ecology the reality that all elements and life are interwoven and interdependent. Thus a new system is needed. This new system should not be in the form of "mock-capitalism," or "conscientious capitalism" to use the terminology of John Mackey (founder of Whole Foods) and Rajendra Sisodia (2013); however, this is the current direction of most of the animal liberation movement. Nonprofit organizations are teaming up with natural, "humane" food corporations such as Whole Foods Markets and Amy's Kitchen vegetarian and vegan convenience foods, but they do not advocate for animal liberation. Animal advocates need to put animal liberation back into the conversation when educating people about veganism and not speak about self-interests such as health and looking attractive or sexy. Animal advocacy, like all social movements, is a battle over cultural values. Beyond challenging consumer capitalism (such as shopping at Whole Foods or buying Amy's Kitchen products), we need to do away with this processed fake-meat mass consumption-based culture, which is based on a capitalist culture of violence and oppression toward other species. This is entirely achievable, but it involves addressing our own oppressive personal behavior as well as wider social systems of domination.

Conclusion

We need to break down our walls of dogma and begin to have truly transformative critical dialogues with those we do not agree with or deem an enemy; however, we should not have these dialogues to control or manipulate, or to generate a media spectacle, but to listen, share, and learn. As a criminologist, I strive to educate and inform law enforcement practitioners and students who want to be involved with the administration of criminal justice about practices and systems that are not punitive, colonial, ableist, racist, classist, ageist, sexist, and anti–LGBTTQIA. We cannot strive to take down a system with no alternatives in place. Police are not machines, and behind this punitive career choice are often working-class people, many of whom want to make their communities safer. The problem is that through the media and school settings, such as in college, and police academies, citizens are taught that the way to make everyone safe is through control, force, weapons, and punitive justice. Consequently, there is no such thing as a non-punitive police officer because this career is based on a punitive model. To use an analogy, if someone knows the way out of a burning building (i.e., the punitive justice system), but does not tell anyone the route, he is to blame if someone perishes in the fire. Some people, because of their identity and status, are forced to engage with police, while others, notably whites most often can avoid police because of their socio-political and economic status. I suggest that those with privilege should consider exploiting their position by educating those in power about racism, domination, and oppressive behaviors and encouraging them to reflect on their own beliefs and practices. Moreover, many anti-racist educators and trainers stress that white people need to speak to white people about racism, as opposed to putting that responsibility on People of Color. Moreover, white people are often more open and honest about their racism when in related company and are more willing to listen and learn from fellow white people, rather than becoming defensive in response to People of Color who promote anti-racist and decolonization education.

Malcolm X once said, "Education is our passport to the future." It is education—not dogma, lack of communication, and shaming others—that will lead to community among disparate groups. Some people, sometimes understandably, critique me for engaging and working with police departments, the military, and the FBI Academy because I write a lot about the ELF and ALF and am involved in social movements. Of course, people should not speak to anyone at all, not just law enforcement, about anything that could aid in getting someone or a group arrested, investigated, repressed, convicted, framed, murdered, or incarcerated. Everything I know about the ELF and ALF is in books, which law enforcement read, so when I speak to them about conflict transformation and their repressive behaviors, I am not naïve about changing all of their minds, but I am interested in sharing my knowledge with others for three reasons: (1) to learn about their punitive, controlling, and repressive educational practices and pedagogy; (2) in hope that speaking truth to power will at least get one or two current or future law enforcement agents to be more critical; and (3) to speak about alternatives to punitive justice. This is not a reformist agenda. For example, I do not support system reforms such as cameras on police or in neighborhoods or cultural sensitivity training; rather, I talk on behalf of Save the Kids (a fully-volunteer national grass-roots organization dedicated to alternatives and the end of the incarceration of all youth and the school to prison pipeline) and other organizations involved in the Ferguson Movement about how punitive justice is dominating and oppressive to people and communities and can never uplift, heal, or empower people and communities.

A just, transformative, equitable, inclusive and holistic community is possible when we acknowledge, educate, share, take accountability and responsibility, and build critical and holistic dialectical bridges against all systems of domination (including those against other species) in hopes of ending police, prisons, property, and punitive justice. Transformative justice was brought about by Black liberationists, Quaker prison abolitionists, and first people in Canada who co-organized the International Conference on Penal Abolition, which is still going. Transformative justice builds on restorative justice, a justice system developed by Mennonites, but was influenced by aboriginal people in New Zealand. Transformative justice addresses three concerns that restorative justice does not: (1) an elimination of all systems of domination; (2) intersectional identity politics when viewing conflict, crime or harm; and (3) being opposed to any form of policing, imprisonment, or punitive justice. Transformative justice is grounded in a voluntary process of healing and accountability that empowers community, promotes individual respect, challenges the socially constructed binary of victim and offender, builds holistic critical education that fosters safer and supportive spaces, collaborates with others using mutual aid, and encourages principles and values built on direct democracy.

REFERENCES

Albert, M. (1997). *Thinking forward: Learning to conceptualize economic vision.* Winnipeg: Arbeiter Ring.
Amster, R., DeLeon, A., Fernandez, L., Nocella, A. J., II., & Shannon, D. (2009). *Contemporary anarchist studies: An introductory anthology to anarchy in the academy.* New York: Routledge.
Ben-Moshe, L. (2013). "The tension between abolition and reform." In *The end of prisons: Reflections from the decarceration movement.* New York: Rodopi. Pp. 83–92.
Berkman, A. (2003). *What is anarchism?* Oakland: AK Press.
Best, S. (2009a). "Rethinking revolution: Total liberation, alliance politics, and a prolegomena to resistance movements in the twenty-first century." In R. Amster, A. DeLeon, L. Fernandez, A.J. Nocella, II, & D. Shannon (Eds.). *Contemporary anarchist studies: An introductory anthology of anarchy in the academy,* (189–199). New York: Routledge.
Best, S. (2009b). "The Rise of Critical Animal Studies: Putting Theory into Action and Animal Liberation into Higher Education." *Journal for Critical Animal Studies.* VII, no. I. Pp. 9–52.
Best, S., & Nocella, II, A. J. (2004). *Terrorists or freedom fighters?: Reflections on the liberation of animals.* New York: Lantern Books.
Best, S., & Nocella, II, A. J. (2006a). *Igniting a revolution: Voices in defense of the Earth.* Oakland: AK Press.
Best, S., Nocella, A. J., II, Kahn, R., Gigliotti, C., & Kemmerer, L. (2007). "Introducing Critical Animal Studies." *Journal of Critical Animal Studies* 5(1), 1–2.
Bodley, J. H. (2005). *Cultural anthropology: Tribes, states, and the global system.* New York: McGraw Hill.
Bowen, J. (2004). "Moving targets: Rethinking anarchist strategies." In Purkis, J. & Bowen, J. (Eds.), *Changing anarchism: Anarchist theory and practice in a global age,* pp. 117–128. Manchester: Manchester University Press.
Chomsky, N. (2005). *Imperial ambitions: Conversations on the post–9/11 world.* New York: Metropolitan Books.
Corrigan, P. W. (2006). *On the stigma of mental illness: Practical strategies for research and social change.* Washington, D.C.: American Psychological Association.

Davis, A.Y. (2003). *Are prisons obsolete?* New York: Seven Stories Press.
Day, R. (2004). "From hegemony to affinity: The political logic of the newest social movements." *Cultural Studies 18*, 716–748.
Dunayer, J. (2004). *Speciesism*. Derwood, MD: Ryce Publishing.
DeKeseredy, W. S., & Perry, B. (2006). *Advancing critical criminology: Theory and application*. New York: Lexington Books.
Del Gandio, J. & Nocella II, A. J. (2014). *The terrorization of dissent: Corporate repression, legal corruption, and the Animal Enterprise Terrorism Act*. New York: Lantern Books.
Dominick, B. (1997). *Animal liberation and social revolution: A vegan perspective on anarchism or an anarchist perspective on veganism*. Retrieved on September 14, 2011 from http://theanarchistlibrary.org/HTML/Brian_A._Dominick__Animal_Liberation_and_Social_Revolution.html.
Ferrell, J. (1997). "Against the law: Anarchist criminology." In D. MacLean and D. Milovanovic (Eds.), *Thinking critically about crime*. Vancouver: Collective Press.
Francione, G. (1995). *Animals property & the law*. Philadelphia: Temple University Press.
Guerin, D. (1970). *Anarchism*. New York: Monthly Review Press.
Gates, J. E. (2014). *Prisons largest mental institutions, study shows*. Retrieved October 1, 2014, from http://www.clarionledger.com/story/news/local/2014/04/09/prisons-largest-mental-institutions-study-shows/7533905/.
Guerin, D. (2005). *No gods no masters: An anthology of anarchism*. Oakland: AK Press.
Hammer, I. (2010). *Why "vegan oppression"' cannot exist*. Retrieved October 16, 2014, from http://veganideal.mayfirst.org/content/why-vegan-oppression-cannot-exist.
Harvey, D. (2006). *Spaces for global capitalism: Towards a theory of uneven geographical development*. New York: Verso.
Harvey, D. (2007). *A brief history of neoliberalism*. Oxford: Oxford University Press.
Kahn, R. (2010). *Critical pedagogy, ecoliteracy, & planetary crisis: The ecopedagogy movement*. New York, NY: Peter Lang.
Klein, N. (2007). *The shock doctrine*. New York: Metropolitan Books.
Kovel, J. (2002). *The enemy of the nature: The end of capitalism or the end of the world?* New York: Zed Books.
Kriesberg, L. (2007). *Constructive conflicts: From escalation to resolution*. Lanham, MD: Roman & Littlefield.
Kristof, N. "Inside a mental hospital called jail." Retrieved October 1, 2014, from http://www.nytimes.com/2014/02/09/opinion/sunday/inside-a-mental-hospital-called-jail.html?_r=0.
Kropotkin, P. (2002). *Anarchism: A collection of revolutionary writings*. Mineola, NY: Dover Publications.
Lewis, R. (2014). "U.S. prisons home to 10 times more mentally ill than state hospitals." Retrieved October 1, 2014, from http://america.aljazeera.com/articles/2014/4/8/mental-illness-prison.html.
Lovitz, D. (2010). *Muzzling a movement: The effects of anti-terrorism law, money & politics on animal activism*. New York: Lantern Books.
Lynch, M. J., Michalowski, R. J., & Groves, B. (2006). *Primer in radical criminology: Critical perspectives on crime, power, & identity*. Monsey, NY: Criminal Justice Press.
Lynd, S., & Lynd, A. (1995). *Nonviolence in America: A documentary history*. Maryknoll, NY: Orbis Books.
Mackey, J., & Sisodia, R. (2013). *Conscious capitalism*. Cambridge: Harvard Business Review Press.

Michalowski, R. J. (1996). "Critical criminology and the critique of domination: The story of an intellectual movement." *Critical Criminology* 7:9–16.

National Alliance on Mental Illness (2010). "NAMI state advocacy 2010: State statistics: Minnesota." Retrieved October 1, 2014, from http://www.nami.org/ContentManagement/ContentDisplay.cfm?ContentFileID=93502.

Nibert, D. A. (2002). *Animal rights human rights: Entanglements of oppression and liberation.* Lanham, MD: Roman & Littlefield.

Nocella II, A. J. (2011). "An overview of the history and theory of transformative justice." *Peace & conflict review* 6, no. 1. Pg. 1–10.

Parenti, M. (1995). *Against empire.* San Francisco: City Lights Books.

Proudhon, P. J. (1840). *What is property? An inquiry into the principle of right and of government.* Auckland: Floating Press.

Purkis, J., & Bowen, J. (2004). *Changing anarchism: Anarchist theory and practice in a global age.* Manchester: Manchester University Press.

Rabinow, P. (1984). *The Foucault reader.* New York: Pantheon.

Ryder, R. D. (1983). *Victims of science: The use of animals in research.* Rev. ed. London: National Anti-Vivsection Society Limited.

Sharp, G. (1973). *The politics of nonviolent action.* Boston: Porter Sargent.

Singer, P. (1990). *Animal liberation.* New York: Avon Books.

Taylor, I., Walton, P., & Young, J. (1974). *The new criminology: For a social theory of deviance.* New York: Harper and Row.

Tolstoy, L. (2010). *The Kingdom of god is within you.* Charleston, SC: Createspace.

Torres, B. (2007). *Making a killing: The political economy of animal rights.* Oakland: AK Press.

Yuen, E., Burton-Rose, D., & Katisiaficas, G. (2004). *Confronting capitalism: Dispatches from global movement.* Brooklyn: Soft Skull Press.

Doing Liberation
The Story and Strategy of Food Not Bombs
DREW ROBERT WINTER

> The name Food Not Bombs states our most fundamental principle: society needs to promote life, not death. Implement the positive and end cooperation with the negative. Live in a world of abundance and stop fearing a future of scarcity. Celebrate with love, not hate; cooperation instead of domination; and compassion, not exploitation.
> —Keith McHenry, Food Not Bombs co-founder

Few organizations can do what Food Not Bombs does. Surprising, given that taking excess food from local bakeries and supermarkets and publicly feeding it to the hungry every week requires only a handful of bodies and almost no money. Yet it is not an easy thing to be at once so radical, yet so uncontroversial—or, to make those who find it controversial to feed the hungry, appear ridiculous. In doing so, FNB members were able to turn a police crackdown on their activities in San Francisco—a process that included hundreds of arrests—into a galvanizing moment that saw an intense outpouring of local support and, over time, the rise of hundreds of FNB chapters across the globe, making it one of the most recognizable and palatable anarchist organizations of our time. Of course this success is in part due to the ever-encroaching capitalist machine that is slowly strangling the Earth's inhabitants—Food Not Bombs is responding to something that demands a response, and its founders would be the first to say so. But few movements against the status quo survive—indeed thrive—with as much resilience.

What follows is the product of a combination of personal experience, traditional research, and interviews with other Food Not Bombs participants—primarily two interviews with FNB's co-founder and perhaps its chief historian, Keith McHenry, in late January 2014. My own experience with Food Not Bombs occurred with the Norfolk chapter in 2010, and its history is likely as unique as just about every other branch. Although a small group fraught with the complexities and tensions that accompany many an organization, my participation in Virginia left me convinced of the transformative power of FNB's simple and inclusive program for community building and worldwide solidarity, with both humans and nonhumans.

The set of simple principles, lack of central leadership, and utterly inarguable main goals (to feed the hungry and "promote life, not death" [FNB, a] create ripe grounds for reproduction, and allow a wide cross-section of the public to take part in these potentially revolutionary activities without being forced to adhere to some or other doctrine. Embedded within the group's simplicity is the ability to maintain a radical organization that promotes community-building, social action, consensus, and earth/animal liberation. The anarchist principles of equality (as opposed to hierarchy), and solidarity (as opposed to charity) have allowed FNB chapters to spring up by the hundreds around the world without a central administration or budget, and the otherwise open-ended nature allows every chapter to articulate itself on its own terms and within their own situated context. This approach has allowed for an organic, bottom-up cultivation of unique but allied ventures, rather than a one-size-fits-all branch dictated from afar by a non-profit administration that is all too often subdued by the whims of its donors, bullied into submission by authorities, and insensitive to the myriad sociocultural forces that must be negotiated on the ground in each case. The result is a process (not an ideology) that unites animal liberation with a host of other issues much more readily championed by the Left—a relationship I believe is necessary, but oftentimes difficult to bridge in North America (Sanbonmatsu, 2011, cited in Kymlicka, 2013). With these unfortunate tensions in mind, the way exploitation and marginalization of many different groups is bound together in the praxis of Food Not Bombs is something to be particularly treasured and examined when developing strategies and campaigns.

What Does Food Not Bombs Do?

The Food Not Bombs process is fairly simple: obtain excess food that would otherwise be thrown out by local stores, cook it with pots and pans donated or purchased with donated money, and serve it to anyone who wants it, while offering free literature and conversation about the problems of the world. It requires no paid staff, no headquarters, almost no monetary donations (minus what's required to procure cooking supplies and folding tables), and—perhaps most importantly—no particular ideological commitment, except the belief that food shouldn't be wasted, and hungry people should be fed. Some chapters are more overtly political than others, taking part in more demonstrations and serving up more literature with their meals. Some are more committed to ideas of animal liberation and veganism than others. But all follow the three principles of Food Not Bombs (see Figure 1):

Figure 1: The 3 Principles of Food Not Bombs

1. The food is always vegan or vegetarian and free to everyone without restriction, rich or poor, stoned or sober.
2. Food Not Bombs has no formal leaders or headquarters, and every group is autonomous and makes decisions using the consensus process.
3. Food Not Bombs is dedicated to nonviolent direct action and works for nonviolent social change [See FNB, b].

Food Not Bombs' history is rich with ties to animal liberation—the founders of the first chapter were entirely vegetarian. Moreover, they counted their four dogs "as equals in the collective." Prominent animal rights activists, such as Andy Stepanian of the SHAC 7, took part in Food Not Bombs, and after leaving prison for his actions against the vivisectors at Huntington Life Sciences, vowed on the news program *Democracy Now!* to return to Food Not Bombs as soon as his probation was up. FNB delivers food to the Sea Shepherd crews whenever they come into port. Keith McHenry, a long-time attendee of the Animal Rights National Conference, found that many people in attendance told him they went vegan and became concerned for animals because of Food Not Bombs. Offering free, meatless food to the public brings people together in the act of eating to create community, which opens up the space to have critical conversations about the world, all the while familiarizing the palette with appealing meat-free cuisine. The organization was founded by anarchists and operates on anarchist principles although it does not formally identify as such. Nor does it formally identify as an animal liberation organization even though many of its members do, and it takes a principled stance against violence to animals. This process of doing rather than saying, or showing rather than telling, is a key to FNB's success as an organization in replicating itself, as well as the ethical ideas behind its founding, even though—and in fact precisely because—those ideas remain unnamed.

A Brief, Selected History

McHenry and other co-founders with Food Not Bombs have extensively covered the group's development in their books *Food Not Bombs* (2000) and its successor *Hungry for Peace: How you Can Help End Poverty and War with Food Not Bombs* (2012), which also offer step-by-step instructions on starting and running your own FNB chapter. Interviews and lectures abound on the internet. The majority of factual and historical information that this chapter draws on is based on two phone interviews in early 2014 with McHenry, as well as his writings and recorded talks. McHenry's accounts differ significantly from the allegations of municipal and police officials (some of which are documented in this essay), but their side has been amply documented in press releases and the popular press. A selection of major events is also available on www.foodnotbombs.net. The autonomous nature of Food Not Bombs chapters and the sheer number of them eliminates any pretense of an exhaustive, authoritative history. What follows is a selected overview of major activities that defined the organization and popularized its concept to reproduce additional chapters across the globe. These events provide necessary context for understanding how FNB has the reputation it has today.

The organization that became Food Not Bombs began from eight residents of Boston and Cambridge, Massachusetts: Jo Swanson, Mira Brown, Susan Eaton, Brian Feigenbaum, C.T. Lawrence Butler, Jessie Constable, Amy Rothstein and Keith McHenry. They would also like to emphasize that their four dog friends—Jasmine, Arrow, Sage, and Yoda—played an important role in bringing the original collective together: Jasmine gave birth to a litter of puppies, cared for by friends who eventually moved in together. The dogs then became crucial to waking members at the appropriate time for their morning walks, which allowed the collective to arrive at bakeries in the early morning to collect food to distribute. Of this initial eight, Keith McHenry is FNB's most visible advocate today, managing foodnotbombs.net and traveling the country to give the oral history of the group. Although adamantly a non-leader, numerous authorities have persecuted him as such with extensive false charges, wiretapping, and even an undercover Interpol agent who managed to get him removed from FNB San Francisco (personal communication, January 31, 2014). Currently blacklisted from work in the United States, McHenry "works" for Food Not Bombs full time as a coordinator and mentor.

The notion of serving food for a radical cause was initially a fundraising effort to help a friend, Brian Fiegenbaulm, arrested during the May 24, 1980, occupation of the Seabrook Nuclear Power Plant. The group decided to hold a bake sale to raise funds for Fiegenbaulm's bail. This attempt failed, but the group tried again. This time, using an old banner with the slogan "It will be a great day when our schools get the money they need and the air force has to hold a bake sale to buy a bomber," the group donned military uniforms purchased from a local army surplus store, and held another bake sale asking patrons to contribute to the purchase of a new warplane. This endeavor fell well short of the $280 million required to purchase a B-1 nuclear bomber, but they were inspired to see their message reach a larger crowd. Over the course of the next year, McHenry was regularly delivering five to six cases of food to a local housing project, salvaged from his job at an organic food coop called "Bread and Circus." Across the street from this project was large, glass building. This was the location where the guidance system for new intercontinental ballistic missiles was being developed. One year after their first protest, on March 26, 1981, the group produced pamphlets revealing that the directors of the Bank of Boston, the Public Service Company of New Hampshire, and local building contractors were all the same people. FNB members dressed as "hobos" and handed out food, saying that current government policies would lead to mass homelessness. They were right—although FNB initially fed many middle class, employed people, the 1980s and the Reagan presidency drastically reduced federal funding for social programs and homelessness skyrocketed. The event fed 70 people, rich and poor, and inspired the nascent group to do Food Not Bombs full time.

Driving around town with the excess food they collected, the group supplied Rosie's Place, a local battered women's shelter, local soup kitchens, and finally the Boston Commons, where they would set up tables and hand out free meals and literature. Local musicians often played to entertain patrons and servers. From this routine the group expanded their actions to include a variety of creative acts of political theatre and art. They produced their own films about U.S. intervention in El Salvador, where it was funding death squads. When a tent was set up beside them asking locals to take the "Pepsi Challenge," FNB decided to hold a "tofu smoothie challenge," proclaiming that "there's more nutrition in this one cup of smoothie than in all the Pepsi on Earth." Handing out brochures on Coca-Cola's hiring of death squads to kill labor organizers in Guatemala was not appreciated, even by their rivals at Pepsi. The corporation sought—unsuccessfully—to have Food Not Bombs removed from the location (McHenry, personal communication, January 31, 2014).

San Francisco

McHenry moved to San Francisco in 1988 and received a grant from American Peace Test, an anti-nuclear weapons group, to serve food to protesters for ten days at a Nevada nuclear testing site. Food was handed out at the site's main gate, while protesters were arrested for camping out to prevent nuclear bombs from exploding. Here, McHenry met another group that had been inspired by their own work in Boston, but called themselves "Bread Not Bombs" in fear of copyright infringement. This worry was quickly quashed by the FNB team and the group's second branch was born. They set up at the entrance to Golden Gate Park from noon until 3 p.m. every Monday—the one day per week when food was not served in the Haight-Ashbury district. The feeding was successful, and one day someone suggested to the members that they obtain a permit from the city to continue the feeding. They submitted a request, but repeated inquiries by FNB members seemed to imply no one at the parks department really knew what they were talking about. These attempts were of little concern to the 45 riot police who, on August 15, 1988, emerged from the woods and arrested nine servers. Despite this attack on the organization, they were immediately besieged with calls from excited and concerned citizens saying things like "How can we get arrested with you guys? This is great!" In response to the crackdown, the group called on people to join in a March, and encouraged demonstrators to bang pots and pans. One patron even brought a self-made painting of the *Star Trek* character Spock— apparently highlighting that police arresting people for feeding the hungry is highly illogical. The march of about 150 people resulted in 29 arrests, with then-nascent news organization CNN capturing footage that spread internationally. Images of the arrests created another, larger surge of support, with people from all over the world calling and writing letters asking how they, too, could get arrested for feeding the hungry. So, the group made a flier— seven steps to starting a Food Not Bombs. The following week, 500 people arrived at the feeding. SFPD public relations officer Jerry Senkir defended the arrests, saying, "There has to be some kind of [police] action. At this point it seems to be a political statement on their [Food Not Bombs] part, not a food give-away issue." In 1989, following additional arrests, SFPD Captain Dennis Martel echoed Senkir's sentiments, saying, "They don't want to feed the hungry, they just want to make an anarchist-type statement and we aren't going to allow it" (McHenry, personal correspondence, January 31, 2014; FNB, c).

Members object to the demand they abolish their message because, they say, they are not an apolitical charity; Food Not Bombs does not offer charity—they offer solidarity. The following week drew 2,000 people, and the police made 54 arrests before giving up (http://foodnotbombs.net/fnb_time_line.html). Facing this losing battle, then-mayor of San Francisco Arthur Agnos created a permit and offered it to FNB in order to stop the arrests. Serving food in Golden Gate Park went unchallenged until Agnos was succeeded by Francis Jordan in January 1992, but the city's homeless were still under attack. Servers began hearing of repeated stories of homeless people being woken in the middle of the night by police and forced to move. In response, an occupation began at Civic Center Plaza, near City Hall, calling it "Tenement Square" in reference to the Chinese occupation of Tiananmen Square. A 24-hour vegetarian restaurant was set up by Food Not Bombs in front of City Hall, portable toilets were brought in, and trash pickup became self-managed (the city called off trash pickup). Poetry readings and concerts were held each day as politicians entered and exited the City Hall. Twenty-seven days later, the mayor announced a solution for the homeless: an abandoned jaguar dealership could be their new home. But only two shopping bags worth of belongings were allowed, it was for men only, there were no mattresses or food, and animals could not be kept there but instead had to be surrendered to animal control, likely to be killed. Seeing this "solution" as unsatisfactory, the Food Not Bombs crew returned to Civic Center Plaza and continued to serve lunch, where sixteen people were arrested and food confiscated. Sensing this would happen in the future, the group devised a plan—they would divide their food, and their servers, into thirds. For dinner, one third of the food was brought out for serving, with the police capturing the servers and taking the food as predicted. Once they had gone, more servers brought out another portion of food and began serving. They, too, were arrested. Finally, the remains of the food were handed out to several hundred people without incident—the police either did not know or were too embarrassed by their own inefficacy to continue arresting people.

This routine continued for about a month, with servers dividing the food into thirds and being hauled off by SFPD each day. Facing imminent burnout, the group decided to invite others to join them, calling their campaign "Risk Arrest One Day Per Month With Food Not Bombs." Nuns and priests came first to be arrested for serving food—awarding the added comedy of seeing cops pat them down for weapons—and were followed by the local carpenters' union, teachers unions, peace groups, and others. The peaceful coalition continued to be arrested twice a day for the crime of feeding the hungry. That is, until the San Francisco earthquake shut down the city, and the police showed up for several meals in a row because Food Not Bombs was the only reliable food provider in the city. FNB proved able not only to ally itself with a diversity of factions, but showed it had the power to make even its arch-enemies dependent upon it.

First International Gathering, Repression, and Pushing Columbus Back Out to Sea

In 1992 the U.S. Congress voted San Francisco the site to celebrate 500 years since Columbus landed in the new world. This prompted American Indian and other indigenous groups to call a meeting to take action against the ceremony. On October 9, 1992, Food Not Bombs held its first international gathering, drawing about 75 people from the roughly 30 chapters then in existence. It was at this gathering where the group's principles—that every chapter would remain autonomous, there would be no leaders, and all food would be vegetarian or vegan—were affirmed by consensus. The following day, the activists served food to American Indian activists who met the ceremonial Columbus's boat as it approached the shore, and pushed him back out to sea. The Niña, the Pinta, and the Santa María—floats for the parade—were then appropriated by Food Not Bombs members and driven away, much to the ire of the Italian American Association who apparently didn't like visitors showing up uninvited and taking things from them. The action was yet another inspiration for more chapters to spring up.

Francis Jordan would take mayoral office in 1992. The former chief of police ran on an anti-homeless platform, and police units began fining and arresting the homeless. The longstanding tent encampment in Gold Gate Park was bulldozed (Mac Donald, 1994). He even received an airplane from the Justice Department equipped with thermal imaging devices to fly over San Francisco and identify homeless people to be rounded up (FNB, d). When this happened, FNB was on the scene. Obtaining a video camera from the American Civil Liberties Union (ACLU), FNB members recorded police ordering homeless people to throw their shoes in garbage trucks, confiscating sleeping bags, and kidnapping their animal companions. One of the most famous scenes caught on tape was an elderly grandmother struggling with police over a photo album, eventually ripping it from her arms to be trashed. This coverage was given to local TV companies and shown on Oakland's Channel 2, infuriating the mayor for making his "Matrix" program appear inhumane. He immediately obtained an injunction against serving food without a permit and ordered the Parks Department to delete the permit process. Predictably, this did not stop FNB, and organizations again heeded the call to risk arrest to feed the hungry. Food Not Bombs responded to the mayor's anti-homeless policies with demonstrations, and eventually began a campaign called "Homes Not Jails" to obtain keys to abandoned houses that were given to homeless families. Squats organized from HNJ have housed thousands of homeless people since 1992 (Corr, 1999, p. 36). But repression of the group continued.

In 1994 FNB asked the Clinton Administration's civil rights division to send federal marshals to protect them from the San Francisco police, who by now were regularly beating them (FNB, e). The request fell on deaf ears, but in 1995, after a mass-arrest during the 50th anniversary of the United Nations near the monument to the Universal Declaration of Human Rights, they received support (FNB, f). Amnesty International wrote letters (FNB, g) to the California governor declaring that anyone convicted would be considered prisoners of conscience. McHenry, among others, attempted to hand-deliver the letter to the city after suffering repeated arrests and beatings, each of which also meant criminal charges. Not only did the supervisor refuse the letter, but she slammed the door on McHenry so hard that it broke glass, cutting his hand. At the hospital he was arrested and charged with assault with a deadly weapon—allegedly breaking the glass himself and attempting to cut the supervisor. Fortunately, occupations of the courthouse and political theatre by members made the trial go nowhere. The case was eventually transferred to a new judge, Lucy McCabe, who dropped most of the charges, the three strikes against him, gave him credit for time served in jail, and allowed him to write his own probation (Brazil, 1995). McHenry was symbolically labeled a felon and decided that his probation would be to forbid him from killing anyone or blowing up any buildings for twelve months.

Many magnificent and terrifying events have occurred during and since the span covered above. Food Not Bombs continues to grow engage in diverse, creative activities: in 2003, FNB Zagreb went to McDonald's and served people with balloons bearing golden arches that read "Eat shit in Croatia," bringing a freshly-killed cow head to highlight the cruelty behind a McDonald's burger; FNB Serbia was serving food while U.S. warplanes were dropping bombs on them; St. Petersburg suffered numerous attacks and beatings from neo–Nazi groups, with a pipe bomb going off at their location that only spared human lives because the members arrived late. Food Not Bombs was something of a joke in Iceland, where poverty was extremely low, indeed nonexistent—until the banking collapse that paralyzed the country. Each feed-in was followed by a march to the Parliament. FNB fed rescue workers on 9/11, protesters at the 1999 World Trade Organization protests in Seattle, and at Occupy Wall Street and innumerable other occupations. They fed the Orange Revolution in the Ukraine, striking farmworkers in Sarajevo, and the workers occupying the window and door factory featured in Michael Moore's "Capitalism: A Love Story." When Hurricane Katrina hit, Food Not Bombs was one of the only sources of relief food, and the Red Cross was directing people to FNB locations. When Czechoslovakia split, Slovakian FNB activists resolved to mitigate problems with stray animals by opening 20 rescue shelters.

The constant, unremitting challenges to FNB members feeding their communities by the State would have quickly broken a centralized and hierarchized organization. Their funding could have been drained, their leaders jailed, their offices raided and equipment confiscated. Cut off from centralized leadership, local branches formulated on the basis of taking marching orders from a headquarters would be aimless and dissolve instantly. But with autonomous cells operating on consensus, groups can share information and coordinate without suffering from any particular bottleneck for material or ideological resources—every group has their own pots, and they maintain their morale with each other, as a collective.

Showing, Not Telling: It's Not What Food Not Bombs Is, But What They Do

Reading through the history of Food Not Bombs, the group's values become readily apparent. Food Not Bombs is not just a group to feed the hungry, although they do that; they are not just a group that fights against unfair trade laws, although they do that; they are not just a group campaigning for an end to poverty, war, environmental disaster, sexism, racism, or speciesism, although they do all of that; they are not just a group of anarchists, although all of their founding members are proudly anarchists and the group is thoroughly anarchist in its structure. There was some debate about whether to identify the group as anarchist, but McHenry said in the end the group decided it would be needlessly alienating. "It's more important to do anarchism than be called anarchist." (This is not a universal: FNBs in the Philippines and Indonesia seem especially fond of the circle-A symbol.) FNB is notoriously effective in recruiting new participants and gaining public support precisely because it is not tied down with a lot of politically-charged labels; the egalitarian values and acts of compassion it embodies are able to reach a wide cross-section of the population without bearing the weight of words chained to decades or centuries of smears and propaganda. They are able to construct a discourse about their activities that seems to fit snugly within the realm of common sense: "Why should it be a crime to feed the hungry?" "How come we can spend as much money on the military as the rest of the world combined, but can't afford to pay our teachers?" "Killing animals is violence." Rather than attempting to sell the public on an ideology, Food Not Bombs is a practice in which people can participate. Thus, that practice of feeding the hungry is the central axis of a pinwheel that simultaneously is receptive to the whole spectrum of agendas, without itself articulating those agendas and driving off the uninitiated. Accordingly, Food Not Bombs does not itself fight for animal liberation as such—it *enacts* a prefigurative politics of animal liberation by filling people up without dead animals, and therefore obviates the notion of exploiting nonhumans for revolutionary purposes. The practices, which are not immediately understood as hostile to the status quo, are experienced in concrete form by participants. This experience helps to inoculate them against the poison that has been attached to the labels for these practices by reactionary propagandists. The truths on which Food Not Bombs bases its actions are practiced as if they are too self-evident to require a name, and that mindset is indeed contagious. When the original eight members started the first chapter of Food Not Bombs, they were all vegetarian and more or less vegan, even though none of them were aware of the word "vegan" at the time. In fact, McHenry recounts, they never even had a collective conversation about vegetarianism—it was merely something so obviously appropriate it didn't require a discussion.

    Within this single non-act is a seed of immense power: the act of behaving as if it's obvious to behave that way. Even the most reactionary rhetoric has not found a way to oppose the central act of FNB—feeding the hungry. It's a concept that is ubiquitously virtuous throughout history and across religions, advocated by every religious figure who hasn't been smeared, painted white, and claimed to support the Republican Party. Even today, as the tendrils of unfettered capitalism and its death prayer of myopic self-interest find ever increasing ways to slither out of our computers, televisions, and ear buds, the idea of arresting people for feeding the hungry is anathema to most of our basic assumptions. Humans are mimetic creatures—we look at those around us and adapt our behavior to them, internalizing behavior around us as normal. Seeing people routinely serving free food—and being arrested for it—is a moment for a spark that can inspire action, just as every mass arrest of Food Not Bombs activists has led to more chapters taking root. They're not preaching an economic system or a philosophical doctrine that may appear affected or arrogant and requires intense study to comprehend; they're not vandalizing property that requires participants to risk their lives; they're not peddling a feeble and uninspired consumer solution or asking for money—they're humbly and selflessly enacting the epitome of preserving life: serving food. A basic human need is being met, and it requires no sacrifice on the part of those who would take advantage of it.

This direct and visible aid to the community not only builds solidarity and saves lives in the moment, but it is a revolutionary tool that has proven crucial in sustaining ruptures in the capitalist fabric; ruptures that have altered the public consciousness, such as Occupy Wall Street and the 1999 shutdown of the WTO that broke open the debate on globalization. Napoleon Bonaparte said an army marches on its stomach. So does a revolution. Tree-sitters blocking loggers need food. Workers occupying a factory or striking need food. Activists marching against police brutality need food. Food is something we all have in common, that makes us all feel better, and that can build a community that is also a coalition to fight the forces arrayed against the oppressed groups of the world. In providing food to a diversity of events, FNB fills a crucial logistical gap, and acquires very real power—the power to dictate the diet of the people they're serving. And it can be fun. When you give someone food, you are in that moment engaging in the very egalitarian mutualism that every system of ethics—including libertarian socialism—sees as its basis. The recipient of some kale salad or mashed potatoes will reciprocate by offering to take a little piece of you along with it—a conversation, perhaps, in which they will feel obligated to hear your view of the world. This is not to suggest that Food Not Bombs will save the world. Quite the contrary, its strength in decentralized autonomy prevent it from attaining that level of power. But the practice is an inspiration to those around it, it creates community, it serves a common need, and it provides logistical support to countless political acts. Serving food is no grand finale, and there are no roars or fireworks. But sometimes, in order to smash the State, you've just got to mash the 'tate.

Acknowledgements

Special thanks to Michael A. Webermann and Keith McHenry for their informative interviews, and Kate Brindle and Larry Butz for offering feedback on the initial draft.

References

Brazil, Eric. (1995). Activist gadfly cuts plea bargain. *San Francisco Chronicle.* February 15. http://www.sfgate.com/bayarea/article/Activist-gadfly-cuts-plea-bargain-3151736.php.

Corr, Anders. (1999). *No Trespassing: Squatting, Rent Strikes, and Land Struggles Worldwide.* Cambridge: South End Press.

Food Not Bombs. (a). *Politics.* http://www.foodnotbombs.net/bookpolitics.html.

Food Not Bombs. (b). *The Three Principles of Food Not Bombs.* http://www.foodnotbombs.net/principles.html.

Food Not Bombs. (c). *Defend our rights.* http://www.foodnotbombs.net/fnb_first_amendment.html.

Food Not Bombs. (d). *The 30th Anniversary Food Not Bombs.* http://foodnotbombs.net/z_30th_anniversary_2.html.

Food Not Bombs. (e). *Letter from U.S. Justice Department to Keith McHenry. Patrick, Deval and Moskowitz, Albert.* http://www.foodnotbombs.net/justice_department_letter.html.

Food Not Bombs. (f). Letter from the United Nations. Möller, Jakob. 1994, January 24. http://www.foodnotbombs.net/UN_letter.html.

Food Not Bombs. (g). Letter from Amnesty International to San Francisco District Attorney. 1994, October 28. http://www.foodnotbombs.net/amnesty_letter.html.

Kymlicka, Will. Animal Rights, Multiculturalism, and the Left. April 2013. Mellon-Sawyer seminar series, Graduate Center, CUNY.

Mac Donald, Heather. (Autumn 1994). San Francisco Gets Tough with the Homeless. *City Journal.* http://www.city-journal.org/article01.php?aid=1368.

McHenry, Keith. (2011, November 4). The History of Food Not Bombs with Keith McHenry. Path on 35th Street in Norfolk, VA. Accessed on YouTube January 2, 2014. https://www.youtube.com/watch?v=Fe4u01fBDiA.

McHenry, Keith. (2011, December 12). The Story of FOOD NOT BOMBS, Part One. El Paso. Accessed on YouTube January 2, 2014. https://www.youtube.com/watch?v=VnAElgf8L3I.

Sanbonmatsu, John (ed.). (2011). *Critical Theory and Animal Liberation.* Lanham, MD: Rowman and Littlefield.

"Nailing Descartes to the wall"
Animal Rights, Veganism and Punk Culture

WILL BOISSEAU AND JIM DONAGHEY

Through bringing together material from numerous bands, zines, patches, leaflets, and newly researched interview material, this essay examines the relationships between punk culture and animal rights/vegan consumption habits. It is argued that this relationship is most strongly and consistently expressed, and most sensibly understood, in connection with anarchism. Examining the overlaps between animal rights/veganism and punk is important in several ways. Firstly, it is a significantly under-researched area—as environmental journalist Will Potter (2011) argues, given the importance that punk plays in the political development of individual activists, it is surprising that "there is a shortage of research into punk's impact on animal rights and environmental activism" (pp. 101–102). Secondly, the themes raised in this essay resonate far beyond the punk scenes from which material is collected: focusing on broader questions of diversity and difference within activist communities, how these differences are managed (even "policed"), the prioritization of certain forms of activism over others, and the role of culture are all issues which cut right to the heart of contemporary activist and community organizing. Thirdly, the topic is of personal importance to the authors, both of whom are writing the essay from the impetus of their own life experiences.

In the first part of the essay the ways in which punk culture and veganism/animal rights coincide will be laid out, to stress the connection's existence and to explore the different ways in which this connection is expressed. Next, the theme of politicization will be raised, examining the link between people's exposure to animal rights/veganism through punk, and the adoption of vegan consumption habits or involvement in animal rights activism. Thirdly, the tension between individual choice and subcultural expectation will be explored, followed by an examination of the supposed dichotomy between consumption and activist politics in animal rights. The essay will conclude by examining how anarchist perspectives cut across and inform these debates in an intersectional manner (Rogue & Volcano, 2012).

This essay is concerned with the *contemporary* UK punk scene, so new primary information collected from interviews by both authors forms the main basis for analysis. All the interviews were carried out in the UK from August 2013 to January 2014 and cover a period of involvement in punk stretching from the late 1970s to the present. The zines considered typically come from self-identified anarchist publications (such as *Artcore*, *Bald Cactus*, *Cargo Cult*, *Last Hours/Rancid News*, and *Ripping Thrash*). From the 1980s onward, animal rights/liberation and vegan praxis have been commonly debated within punk fanzines. Grounded theory informs the interview method, and is a fruitful approach for anarchist-associated themes in general for several reasons. For example, interviewees, and the data they offer, are given primacy over imposed theoretical abstractions. Indeed, as Strauss & Corbin (1998) argue, this approach "means openness, a willingness to listen and to 'give voice' to respondents" (p. 43) and "the need to get out into the field to discover what is really going on" (p. 9). This approach, then, helps prevent the foisting of ideological preconceptions onto a research topic, or the warping and misrepresentation of interviewees' testimony to suit particular biases, while valuing the critical analyses generated from immersed and insider perspectives.

The research also draws on the principles of Critical Animal Studies (CAS). CAS promotes collaborative work that rejects "pseudo-objective academic analysis" and instead aims to produce work that links theory to practice and the university to the community, while advancing a "holistic understanding of the commonality of oppressions" and championing a politics of total liberation (Nocella et al., 2014). This commitment to avoid exploitation of interviewees, while emphasizing bottom-up theory construction, makes this approach highly compatible with an anarchist studies position. Most of the names of interview respondents have been changed to protect anonymity, and the interviewees have been extended a pre-publication opportunity to veto or amend any of the comments attributed to them. This ensures that respondents feel fairly represented, helps to prevent any basic errors, and is also important from a basic respect for individual privacy, particularly because of the sensitive nature of some of the activism discussed, and the background of harsh repression meted out to the animal rights movement over recent years.

Animal rights and veganism in punk

> *UK hardcore and animal rights went hand-in-hand.*—Interview respondent George [24/11/2013]

Punk and veganism/animal rights are undoubtedly connected. This is expressed through the lyrics and imagery of punk bands, the editorial and interview content of zines, numerous benefit gigs and record releases for animal activist causes, and in the overlap between punk and veganism in cafés, social centers, Food Not Bombs chapters, and hunt saboteur (hunt sab) groups. This is not to say that *all* punks are vegan, or that *all* vegans are punks—but the prevalence of this connection cannot be ignored and is particularly striking when considered in conjunction with anarchist and intersectional politics.

Literature dealing with punk pays scant attention to vegan/animal rights issues in general. The majority of books written about punk follow very narrow, singular narratives which consider punk as a brief moment of the late 1970s, and even within that time period only focus on commercially successful bands. Such a focus ignores the emergence of animal rights in punk, which Alastair Gordon (2005) identifies

> on the *Stations of the Crass* record [1979] with the track "Time Out" where comparisons are made to human and animal flesh. Animal rights became a central ethical theme over the next decade.... There were numerous anarcho records voicing animal rights issues such as the promotion of vegetarianism, anti hunting and anti vivisection themes [p. 112].

The anarcho-punk scene held animal rights as a central theme, so those accounts of punk that get beyond 1979 *do* frequently mention veganism and animal rights, but even here it is often as a brief mention within a list of other political engagements. The blurb to Roy Wallace's *The Day the Country Died* documentary is typical: "Many anarcho-punks are supporters of issues such as animal rights, feminism, the anti-war movement, the antiglobalization movement, and many other social movements" (Wallace, 2007). Mike Dines' (2004) thesis discusses a "'punk rock' resistance that accompanied the expansion of protest into areas such as animal rights, feminism and environmental issues" (p. 214). Similarly, Tolga Güldallı (2007) writes of punk's "anti-fascist, anti-capitalist, anti-militarist, anti-authoritarian, anti-sexist, anti-homophobic, deeply ecological, pro-animal rights 'ideology.'" This understanding of veganism and animal rights in conjunction with other radical politics is valid and useful. However, it is worthwhile to examine punk's adoption of veganism and animal rights positions in isolation as well—especially because, for many, animal rights is an issue of prime concern. Interview respondent Ryan, who has been involved in the Belfast anarchist and punk scenes since the early 1980s, recognizes that "animal rights was always a very very key type of thing. But it was one of the things that, for me, it became almost too exclusive ... *it came at the top* of all the people's chains" (Interview, 08/10/2013, emphasis added).

When *Last Hours* (2006) zine attempted to compile a "Punk Rock Census" they found that 54.6 percent of the 306 respondents were either vegan or vegetarian, as compared to less than three percent of the total UK population (VegSoc). That the survey even asked about dietary practice reveals that some connection is presumed, and the high number of respondents who did not eat meat further demonstrates the connection. The musical and artistic output of bands adds more weight to the evidence of the connection between punk and animal rights. There are far too many examples to cover exhaustively here, but a few selections will serve to illustrate some typical approaches. Among the numerous anarcho-punk (and other punk sub-genre) bands to embrace animal rights and veganism in the 1980s, Conflict stood as a totem. To supplement their lyrical exhortations they projected video footage taken from inside abattoirs onto screens behind the stage as they performed. They also exalted the animal liberation activist movements of the 1980s. As Mike Dines (2004) writes:

> Much of [Conflict]'s material provides a "call to arms" in the fight against butchers, the police and government structures alike. "This is the A. L. F [Animal Liberation Front]" a track on *The Ungovernable Force* (1986) particularly highlights such an idea. "What does direct action mean?" begins the track. "It means that we are no longer prepared to sit back and allow terrible cruel things to happen," proclaiming "direct action in animal rights means causing economic damage to those who abuse and make profits from exploitation" [pp. 232–233].

Benefit gigs and record releases provide a poignantly material connection between punk and animal rights. Here, the everyday cultural production processes of punk are turned toward activist causes. The 2013 North London punx picnic was a benefit for the FRIEND animal sanctuary in Kent (http://www.friendsanimalrescue.org.uk/), and was organized by an active animal liberationist and hunt saboteur. This individual had in fact been recently incarcerated for his animal liberation activities as part of SHAC (Stop Huntingdon Animal Cruelty). A benefit CD was released called *Prisoners of War*, and the songs included cover a range of political themes, pointing again to the interconnectedness of activist struggles associated with punk. One former punk rock hunt sabber, Jon of Active Distribution, started a tape distribution called "Lively Tapes" which he "made ... a benefit for the Swansea hunt sabs" (Interview, 19/09/2013). In all these cases the role of the benefit is two-fold: as a material fund-raiser for activist causes; and as propaganda and information (and even as entertainment too).

Punk-engaged social centers are overwhelmingly vegan, and also anarchist. Examples include the Warzone Centre in Belfast, the Cowley Club in Brighton, the Sumac Centre in Nottingham, the 1in12 Club in Bradford, Kebele in Bristol. Interview respondent Liam, a current member of the Warzone Collective in Belfast, commented, "we do operate a vegan café, which obviously results in discussion and opportunities for anyone who maybe wouldn't have eaten anything vegan before to come and eat it and realise it's fucking nice [and] a lot better for ye than the crap that people eat" (Interview, 06/10/2013).

The connection between punk and animal rights is also recognized by animal rights activists who are not punks. Simon, the current chair of the Hunt Saboteurs Association, acknowledges that "there's always been that push within the punk movement to support animal rights, and because the punk movement is by its very nature anarchist—they push towards organisations like us and not the more [mainstream] organising groups." The connection persists to the present, emerging at the end of the 1970s when there were "anarchists coming out of the punk movement, so there's always been that sort of angle within hunt sabs, because it doesn't involve any authority, it doesn't involve anyone telling you what to do, anybody can get out and do it" (Interview, 25/04/2014). Hunt sab groups and Food Not Bombs chapters are frequently populated by punks: at least three of Gordon's (2005) interview respondents were involved as a direct result of being in a punk scene (p. 89), and interview respondent Jon Active remembered "it was, hunt sabbing during the day and then punk rock at night." "We used to go hunt sabbing ... and then we'd [find out] 'right, where's the gig' ... 'cause the van was hired for 24 hours, so we [would] go to a gig anywhere we could potentially drive to, get to the gig, drive back that fuckin' night, wow jesus, and then take the van back the next morning" (Interview, 19/09/2013). Ryan, discussing the make-up of political groups during the 1980s in Belfast, commented that "in terms of animal rights [it was] almost exclusively punks" (Interview, 08/10/2013). This connection continues today, and even where personal involvement in the punk scene has lessened, animal rights activism continues. Tommy, who organises punk gigs in London and has been heavily involved in the animal liberation movement, notes "in a group, an animal rights group, you're thinking 'what kinda music are they into?' And suddenly you're talking to 'em about Crass and ... they know all the old bands ... so yeh, in the animal rights scene there are a lot of so-called 'ex-punks'" (Interview, 19/10/2013).

There is, then, an undeniable connection between animal rights/veganism and punk. As already intimated above, this relationship is not straightforward, so attention must be paid to the complications that are thrown-up, looking particularly at politicization through punk, the tensions between subcultural expectations and individual choice, and the supposed dichotomy between activist engagement and "mere" consumption habits.

Politicization Through Punk

> *It's just what you did, which sounds horrible and trendy, but it's true. You became punk, you found out about animal rights and you quit meat.*—Interview respondent Phil Chokeword [19/01/2014]

One of the key assertions here, and a main explanation of their relationship, is that an exposure to punk culture encourages people towards veganism/animal rights. Paul Gravett describes this consciousness raising effect, going from growing up "in a right wing Tory working class family" to involvement in campaign groups such as London Animal Action through "the influence of punk music" (Interview, 07/12/2013). Isy Morgenmuffel, who was active in the Cowley Club, believes that "punk rock is a great entry point to lots of rebellious ideas," but this does not mean that *all* ideas will be meaningfully adopted by participants (Interview, 17/12/2013). For Phil Chokeword, involvement in the South Coast hardcore punk scene during the late 1990s coincided with a time of "finding out about a lot of political issues for the first time as well as developing really strong ideas about DIY culture and politics" (Interview, 19/01/2014). Many of these ideas were intertwined with anarchist politics, but it was through discussions with fellow punks, rather than studying anarchist or animal rights literature, that Phil adopted a vegetarian diet.

Of course the process of politicization is by no means simple, and politicizing effects can emerge from any number of sources, mainstream as well as alternative. Paul, who became an anarchist, "never actually read much by anarchists in the early days. My main source of reading ... was the *New Musical Express*" (Interview, 07/12/2013). Similarly, Roger Yates, who was active as a press officer for the Animal Liberation Front (ALF) became interested in animal rights in 1977 when he "saw an article in a music paper" which focused on the anti-bloodsports movement (Interview, 11/12/2013).

The music press was particularly important for spreading alternative ideas; indeed DIY zines, which habitually feature animal rights issues, remain a key method by which punks can spread ideas from scene to scene. The process of politicization is further complicated because many activists are already interested in animal rights, and other radical politics, before they are attracted to punk. Isy, for instance, became vegetarian partly inspired by The Smiths, but through her involvement in leftist politics she came into contact with "anarchist vegans who I felt affinity with. I ended up much less involved with animal rights and more with community organising," and it was only through this process that Isy became involved with DIY punk (Interview, 17/12/2013).

Interview respondents Tommy, Megan, Oisín, and Sonia were all also already vegetarian before becoming involved in punk. Tommy describes the relationship between animal rights and punk in his own politicization as "a bit like a circle. I was already into animal rights ... and then I discovered these bands who were as well ... like a lot of other people it got me more involved into animal rights ... both fed off each other really with me, um both things been a big part of my life" (Interview, 19/10/2013). Those who are already vegetarians or interested in animal advocacy when they become involved in punk are encouraged to become vegan, get more active in direct action politics, and feel a sense of cohesion within punk scenes that is lacking in mainstream society. Further, the politicizing relationship between veganism/animal rights and punk operates *in both directions*—suggesting a very strong, if complicated, relationship.

Politicization through punk typically involves an awareness of animal liberation. Since the growth of anarcho-punk in the late 1970s and early 1980s, bands would often "include in their records information and images of the horrors of animal use and abuse" (O'Hara, 1999, p. 134). Gordon (2005), in his study of the Leeds and Bradford DIY scenes, found that one of the most "salient demonstrations of commitment" to the punk *lifestyle* was a vegetarian diet. Indeed, "the most striking similarity ... was that *all of them* were, or had at some time in their subcultural careers, been either vegetarian or vegan" (p. 89, emphasis added). However the politics of punk are not confined to animal issues, and as such, punk has acted as a site of discourse between anarchism and animal liberation. Interview respondent Liam said, "Personally speaking, for me, it definitely comes from ... an anarchist viewpoint, because it was lot of the early bands I listened to ... that sort of got me into that way of thinking, of vegetarianism." He continues:

> [I]t was definitely started by punk bands [but thereafter] it's something I just continued on myself because I realised that my veganism was more about poverty than actual ... rights for animals, where I realised that like vegetarianism just wasn't enough.... To be totally honest I think protest politics is kinda flawed but I can see no other way around like making myself feel OK about my diet. Like I can't partake in that, so that includes like ethical eating, like not just what I'm eating, but where it comes from [Interview, 06/10/2013].

Liam's initial exposure to animal rights through punk was augmented by his exposure to, and involvement in, anarchist politics, and became part of an overarching critique of oppression, combining veganism with an economic critique.

Punk has a clear politicizing role, and many people exposed to animal rights and veganism continue their activism after ending their involvement in punk scenes. This suggests that while punk has a politicizing role for young activists, working as their first point of contact with radical activism, it is not regarded as a significant end in itself. Former ALF activist Roger Yates argues that whereas some animal rights activists "seemed to have a deep and informed commitment to anarchism," "others simply liked the symbolism and antiauthoritarianism involved" (Interview, 11/12/2013). For Roger "punk music and the lyrics were probably more influential than the written anarchist texts." Clearly, punk is significant for radicalizing young anarchists and familiarizing them with animal rights arguments, but this seems to suggest that punk is merely concerned with "symbolism" rather than a "deep and informed commitment." Contrary to this, many punks see themselves as involved in "a counter culture that has strong anti-capitalist values" and believe punk is more than just a gateway for people to pass through before entering more serious political activism (Interview, 19/01/2014).

Of course, there is a degree of difficulty in gauging the commitment and reasoning of those who adhere to the norms of any scene or movement. If a person desires to become a member of a scene, then they will adopt the norms of that scene. This may be understood as politicization, and exposure to a valuable culture—but it may just be, as interview respondent George (who grew up around the Liverpool punk scene in the 1980s, and now resides in Manchester where he is editor of a widely read zine) suggests, that "people in life just go with the flow, y'know, so, a lot of people in life go with what their … social group do," resulting in empty rhetoric, "punks around the time [the '80s] … used very political language while not themselves being committed to the politics" (Interview, 24/11/2013). The important thing was to belong to "the culture." Even Oisín, who plays in a London-based band, and who is vegan, suggests that hard-wrought political consciousness isn't always the driving factor:

> We've played benefits for everything. Half the time we don't even know what we're playing benefits for. The fucking transsexual badgers in fucking Somerset or something like that, y'know [Interview, 19/10/2013].

This can result in a superficial engagement with a scene's underlying political motivations. George talks about "quite conservative kids who were into way-out music, y'know. And then grew up, grew out of it" (Interview, 24/11/2013). Once their involvement in the scene ends, so too does their adherence to the norms of that scene. Ex-punks *can* become ex-vegans, but as Tommy and Roger mentioned above, this isn't always the case—many "ex-punks" carry on with meaningful political engagement after they exit a scene.

It seems overly ambitious to demand that all the members of a particular community must arrive at a thoroughly considered position of every issue of their everyday lives. It is true that in the case of veganism and punk this usually involves a change of diet and lifestyle, where one might expect some thought to have gone into the transition. But adhering to a cultural norm can be played out as praxis without much hand-wringing reflection. Consider the myriad behaviors that are culturally specific to contemporary capitalism, behaviors that, for many, are simply accepted as ways of life—as *normal*. If veganism were to became a normative value in a mainstream hegemonic society, then people would *just be* vegan—they might not ever agonize over the ethics of consuming another living creature, but the suggestion to do so would seem preposterous. If some people in punk scenes fail to make an ethical, deep-seated commitment to veganism, but only play it out as a cultural norm, this does not necessarily undermine the value of that action entirely. It is also frequently the case that those who initially stop eating meat for purely cultural reasons later develop a more considered commitment to animal rights in general. A cultural motivation need not be considered void.

Nor is it the case that all activists who are focused on "more radical" activism have ceased their engagement with punk culture—many remain involved. Punk does not just have an initial politicizing effect, it also provides the intellectual and cultural support to ensure that activists remain politicized, motivated and undefeated. In Adam's case "the more political stuff probably came through Conflict. Eh, and I remember getting albums that had contact addresses for different sorta anarchist groups and organisations. That, I suppose, was maybe, maybe the first step in terms of looking at anarchism more politically. Y'know, as opposed to just listening to music that I liked and I identified with, and I agreed with a lot of" (Interview, 28/08/2013). Jon Active was on the supply-side end of this propagandizing relationship: "I did [the distro] for the same reason I mentioned before basically. I knew that I really wanted to communicate all that stuff, those ideas, and I wanted to make some money for the hunt sabs selling the tapes, and I wanted to, y'know get more people interested in going hunt sabbing ... and all the other stuff which we were doing" (Interview, 19/09/2013). Punk commodities, in addition to being entertainment and offering inspiring invective against any number of oppressions, actually facilitate engagement in the anarchist movement by providing opportunities for listeners to *get involved*. As Elizabeth Cherry (2006) discovered, those involved in punk are more likely to remain politically active as vegans than those outside punk who lack the support structures that are entrenched within punk culture:

> There are both relational and cultural differences in the social networks of these punk and non-punk vegans. While the punks found support for veganism in their everyday lives through friends or music, the non-punks did not have such support, or had support that did not encourage them to maintain a strict vegan lifestyle [pp. 164–165].

Even if participants no longer believe that "punk rockers would be at the vanguard of a peaceful anarcho revolution" (*Ripping Thrash*, #24, p. 7) they may remain active partly to encourage those newly interested in the scene to consider radical environmental and animal rights politics, and also because punk is a prefigurative example of the society they wish to see in action—cooperative, non-hierarchical, and internationalist. Punk has often met the charge of merely preaching to the converted, of singing about animal issues to those who are already vegan, but as Kismet HC explain, "animal exploitation never goes away ... yet there are new faces emerging into the scene every day and maybe 'this song' will touch them and make them think" (*Ripping Thrash*, #24, p. 8).

Subcultural Expectations and Individual Choice

A picture has emerged of punk scenes as spaces or communities where veganism is normative, in contrast with mainstream social situations where veganism is seen as "other." As a norm, then, there is a degree of expectation for members of a punk scene to adhere to a vegan diet. This raises issues of how this norm is upheld or "policed," and also the implications of people "going with the flow" and adopting a vegan diet without any real deep-seated commitment to animal rights. This essentially boils down to a tension between subcultural expectations and individual choice, and this tension is felt particularly sharply in punk because of the importance attached to personal freedom.

Jack, who grew up in the midlands, but is now involved in anarcho-syndicalist activism in Glasgow, recalls "a big emphasis on moralism, and a big emphasis on lifestyle [in the 1980s anarcho-punk scene]. I wouldn't say *lifestylism*, but just having an alternative lifestyle." "[A]lmost like developing a new genre of hippie-punk, right?" (Interview, 14/08/2013). This points to the sense in which veganism came to be part of the normative values and lifestyle practices of many punk scenes. These scenes nurture vegan consumption choices and offer a space for vegans to socialize with other vegans, and have some reprieve from the stresses of having to remain ever-vigilant in an animal consuming society. Punk scenes reinforce the vegan norm through the cultural reproduction of everyday practices (serving vegan food, beer, etc.), and can also (re)inspire the commitment to this consumption choice. Gordon's (2005) research uncovers the importance of subcultural community in this regard. His interview respondent, Mr. C, "was explicit how his choice to become a vegetarian was both a combination of the need to impress his girlfriend at the time and his investigation of the anarcho-punk genre.... Mr. C shows how the level of commitment *is both a combination of peer pressure and the input of the political statements* of the genres of punk he was investigating" (emphasis added, pp. 89–90). Interview respondent Megan, who puts on feminist punk gigs in Brighton, revealed a very similar motivation. "I'd wanted to go vegan for many years but had always relied heavily on processed foods so I thought it would be too difficult, but when I was forced into a position where I had to learn how to cook [as part of a vegan household] I saw how easy it would be and then the transition to full veganism was easy" (Interview, 17/12/2013). Laura Portwood-Stacer (2013), in her investigation into the contemporary anarchist movement in the U.S., identifies the performative and "identificatory motivations" in this dynamic (p. 41). Her interview respondent, Aaron, describes the importance of subcultural community:

> You literally live with other people who call themselves anarchists, who have a similar frugal punk-y lifestyle, and you put a lot of time into creative projects, and into discussions about what it means to live out your politics etc. You're in close proximity, and if anybody suddenly stops being vegan it's a big deal. And I think the same is true as far as political identity. It's easier to maintain a very abstract identity like "anarchist" when you have other people to orient yourself around, other compass points [Portwood-Stacer, 2013, p. 88].

Further, veganism is considered as "other" in mainstream society, so adopting this as a normative value helps to site the counter-culture outside of that cultural hegemony. It is a statement of identity, and a statement of resistance.

It is clear that this sense of cultural identity and belonging are important to participants in punk scenes, particularly where vegan consumption choices are concerned. Phil directly contrasts the role of this cultural identity with the importance placed on personal freedom, believing a sense of cohesion to be more important:

> I don't feel like it's realistic to build a community based on people who are all doing and believing different things. There has to be shared values at least so that people can hang out and co-exist. One of the shared values could be a belief that exploitation of animals is wrong. If you go strongly against that value, is there a place for you in that community? Go off and find somewhere that is more to your liking, don't hang around antagonising me. I don't have a problem with taking that stance on individualism to be honest [Interview, 19/01/2014].

It might be expected that this subcultural identity will be defended against normative transgressions ("policed"). However, the idea of creating some kind of rule or law by which members of these scenes should abide directly infringes on the ideas of personal freedom held by participants in these scenes, and is likely to generate conflict. Nonetheless, when compared with something like a safer spaces policy, a shared commitment to challenge mainstream relations to nonhuman animals appears consistent (Website of the Coalition for Safer Spaces). Indeed the emphasis on conflict resolution and being "welcoming, engaging and supportive" are key elements of a safer spaces policy that punk scenes might take into consideration when thinking about how to maintain a vegan norm, without resorting to alienating behavior to police this (Website of the Coalition for Safer Spaces). As the CrimethInc. ex–Workers Collective puts it "a big YES! to do-it-yourself punk rock and all other expressions of rebellion and independence, and a little no to subcultural isolation and provincialism" (*Rolling Thunder*, 2007, p. 3). This dynamic is recognized by Gordon (2005) as well:

> DiY [and vegan] purists have been accused of being inward-looking, preaching to the converted and being subculturally elitist with little chance of ever reach-

ing to the broader body of people whose support would make DiY a significant political tool of empowerment. The purists in turn accuse those who defect of intellectual slack-mindedness, political populism and ethical bankruptcy. The dilemmas strike deep [p. 270].

This insular, or ghettoized, perspective is problematic—especially if propaganda, information, and politicization are considered to be of importance. Portwood-Stacer (2013) emphasizes the communicative motivation of veganism, and its prefigurative potential, which "rests on implicit assumptions about the capacity of small-scale actions to work as theatrical spectacles which publically represent political ideologies and convince others of their correctness" (p. 41). Inevitably, in trying to attract new people to animals rights and veganism, it is essential to talk to non-vegans and people who are not familiar with animal rights issues. This means welcoming them into your scene in order to expose them to alternatives, and open them up to the cultural norms practiced by punk scenes. As "best practice" this might achieved with calmly weighted discussion, support and encouragement (as suggested by safer spaces policies), but is often played out as shunning, aggression, and even violence. Those who employ the latter approaches are labeled as "vegan police," a pejorative term for those individuals who aggressively chastise others for not adhering to the scene norm of veganism. "The ostensible purpose of ['calling someone out'] is to raise consciousness among one's fellow anarchists [or vegans] and to encourage each other to stay committed to their shared political project" (Portwood-Stacer, 2013, p. 88). Jack identified this issue: "they would have like frowned upon [mere] vegetarianism, right? Same as if you were like wearing like leather boots and stuff, y'know?" (Interview, 14/08/2013). Again, Gordon's (2005) respondent Mr. C echoes these views:

> There has been a vegan police element which I've remembered. I remember from the days doing hunt sabbing that people would be like fucking going into people's kitchens and looking in people's cupboards and going "what the fuck is this in your cupboard?" That is just ridiculous like [p. 128].

Ryan spoke about the implications this "policing" attitude could have:

> People who were involved in the original anarcho-punk movement will tell you it became so rigid with people who were thinking that you *had* to be vegan … there was like all these kinda rulebooks … from people that hadn't read too much, or hadn't really looked at any details about … the bigger picture.… Anarcho-punk bands were doing this as well … so they were getting this em, half-baked anarchism from bands who obviously didn't know what they were talking about.… A lot of people will say that *they left the anarcho-punk scene because of this rigidity* that kind of formed in it [Interview, 08/10/2013].

Gordon (2005) describes this focus as "a symbolic site for the politics of cultural elitism" (p. 128). So by enforcing the scene's vegan norm, possibly from an urge to protect the scene's identity or in a ham-fisted attempt to encourage somebody to become vegan, this "policing" in fact pushes people away from scenes and communities where they might be exposed to useful ideas and cultures. Conscious of this dynamic, interview respondent Megan tries to "live and let live" around vegan issues (Interview, 17/12/2013). Oisín, follows a similar logic:

> I'm pretty much like live and let live, I'm not gona start going up and [saying] "you fucking cunt, you're eating meat." I've never been like that. I'd have no fuckin' friends if I did, y'know [Interview, 19/10/2013].

One of Oisín's bandmates eats meat, and he says, "Yeah I'll wind him up about it, but it's nothing serious" (Interview, 19/10/2013). Even though both of these interview respondents are vegan, and have both been vegetarian since a very young age prior to their joining in the punk scene, they don't want to alienate people by preaching. This tension is not easily resolved—and indeed, there is nothing to suggest that it *should be* resolved. As well as this internal critical dialogue, there are also criticisms leveled at punk's engagement with veganism/animal rights from outside the culture.

Consumption and Activism

Tied in with the accusation that veganism is a subcultural expectation is the question of whether some punks' concern with animal issues is "proper" activism or "mere" consumerism. Moreover, when capitalist companies can happily produce vegan alternatives, and big-brand celebrities willingly endorse a version of veganism, it may be argued that this dietary habit is unconnected from any political critique whatsoever.

Certainly, some anarchists involved in animal rights treat punks with suspicion, viewing it as a secondary, ill-informed activism. Urban myths of inebriated punks eating ham sandwiches on hunt sabs abound. One activist, who founded Re-Pressed anarchist distro, often saw "the punk scene being no use at all, just a load of pissed up knackers … or over obsessive straight edge vegan fascists" (*Cargo Cult*, p. 13). However, even with this qualification, it is difficult to deny that punk produces "great practical examples of anarchy in action" and surges of political activity including involvement in anti-fascist action and hunt sabotage (*Cargo Cult*, p. 13). Anarchist punks often attended national animal rights demonstrations, contributing significantly to the anarchist presence (Interview, 07/12/2013).

There are numerous examples of punks putting animal rights theory into action. As well as promoting veganism/animal rights within DIY shows, and writing proselytizing animal rights lyrics, members of punk bands regularly work with local animal rights groups. Discussing the situation in the 1980s, interview respondent George considers that "if punk was affiliated with anything politically, it was animal rights.... The Animal Liberation Front were kind of very active, and it was a time of ... very little surveillance. So you'd get grubby punks throwing bricks through ... butcher-shop windows and things like that, and punk was far more aligned to that I think" (Interview, 24/11/2013). Kismet HC regularly ran "street stalls collecting money for animal aid & petitions against fur trades, circuses, HLS [Huntington Life Sciences]," and Leeds hardcore band Indictor regularly protested outside Covance Laboratories in Harrogate and Harvey Nichols, who sold fur, in Leeds (*Ripping Thrash*, pp. 6–14; *Bald Cactus*, 22, p. 16). In Brighton, punks supported the Anarchist Teapot, which began life as a "string of squatted cafes" and soon turned into a vegan mobile kitchen for mass catering at demonstrations. The Cowley Club, also in Brighton, took inspiration from the social centers of the Spanish revolution, and work to provide a "community-focused space with resources" and also hold veganism/animal rights as a key tenet (Interview, 17/12/2013). In London, punks were involved in London Animal Action's vegan fayre, although perhaps this does not rule out the charge of veganism being a mere consumer activity (*Rancid News*, p. 18).

Of course there are some punks who are simply not interested in animal rights. Even at the Barry Horne Memorial Gig, put on to honor the memory of the ALF hunger striker and to raise funds for animal liberation magazine *Arkangel* and other animal rights causes, some audience members "were there to see Conflict and the Subhumans and probably got a big Mac after the gig" (*Bald Cactus*, 20, pp. 4–7). This *perceived* attitude has led some activists to question the sincerity of the punk scene's commitment to animal advocacy, dismissing it as empty posturing at worst, and vegan consumerism at best. Some members of South Coast hardcore punk band Pilger, whose lyrics encouraged listeners to "think about what you eat," believed that "what we buy and where we buy it shapes the world"—they commended the fact that there were no longer "animal fats in Mr. Kipling's cakes" (*Artcore*, 2005, p. 11). But taken in isolation, such an attitude amounts to little more than supporting cruelty-free capitalism.

Ryan Gunderson (2011) believes the animal rights movement, and it would seem this could apply to certain punk scenes, have allowed themselves to be co-opted by cruelty-free capitalism, to the extent that activists "*consume their identities as pseudo-political achievement*" (p. 269). Rather than questioning structures of society and making links between varying forms of oppression, vegan consumers are willing to accept the "chocolate laxative" offered by capitalism. For Gunderson (2011), individualist ethical consumerism is not just limited and ineffective, it also "*halts social justice movements from pursuing radical means of altering society* because they have been co-opted"

(p. 269, emphasis in original). Critics of vegan consumerism believe that it does not offer a "critical assessment of social domination," that it only challenges one aspect of hierarchical domination while seemingly allowing for "animal-free workhouses" to continue, and that it adopts the capitalist system's way of conceptualizing change—through consumer power (*A Murder of Crows*, pp. 74–80). Of course, this criticism implies that ethical consumerism is not linked with a wider desire to change social institutions and challenge the economic system, which is not necessarily the case. The punk commitment to providing vegan meals, or sharing recipes, could be interpreted as vegan outreach in a capitalist society, and by sharing food or working in conjunction with Food Not Bombs punks can also work to subvert capitalist economic practices.

Peter Gelderloos (2011) (who seems to believe that merely wanting to eat adequately amounts to rampant consumerism) argues that "every vegan ... is actively supporting capitalism by participating in a great smoke screen which hides the true nature of how the present economic system actually functions" (p. 4). Rather than providing an insightful anarchist perspective, these criticisms of the "naïve vegan novice out to change the world" are often patronizing and offer no solutions to creating the better world their authors claim to seek (Gelderloos, 2011, p. 17). Considered alongside the veganism of Bill Clinton, Bill Gates, Jay-Z and Beyoncé (Barford, 2014), punk veganism might be considered as merely part of the rising global consumer trend for vegan diets. Some vegan activists, who have often emerged from the punk scene, even consider that their actions do not amount to a political activity. For instance, the Pogo Café was run "as a workers collective where everyone involved has a joint say," the collective "started as Emmaz ... the origins are in the punk rock community, who then joined with people from the animal rights community and the group got bigger" (*Last Hours*, 2006, pp. 74–75). Despite this, some Pogo Café volunteers believed that the collective "don't really have any politics" (*Last Hours*, 2006, pp. 74–75). *Subversive Energy* (2012), a group influenced by Max Stirner, promote stealing or "freeganism" "in an attempt to subvert the consumer-product relationship ... [and] undermine the transfer of resources" of the capitalist system (p. 5). Indeed, punks frequently engage in skipping (known as dumpster diving in the U.S.) to provide for mass catering and Food Not Bombs initiatives. The fact that punks have so often combined activism with their dietary practice disproves any claim that they are merely engaged in consumerism. This link between dietary habits and activism separates veganism in the punk scene from the growing international trend. Another key difference is the tendency of punks to combine veganism with a critique of capitalism and—most significantly—with an anarchist engagement. Punk animal advocacy most readily and consistently emerges in connection to anarchism.

Conclusion

> *This is only one issue, it's a big issue, it's an important issue. But it's a single issue or several issues, which all have the same kind of cause, they all come from the same kind of capitalist, patriarchal, church and state system y'know, which looks at everything as product, including animals.*—Interview respondent Ryan [08/11/2013]

As mentioned above, veganism and animal rights are generally included among a list of other political engagements connected to punk scenes. Megan echoes Ryan when she says, "everything's kinda like interlocked, and these whole overarching systems of oppression, and they kind of intersect, and intersectionality's great as a theory" (Interview, 17/12/2013). This intersectional understanding is underpinned by an anarchist political philosophy, and as repeatedly suggested throughout the chapter, it is from this understanding that the relationships between veganism/animal rights and punk culture make sense. Jon Active recalls the practical implications of this struggle against a wide range of oppressions. "It wasn't just hunt sabbing … there was going to the … nuclear bases, going to Upper Hayford, and goin' to Greenham Common…. And of course the anti-fascist stuff, and then there was the um … Public Order Act, whenever that was…. Those kind of demos, and then the … anti–McDonald's stuff" (Interview, 19/09/2013).

However, the relationship between anarchism and animal advocacy fluctuates and there are anarchists who deny that animal rights has anything to do with their politics. Although the Class War Federation once believed that "animals are the lowest class imaginable" and "abolition of Class Slavery means freedom for all animals" (*Class War*, n.d, p. 4) a later pronouncement in their book *Unfinished Business* states that they do "not think that music, drugs or fashion will change the world. The Federation has no links with, or interest in, the animal rights movement" (Class War, 1992, p. 13). Some anarchists reject veganism as a consumer activity while others believe that "anarchism is a life without structure or authority, therefore my diet follows neither of these" or that an emphasis on a seemingly restrictive diet makes it difficult to organize with community groups outside of the anarchist movement (Anarchist Survey). Some anarchists reject the concept of "rights" while others deny that nonhuman animals are suitable candidates for liberation because they can less clearly engage in their own liberation struggle (Franks, 2006, p. 119). Interview respondent Adam, who was exposed to anarchism in the late 1980s Belfast punk scene, and who was vegetarian for a large part of his life, is now involved in anarcho-syndicalist activism and now doesn't consider animal rights as "necessarily intrinsic to anarchist politics" (Interview, 28/08/2013). However, he is critical of the polarization that often occurs in the anarchist movement over the animal rights issue. "In my experience the people that argue about this are, on one side, people that only give a fuck about wee fluffy animals, and don't really care about exploitation of people ... there's something about them that's misanthropic. Uh, and on the other extreme you have people who have come through that sorta thing, who are fucking overly embarrassed about it, who think 'aw, we have to be so materialist about everything.'" In Adam's opinion this lifestylist/workerist dichotomy is based on "stupid fucking arguments."

> If you join an anarcho-syndicalist organisation, or an anarcho-communist organisation for that matter, I don't think there is any contradiction in having a debate and putting forward some sort of approach to agricultural industry and the way animals are treated and the way they're farmed and processed and all the rest of it.... I would like to think people would generally agree at that level.... Really, I mean given the state the world's in, right, people can come together and agree that the way they're organised is to do certain things. And if people want to do stuff that is also more about hunt sabbing, or more about some sort of vegan or vegetarian activism, or not, they can do that outside the framework of that type of organisation. And they should not be berated or made to feel like idiots over it, at all. Uh, and I think that the whole lifestyle/class debate does that, and I think it's fucking ridiculous [Interview, 28/08/2013].

There is, then, a deep and strongly expressed connection between animal rights/veganism and punk culture. This relationship is best understood in conjunction with anarchism and an intersectional opposition to all forms of domination. As Canadian anarchist punk band Propagandhi (1996) convey in the song that gives this essay its title: "I have recognised one form of oppression; now I recognise the rest." The complications and tensions discussed here ensure that these issues will continue to be debated and discussed within punk scenes (the more the better!). It is hoped that this analysis can be a useful contribution to those debates, as well as introducing outsiders to this important subject area, and indeed, to the importance of veganism and animal rights more widely.

REFERENCES

Anarchist Survey. [Last accessed 14/04/2014, http://www.anarchismdocumentary.net/survey/.]
Artcore. (Spring 2005). Pilger interview. No. 22. 11.
Bald Cactus. (n.d.). Active Slaughter interview. No. 20. 4–7.
Bald Cactus. (n.d.). Indicator interview. No. 22. 16.
Barford, V. (2014). "Rise of the part-time vegans." *BBC News Magazine*. [Last accessed 08/04/2014, http://www.bbc.co.uk/news/magazine-25644903.]
Cargo Cult: DIY punk fanzine. (n.d.). No. 4.
Cherry E. (2006). "Veganism as a cultural movement: A relational approach." *Social Movement Studies: Journal of Social, Cultural and Political Protest* 5, no. 2, 155–170.

Class War. (n.d.). unnumbered, 4.
Class War Federation. (1992). *Unfinished business ... The politics of Class War.* Edinburgh: AK Press.
CrimethInc. ex–Workers' Collective. (Spring 2007). *Rolling thunder: An anarchist journal of dangerous living.* No. 4. 3.
Dines, M. (2004). "An investigation into the emergence of the anarcho-punk scene of the 1980s." ARICAS, School of Media, Music & Performance, University of Salford, Salford, UK, PhD Thesis.
Friends Animal Rescue. http://www.friendsanimalrescue.org.uk/.
Gelderloos, P. (2011). *Veganism: Why not: An anarchist perspective.* [Accessed at The Anarchist Library—http://theanarchistlibrary.org/library/peter-gelderloos-veganism-why-not.]
Gordon, A. (2005). The authentic punk: An ethnography of diy music ethics. Loughborough University, PhD thesis.
Güldallı, T. (2007). "Being punk in Turkey." In Boynik, S., & Güldall, T. (eds.). *Türkiye'de punk ve yeraltı kaynaklarının kesintili tarihi 1978–1999* [An interrupted history of punk and underground resources in Turkey 1978–1999]. Istanbul: BAS. http://www.turkiyedepunkveyeraltikaynaklarininkesintilitarihi.com/tolga-guldalli-being-punk-in-turkey.php.
Gunderson, R. (2011). From cattle to capital: Exchange value, animal commodification, and barbarism. *Critical Sociology*, Vol. 39. No. 2. 259–275.
Franks, B. (2006). *Rebel alliances. The means and ends of contemporary British anarchisms.* Edinburgh: AK Press.
Last Hours. (Summer 2006). "Punk rock census." 13.
Last Hours. (Summer 2006). Pogo Café interview. 74–75.
A Murder of Crows. (2007). No. 2. New York. [Accessed at The Anarchist Library—http://theanarchistlibrary.org/library/various-authors-a-murder-of-crows.]
Nocella II, A. J., Sorenson, J., Socha, K., & Matsuoka, A. (Eds.). (2014). *Defining Critical Animal Studies.* New York: Peter Lang.
O'Hara, C. (1999). *The philosophy of punk: More than noise!* Edinburgh: AK Press.
Portwood-Stacer, L. (2013). *Lifestyle politics and radical activism.* New York: Bloomsbury.
Potter, W. (2011). *Green is the new red: An insider's account of a social movement under siege.* San Francisco: City Lights.
Propagandhi. (1996). "Nailing Descartes to the Wall/(Liquid) Meat is Still Murder," *Less Talk, More Rock.* Fat Wreck Chords.
Rancid News. (July/August 2004). No. 7. 18.
Ripping Thrash # 24; A Network of Friends # 3 (n.d., c. mid–2000s). Kismet HC interview. 6–18.
Rogue, J., & Volcano, A. (2012). Insurrection at the Intersection. In Dark Star. (Ed.). *Quiet rumours: An anarcha-feminist reader* (pp. 43–46). Edinburgh: AK Press.
Strauss, A., & Corbin, J. (1998). *Basics of qualitative research: Techniques and procedures for developing grounded theory.* London: Sage.
Subversive Energy. (2012). *Beyond Animal Liberation.* [Accessed at The Anarchist Library. http://theanarchistlibrary.org/library/subversive-energy-beyond-animal-liberation.]
VegSoc. "Department of Health and Food Standards Agency (FSA)—National Diet and Nutrition Survey." https://www.vegsoc.org/sslpage.aspx?pid=753 [last accessed 11/08/2014.]
Wallace, R. (dir.) (2007). *The Day the Country Died—A History of Anarcho Punk.*

London: Cherry Red. Available free online at http://fuckcopyright.blogspot.com/2009/04/day-country-died-2007.html

Website of the Coalition for Safer Spaces, including resources and information on developing a safer spaces policy. http://saferspacesnyc.wordpress.com/ [last accessed 17/04/2014].

Part II
Intersections

"Anarchism has but one infallible, unchangeable motto, 'Freedom.' Freedom to discover any truth, freedom to develop, to live naturally and fully."
—Lucy Parsons

"By anarchist spirit I mean that deeply human sentiment, which aims at the good of all, freedom and justice for all, solidarity and love among the people; which is not an exclusive characteristic only of self-declared anarchists, but inspires all people who have a generous heart and an open mind."
—Errico Malatesta

"You cannot buy the revolution. You cannot make the revolution. You can only be the revolution. It is in your spirit, or it is nowhere."
—Ursula K. Le Guin

Intersectionality, Species and Social Domination

Erika Cudworth

An anarchist society is one "which organizes itself without authority" (Ward, cited Marshall, 1992, p. 42). Hierarchical and exclusive forms of social organization are usually understood by anarchists to be forms of domination. It is unsurprising then, that the history of anarchist thought and practical political engagement demonstrates a concern with an eclectic range of dominations—around "race," ethnicity and nation; caste, class and wealth; formations of sex, sexuality and gender; colonialism, imperialism and warfare amongst others. These forms of social domination have been at least as significant in anarchism as the focus on the state and governance; for some scholars and activists, more so. This concern with challenging multiple sites of power has led to anarchism being presented implicitly as a challenge to dominatory power. Alternatively, the coupling of anarchism with other explicit challenges (anarcha-feminism, anarcho-communism, green anarchism, queer anarchism and so on, or multiple chains thereof!) illustrates the eclecticism of the anarchist challenge. We might say, therefore, that anarchism is highly open to intersectionality, if not already characterized by it.

The term "intersectionality" is now widely used. Its origins are feminist, specifically, black feminist scholarship's attempts to theorize the overlapping qualities, as well as the tensions between formations of "race" and gender (see Crenshaw, 1991). The empirical and theoretical exploration of the ways different kinds of domination impact on one another has been a feminist preoccupation since the mid-1970s, and this has included, for some, an interrogation of the binary distinction between "human" and "animal" (for rather different accounts, see Adams, 1976; Haraway, 1989). This has gone against the presumption of academic social science that we are "supposed to study people, not other creatures" (Kruse, 2002, p. 375). Arnold Arluke (2004) has noted that it is not only mainstream scholarship which has been characterized by "androcentrism" (as he puts it). Radical and critical scholarship has also been highly resistant to the study of nonhuman animals, shaped by the belief that studying animals lessens or undermines the notion of oppression. This essay challenges anarchism to think about species seriously as a form of social domination, and reflect on the humanocentrism and human exclusivity that characterizes much of both historical and contemporary scholarship. It is not my intention to document this here, rather, to suggest that the openness of anarchism to considering multiple forms of domination means that it is well-suited to develop powerful critiques of the human domination of other animals.

We begin with a consideration of two anarchist contributions to debates on human relations with other animals. First, Kropotkin's contribution to understanding species in terms of differentiations rather than differences and his notion that we are co-constituted in "federations" of life with nonhumans. This conceptualization links him to contemporary scholars in animal studies who question hierarchical models of species distinction. While owing much to Kropotkin, and also being highly attentive to the "linked hierarchies" of intra-human domination and the necessity of challenging the exploitation of non-human nature, anarchist political ecologist Murray Bookchin held fast to the dichotomy between humans and all other animals. While I will endorse Bookchin's wide-ranging understanding of the linked emergence of hierarchy and the necessity of challenging multiple forms of social domination, I critique his "humanocentrism" (Bekoff, 2002).

Other kinds of critical political theory, particularly feminism, have effectively problematized such distinctions and have longstanding engagements with ideas about linked hierarchies and dominations. Some, such as Carol Adams and Val Plumwood, have developed approaches to human relations with non-human animals framed by what is now commonly referred to as "intersectionality." My intention is to draw on feminist influenced accounts of human relations with nonhuman animals as constituted by relations of intra-human oppression and exploitation in arguing that in seeking to challenge varied forms of domination, anarchism must also attend to the domination of nonhuman animals. The essay closes with the examination of some anarchist work which foregrounds the intersectionalised oppression of humans and other animals. I will argue that while ideas of intesectionality and social domination are increasingly engaged with both anarchism and animal liberation discourse, there is a significant way to go. I argue that both anarchist theory and anarchist politics—opposed as they are, to a range of dominations that they see as interlinked and interdependent—are compatible with a politics which contests the human oppression and exploitation of nonhuman animals.

Glimpses of the NonHuman in Some Anarchist Thought

The Western conception of the human as an autonomous, rational being able to make decisions and choices about actions has only developed alongside, and in contradistinction to, the "animal." These conceptions of autonomy and rationality have been important to all Western left political projects, including anarchism. It is not my intention to give a comprehensive overview of the way species has, or rather more often, has not, featured in the history of anarchist thinking. Rather, I want to consider two well-known anarchist writers for whom species and species relations have featured. Neither Kropotkin nor Bookchin are referenced much in work within "animal studies," but certainly they have a contribution to make. They also, of course, link anarchism to critical perspectives on humanocentrism.

In addition to his work as a political theorist and revolutionary, Kropotkin (1842–1921) was a geographer and a biologist who challenged the ways in which Darwin's theory of evolution had been interpreted. Kropotkin argued that the metaphor of the survival of the fittest had become the central way in which evolutionary theory had been explained. The focus on competition over-stated one aspect of evolution, ignoring the significance of co-operation within species; rather, "sociability is as much a law of nature as mutual struggle." (Kropotkin, 1987a, p. 24). Starting with an examination of nonhuman animals Kropotkin claimed that "natural selection continually seeks out the ways precisely for avoiding competition as much as possible" (1987a, p. 72). He noted how few animal species exist by directly competing with each other compared to the numbers who practice "mutual aid," and that those who do are likely to experience the best evolutionary prospects. Given this, it is therefore unlikely that humans should have flourished so successfully without co-operation (1987a, p. 74). Sociability is inherent in the success of humans as a species (1987b). Drawing upon the work of anthropologists, and the observations of Darwin, Kropotkin argued that from the earliest times, humans were social rather than individualistic, and dependent on "the support they found in their surroundings" (1987a: 154). Contemporary biologists might describe this in terms of co-evolution—natural systems developing as a result of interactions with their "environment" and the incredible variety of nonhuman life forms therein (Kauffman, 1993). Mutual aid has been, Kropotkin argues, a feature of human existence that has widened its reach, ultimately potentially to the whole human species and beyond its boundaries (1987a, p. 234). The story of evolution in Kropotkin is not one of a path towards fixed things, but a process of relationships and linked becoming. Species is not a fixed taxonomy but about the recognition of what Darwin calls "differentiations." *Mutual Aid* stressed the process of evolution as one where successful adaptation and exploitation of evolutionary niches is secured by species' propensity for co-operation and solidarity or what biologists might now refer to as symbiogenesis (Margulis and Sagan, 2002, p. 205). This order can be spontaneous and progressive. As Marshall notes, anarchists "consider society to be a self-regulating order which develops best when least interfered with" (1993, p. 13), and this order, in Kropotkin, is not human-exclusive.

Many of Kropotkin's ideas are elaborated in the work of Murray Bookchin, who has been instrumental in linking anarchism to green social and political thought in the development of "social ecology." In his best known work, *The Ecology of Freedom*, Bookchin gives an account of the emergence of social hierarchies. These emerged with, first, the oppression of women, proceeding to the exploitation and oppression of other groups of humans, socially stratified according to age, "race," class and sexuality (2005, p. 24). The notion of overlapping and intersected forms of social domination which are systemic and co-constituting is clearly compatible with an intersectionalised analysis of social domination. In addition, Bookchin's understanding of the hybridized and amorphous nature of contemporary political systems embedded firmly in the social fabric and constantly in the processes of arranging and rearranging social life—can be given a posthumanist reading (see in particular Bookchin, 2005, pp. 191–200). However, although Bookchin is to be applauded for his conception of humans as in and of nature, he holds to a problematic human exclusivity when it comes to considering relations between human and other species. He cannot account for human domination of other species, domination that for some feminist scholars (such as Fisher, 1979) predated, and was the model for, the oppression of women.

A key reason for this lies in the distinction Bookchin makes between "first" and "second" nature. For Bookchin, humans as a species have developed to an exceptional degree such that they have produced a "second nature," that is, a "uniquely human culture, a wide variety of institutionalized human communities, an effective human technics, a richly symbolic language, and a carefully managed source of nutriment" (Bookchin, 1990, p. 162). This is a development out of "first nature," or "nonhuman nature." An important distinction between human and nonhuman nature is hierarchy, "institutionalized and highly ideological systems of command and obedience," which are an "exclusive characteristic of second nature" (Bookchin, 2005, p. 26). Hierarchy is not a defining feature of second nature (human culture), but one that has emerged historically. Earlier, societies were non-hierarchic, and characterized by mutualism, where care was taken for all members of society, without attributing particular status to differences between its members. Over time, Bookchin suggests that hierarchic relations emerged related primarily to gender, age and lineage, developing into the range of hierarchic distinctions that typify the contemporary world. Our current malaise is a result of an evolutionary history containing two competing logics—that of spontaneous mutualistic ecological differentiation, and that of social domination (Light, 1998, p. 7). Similarly to Kropotkin, Bookchin considers that species exist in relations of mutual interdependence and co-operation and the concept of species co-evolution and 'federations' of life forms, runs through both *Mutual Aid* and *The Ecology of Freedom*.

However, Bookchin's Enlightenment narrative in *The Ecology of Freedom* tells of an evolution to a higher level of consciousness culminating in a state of "free nature" in which intra human hierarchies are dissolved and the domination of the environment is no more—it is inferred by this that animals will be liberated through our Enlightened protectionism which enables other species to flourish. However, the human domain remains unique and distinct (Bookchin, 2005, p. 458). While I would concur with Bookchin that the human world has certain unique properties, the hard distinction of human worlds from those of all other species is an unnecessary and humanocentric move. Bookchin is careful to track the development of different forms of intrahuman domination, their distinct qualities and co-constituted aspects. When it comes to the human domination of "first nature," however, there is a reductionist argument made that the end of intra human domination will simply result in the demise of the exploitation and oppression of nonhuman beings.

This said, both Kropotkin and Bookchin provide us with a useful legacy that might be drawn into critical work in animal studies. For example, the insight that many species have overlapping forms of "species life" with humans, with certain needs, forms of sociality and ecological and cross-species dependency; the challenge in Kropotkin of the presumption of human separateness from "other" animals, arguing that we should think about "differentiations" rather than differences. Differentiations of species, and particular social, economic and ecological contexts give rise to different kinds of human animal relationship that sociological animal studies has been concerned with, such as the use of certain nonhuman animals as laborers of various kinds; as food and resources; as "companions"; as human entertainment, and so on. We might best understand these socially constituted categorizations as carrying relations of human power, and that power is very often not benign. The next section considers the idea of species as a political category and the notion of species difference as a form of social domination. Bookchin's conceptual framework of linked domination makes its presence felt here as the domination of species has been seen to be bound up with intra-human forms of domination.

Intersectionality and Dominations

Peter Singer is a much associated with the use of the terminology of "liberation" and "oppression" to describe human relations with animals. The key concept underpinning Singer's contributions is "speciesism," discrimination based upon species membership. The undoubted strength of theorizing as Singer does, in terms of the interests of nonhuman animals, has been to set an agenda in which the lives and well-being of nonhuman animals is analytically foregrounded. To consider "species" as a problematic, socially constituted and oppressive category has been a highly important innovation, problematizing the certainties and the qualities of human power. Decades have passed since arguments were made for the sentience of animals and the irrationality of the ways in which humans treat them, yet fundamental changes in human relations with nonhuman animals have been negligible. Singer scorns the suggestion that a failure of his position on animal liberation was that he did not attend to the intersection of the oppression of nonhuman animals with some of those animals we call human (Cudworth, 2011a, p. 56). Yet this has been the problem.

Other work in animal studies has usefully stressed the operationalization of speciesism as a discourse of power rather than a form of discrimination. These accounts are often intersectional; considering the ways in which the discourse of species is constituted with other discourses around human difference and domination. Cary Wolfe, for example, is clear that while "the violent effects of the discourse of speciesism fall overwhelmingly in institutional terms, on nonhuman animals" (Wolfe, 2003a, p. 6), the "discourse of animality [has] historically served as a crucial strategy in the oppression of humans by other humans" (Wolfe, 2003b, p. xx).

This questioning of the way in which overlapping discourses co-constitute forms of Othering has a long legacy in feminist and postcolonial theory, and in particular in ecofeminist work. Some of those attempting to understand the cross cutting of multiple social inequalities with gender, have used the term "intersectionality" to emphasize the ways social differences and dominations are mutually constitutive. The effects of, for example, "race" for gender are not simply an overlapping of inequalities. Gender relations, through intersection, change the properties of "race" (McCall, 2005; Phoenix and Pattynama, 2006). While the term "intersectionality" emerged from black feminism in the U.S. (Crenshaw, 1991), this focus on multiple inequalities and forms of social domination has been a characteristic of socialist feminist writing (Walby, 1990, 2009, 2011, p. 125–46) as well as ecofeminism (Cudworth, 2005; Sturgeon, 2009).

From the early 1970s ecofeminists suggested that cultural discourses carry binary normalizations that construct a dichotomy between women and "nature," including the multifarious species of nonhuman animal, and male-dominated, Western, human culture. The arguments presented often drew on a form of standpoint epistemology: gender roles constituted through such discourses (such as social practices of care) render women in closer material proximity and relation to the environment and nonhuman animals (Salamone, 1982). Additionally, it was contended that women may empathize with the sufferings of animals as they have some common experiences, for example female domestic animals are most likely to be "oppressed" via control of their sexuality and reproductive powers (Benny, 1983). Others examined the speciesism of linguistic practices and the links between this and our gendered and radicalized use of language (Dunnayer, 1995; Adams, 1990, 2003); or looked at the interrelations between gender and the environmental and species impact of colonial practices (Lee Shanchez, 1993; Shantu Riley, 1993). Such writing has been influential in alerting us to the intersectionalised qualities of oppression. However, there is often a tendency in this literature to deploy an all-encompassing theory of gender relations to explain intersected oppressions. For example, Suzanne Kappeler has asserted that patriarchy is "the pivot of all speciesism, racism, ethnicism, and nationalism" (1995, p. 348). Val Plumwood sees gender, nature, race, colonialism and class as interfacing in a "network" or "web" of oppressive relations (1993, p. 2, 194). Ultimately however, forms of domination have "a unified overall mode of operation, forming a *single system*" with a "common structure and ideology" (1994, p. 79, my emphasis). These approaches provide a powerful analysis of the ways the social system of gender relations is co-constituted through ideas and practices around 'nature' and species relations. However, there is a tendency towards conflation in ecofeminist accounts, inviting criticism for an over-general use of a theory of patriarchy, which is presumed to account for a wide range of oppressive relations.

David Nibert's work has been important in foregrounding an analysis of capitalism in understanding our relations with nonhuman animals. Nibert (2002, p. 7) explicitly uses the concept of oppression in relation to the historical development of human relations with nonhuman animals. He argues that social institutions are foundational for the oppression of animals—not the individual attitudes and moral deficiencies implied by Singer. Nibert isolates three elements in his model of oppression. First, we have economic exploitation where animals are exploited for human interests and tastes; second, power inequalities coded in law leave animals open to exploitation; and third, this is legitimated by an ideology of speciesism which naturalizes the oppression of animals in its many forms. Contemporary cultural processes and institutional arenas through which animals are exploited and oppressed—zoos, the breeding and keeping of "pets," the "use" of animals in research, hunting, farming and slaughter are explained in terms of profit creation, corporate interest and the generation and sustaining of false commodity needs. Nibert acknowledges his debt to ecofeminist writers and his understanding of the concept of oppression is very much influenced by its use in feminist theory (such as Young, 1990). Nibert even appears to endorse a model of interacting systems of oppression: *"the arrangements that lead to various forms of oppression are integrated in such a way that the exploitation of one group frequently augments and compounds the mistreatment of others"* (Nibert, 2002, p. 4, original italics). Disappointingly however, the overriding thesis is that the human oppression of other animals is caused and reproduced by relations of capitalism (2002, p. 3). While I concur with Nibert on the oppression and exploitation of domesticates in animal agriculture, an explanation based on an analysis of capitalism does not capture the range of interlinked processes involved. We must also consider the ways in which for example the intersection of colonialist and patriarchal relations is particularly marked in the farming of animals for food.

In the contemporary West, the meat industry is patriarchally constituted. Farmed animals are disproportionately female and are usually feminized in terms of their treatment by predominantly male human agricultural workers. Farmers disproportionately breed female animals so they can maximize profit via the manipulation of reproduction. Female animals that have been used for breeding can be seen to incur the most severe physical violences within the animal food system, particularly at slaughter (Cudworth, 2008). Female and feminized animals are bred, incarcerated, raped, killed and cut into pieces, in gargantuan numbers, by men who are often themselves subjected to highly exploitative working conditions (Eisenitz, 1997, 85). These working conditions are structured by the gendered division of labor and also characterized by a culture of machismo (Cudworth, 2008, for further discussion see Alexis, this volume).

Furthermore, operations of local, regional and global networks of relations shaped the development of animal food production, and the production and consumption of animals as meat was an historical process in which systemic relations of species are constituted with and through relations of colonialism. In the eighteenth and nineteenth centuries, European countries established the global international system of meat production. Britain and Germany in particular invested heavily in land and later also factories in South America, primarily in Argentina in the eighteenth century, and in Brazil in the nineteenth (Velten, 2007, p. 153; Rifkin, 1994, pp. 145–7). The colonial model of meat production was further enabled by the development of refrigerated shipping which made it possible to ship "fresh" meat to Europe from the U.S., South America and Australasia (Franklin, 1999, p. 130). This enabled Europeans to consume greater quantities of meat, but in order to make best use of the potential market in Europe the price had to be minimized by intensifying production and saving labor costs through increased mechanization, processes which led to the development of intensive agriculture in Europe and the U.S., models of production now spread across the globe with corporate interventions in Asia, Africa and the Caribbean (Cudworth, 2011b).

Finally, as social and natural systems are co-constituted, we must also consider the impact of farmed animal agriculture on the worlds of other species and things. As is becoming increasingly recognized, industrialized animal agriculture is a driving force behind contemporary and pressing environmental problems that we face—deforestation, water scarcity, air and water pollution, climate change and loss of biodiversity (CIWF, 2002; Steinfeld et al., 2006; World Bank, 2001). Thus while farmed animal agriculture is an integral element of a social system of species relations in which domesticate nonhuman animals are oppressed, it is also constituted by relations of capital, colonialism and patriarchy and shaped in important ways by intra-human difference.

What is required therefore is as full an analysis of social intersectionality as we are capable of. We need an analysis of social difference, inequality and domination in terms of relational systems of power. We also need an analysis of the social practices and institutions which constitute, reproduce and rearticulate the relations of species specifically. The oppression of non-human animals is co-constituted by relations of capitalism, colonialism and so on but is not reducible to them.

Anarchism and Human Domination

Analyses of intersectionality and domination have therefore been used to understand our relationships to animals, but rarely in explicitly anarchist ways. In this section, I consider the more academic intervention of Bob Torres (2007), who applies Nibert's model of animal oppression to the case of highly industrialized capital-intensive agriculture in the global north, and in doing so, explicitly links it to anarchist politics. I also look at the important pamphlet by one of the contributors to this collection, Brian Dominick (1995, 1996, 1997). Dominick's *Animal Liberation and Social Revolution* outlined the similarities in perspective between anarchism and veganism, broadly defined in terms of living a life which is as compassionate as possible towards animals, including of course, human beings. For Dominick, veganism is anarchist praxis.

Capitalism has, as Torres rightly suggests, "deepened, extended and worsened our domination over animals and the natural world" (2007, p. 3). Animals are largely understood as laborers—producing commodities such as milk and eggs and becoming commodities such as meat and leather. Animal labor within capitalism is slave labor. In the commodities of meat, milk and eggs, complex chains and networks of productive forces and relations can be found (2007, pp. 36–38). Animal labor is also alienated labor if we consider the alienation from the products of labor, of breeder animals separated from their young, for example; and the alienation from productive activity, for example in the dull existences of meat animals whose labor is to eat, in order to become meat. Animals are also alienated from members of their species in the ways they are contained and separated, and alienated from their "species-life" in being unable to fulfill natural behaviors such as foraging, play and nest building. Torres argues strongly against the use of animals in agriculture however high standards of welfare might be for although "some forms of dominance are 'nicer' than others, exploitation is still exploitation in the end" (2007, p. 44). Animals are not exploited in the same way as human beings in the labor process, however. The classed and radicalized composition of the labor force in animal agriculture and the meat industry and the alienated conditions of labor are deeply problematic (see 2007, pp. 45–49). Animals demonstrate a different kind of embodied labor. Their bodies not only are exploited by working for us in order to produce animal food products, their bodies are *themselves* commodities, as he puts it: "They are superexploited living commodities" (2007, p. 58). Animal lives and bodies are a means to profit creation within capitalism. In addition, animals are property, and this relationship of ownership over animal bodies is essential for the extraction of profit. Torres' analysis here is much influenced by anarchist writing, in particular the ideas of Proudhon and Kropotkin. The value created by labor and embodied in private property is not fully recognized—and in the case of animals, is not recognized at all. Animals-as-property means that, in the case of animal agriculture for example, animals are "sensate living machines" for the production of commodities (2007, p. 64). But the condition of animals is one of slavery—they can exercise no choice in their lives and can never leave the place of production, unlike humans in the wage production system of capitalism. For Torres, capitalism remains the key analytical device throughout, and his analysis of human relations with nonhuman domesticate animals is conceptually underpinned by notions of property relations and commoditization.

Torres also draws strongly on anarchist ideas about interlinked dominations, those of Bookchin in particular. Torres sees critique of domination and a contestationary politics of non-domination as key to anarchist politics (Torres, 2007, pp. 85–7). While Bookchin's own contribution to debates on the status of nonhuman animals is limited and problematic, the simple but vital notion that human domination is intersectionalised is key to an anarchist embrace of projects of animal liberation. Yet as Torres points out, the domination of the nonhuman animal world is an instance of highly normalized and everyday oppression in which most Western humans are much invested.

It is also, as I have tried to demonstrate here, crucial to understand our relations with nonhuman animals as integrated into intra-human exploitative and oppressive structures.

The analyses of linked dominations and of the politics of non-denomination could have played a greater role in Torres' analysis however. While he allows that the histories of exploitative systems are different and differentiated (2007, p. 156), and that the oppression of animals can exist before and beyond capitalism, his analysis of the oppression of animals, however, becomes focused very much on one systemic cause:

> If we're to be successful in fighting oppression—whether based on race, class, species or gender identity—we're going to need to fight the heart of the economic order that drives these oppressions. We're going to have to fight capitalism [2007, p. 11].

This is, ultimately, a reductionist position and a more intersectionalised analysis requires the broader notion of multiple domination, such as is found in Bookchin. This broader perspective comes through strongly in the pamphlet by Brian Dominick which argues that contesting domination is key to vegan politics. Dominick calls for anarchists to recognize the imposition of social categories on animals. Nonhuman species are not "less" than humans, rather, this hierarchy is constantly reproduced by the active dehumanization of animals and the reinforcement of separation. This hierarchy is political, and anarchists sensitive to the naturalization of categories of oppression (in terms of gender or "race" or ability and so on) should be attuned to those generated by the politics of species domination. In addition to an objection to hierarchy, anarchists are called to oppose the exploitation, violence and alienation experienced by nonhuman animals (in animal agriculture, vivisection, the pet industry etc.) as well as the alienation of many human laborers in such industries, and avoid as far as possible, the consumption of products based on the exploitation and suffering of animals. The intersectionalised nature of the domination of animals means that veganism becomes part of the multi-faceted resistance to the dominant social paradigm that is anarchism:

> Only a perspective and lifestyle based on true compassion can destroy the oppressive constructs of present society.... This to me is the essence of anarchy. No one who fails to embrace all struggles against oppression as his or her own fits my definition of an anarchist.

On reflection, in an afterword to the third version of *Animal Liberation and Social Revolution*, Dominick softens this line and suggests that while social revolution is needed in all spheres of domination, including our relations towards nonhuman animals, we must see compassionate living as a process rather than an end state. It is an ideal to which few if any of us will realize, but a struggle to be engaged with. Indeed, the struggles in countering multiple dominations and oppressions in daily life mean that our political choices are always compromised and complicated (see Brian Dominick's reflective discussion on his earlier writing in this volume).

Bookchin has nothing but contempt for what he calls "lifestyle anarchism," but Dominick makes very clear that veganism is not about a "lifestyle choice." Rather, Dominick rejects the dichotomous positioning of social change against "lifestyle." The way he understands veganism as resistance to exploitation makes his argument closer to that of advocates of revolution in everyday life. It is to be understood as part of a process of human liberation which enables us to free animals from exploitation and oppression. What "agency" nonhuman animals might have is a topic of keen debate in animal studies. In the social sciences, agency has been attributed to beings with desires, intentions and wills and this definition certainly applies to some nonhuman species, certainly to those animals within agricultural complexes and many of those kept as pets in the West. Many species, particularly domesticates, have a sense of selfhood. They can exercise choice and communicate with humans and other species (however much the content may be open to interpretation) as fellow agentic beings. Yet what might constitute "liberation" for other species we might never know. Indeed, our very language of "liberation" is both humanist and human-centered. Yet as Carol Adams and Marjorie Proctor-Smith note, while animals "cannot fight collectively against human oppression, ... the lack of struggle cannot be taken as absence of resistance or acceptance of domination" (1993, p. 309). In his afterword Dominick wisely eschews the term liberation for animals in favor of terms such as freedom from exploitation and violence which he sees as essential to the anarchist project of freedom for all. It is here, I think, that anarchism might usefully revisit notions of freedom, autonomy and liberation with a critical and posthumanist eye.

Conclusion

I have argued that there is the potential for a fruitful dialogue between critical approaches in animal studies and anarchist political thought. In the work of anarchist social ecologists such as Kropotkin and Bookchin, the critique of naturalized hierarchies and the embedding of social systems within "natural" systems are fore grounded. What is perhaps most significant in terms of their placing in the anarchist tradition however, is their analysis of patterns of hierarchy and domination which usurp, distort and reconfigure human relations, but also, particularly for Bookchin, structure our coexistence with nonhuman natures.

Anarchism has been relatively open to multifaceted struggles against different forms of social domination. The analysis of the power relations of domination has often been characterized by what is often now referred to as "intersectonality"—an examination of overlapping formations and practices of domination and interconnected relations of power. The insights of feminist, critical race and postcolonial theory have been of great significance here and have impacted on anarchist scholarship and work in animal studies. I have suggested that anarchism must embrace both the notion of species hierarchy as a form of social domination in which oppression and exploitation are naturalized, and an understanding that species relations are implicated in forms of intra human social domination.

To place both the struggle against multiple injustices and the attempt to live well as part and parcel of the same struggle has been an element of radical politics for centuries. As those such as Dominick and Torres have rightly suggested, living well with both human and nonhuman animals is a political as well as personal struggle in a context of multiple and entangled forms of domination. And that struggle would best be in the service of *all* the creatures with whom we human animals share this planet.

REFERENCES

Adams, C. J. (1976). "Vegetarianism: The inedible complex." *Second Wave* 4(4): 36–42.
Adams, C. J. (1990). *The sexual politics of meat.* Cambridge: Polity.
Adams, C. J. (2003). *The pornography of meat.* London: Continuum.
Adams, C. J., and Proctor-Smith, M. (1993). "Taking life or taking on life? Table talk and animals," in C. J. Adams (ed.), *Ecofeminism and the sacred* (pp. 295–310). New York: Continuum.
Arluke, A. (2004). "A sociology of Sociological Animal Studies." *Society and Animals* 10(4): 369–374.
Bekoff, M. (2002). *Minding animals: Awareness, emotions and heart.* Oxford: Oxford University Press.
Benny, N. (1983). "All one flesh: the rights of animals," in L. Caldecott and S. Leyland eds., *Reclaim the Earth* (pp. 141–151). London: Women's Press.
Bookchin, M. (2005). *The ecology of freedom: The emergence and dissolution of hierarchy.* Edinburgh: AK Press.
Bookchin, M. (1990). *The philosophy of social ecology: Essays on dialectical naturalism* Montreal: Black Rose Books.
Caldecott, L., and Leyland, S. (eds.), (1983). *Reclaim the earth.* London: Women's Press.
Collard, A., with Contrucci, J. (1988). *Rape of the wild: Man's violence against animals and the earth.* London: Women's Press.
Compassion in World Farming (CIWF). (2002). *Detrimental impacts of industrial animal agriculture.* Godalming, Surrey: CIWF.
Crenshaw, K. W. (1991). "Mapping the margins: Intersectionality, identity politics, and violence against women of colour." *Stanford Law Review* 43(6): 1241–99.
Cudworth, E. (2008). "Most farmers prefer Blondes"—dynamics of anthroparchy in animals' becoming meat." *The Journal of Critical Animal Studies* 6(1): 32–45.
Cudworth, E. (2011a). *Social lives with Other animals: Tales of sex, death and love.* Basingstoke: Palgrave.

Cudworth, E. (2011b). "Climate change, industrial animal agriculture and complex inequalities: Developments in the politics of food insecurity." *Science and Society* 2(3): 323–334.
Dominick, B. *Animal liberation and social revolution: A vegan perspective on anarchism and an anarchist perspective on veganism.* New York: Critical Mess Media.
Dunayer, J. (1995). "Sexist words, speciesist roots," in C.J. Adams and J. Donnovan, eds., *Animals and Women* (pp. 11–31). Durham: Duke University Press.
Eisnitz, G. (1997). *Slaughterhouse: Shocking tales of greed, neglect and inhumane treatment inside the U.S. meat industry.* New York: Prometheus.
Fisher, E. (1979). *Woman's creation: Sexual evolution and the shaping of society.* Garden City, NY: Doubleday.
Franklin, A. (1999). *Animals and modern cultures: A sociology of human-animal relations in modernity.* London: Sage.
Gellatley, J. (1994). *The silent ark: A chilling expose of meat—the global killer.* London: Thorsons.
Haraway, D. (1989). *Primate visions: Gender, race and nature in the world of modern science.* London: Routledge.
Kappeler, S. (1995). "Speciesism, racism, nationalism ... or the power of scientific subjectivity," in C.J. Adams and J. Donovan, eds., *Animals and women: Feminist theoretical explorations* (pp. 320–352). Durham: Duke University Press.
Kauffman, S. (1993). *At home in the universe: The search for laws of self-organization and complexity.* Oxford: Oxford University Press.
Kropotkin, P. (1987a). *Mutual aid.* London: Freedom Press.
Kropotkin, P. (1987b). *The state: Its historic role* London: Freedom Press.
Kruse, C. R. (2002). "Social animals: Animal studies and sociology." *Society and Animals* 10(4): 375–379.
Lee-Sanchez, C. (1993). "Animal, vegetable, and mineral," in C. J. Adams, ed., *Ecofeminism and the sacred* (pp. 207–228). New York: Continuum.
Light, A. (1998). "Bookchin and/as social ecology," in A. Light, ed., *Social ecology after Bookchin* (pp. 1–23). New York: The Guilford Press.
Le Duff, C. (1999). "At the slaughterhouse, some things never die," reprinted in Wolfe, C. ed. (2003). *Zoontologies: The question of the animal* (pp. 183–198). Minneapolis: University of Minnesota Press.
MacDonald, M. (2010). "Foodprints" in *The future of food*, special issue of *Resurgence* (pp. 32–33) no. 259, March/April.
Mason, J., and Finelli, M. (2006) "Brave new farm?," in P. Singer, ed., *In defense of animals: The second wave* (pp. 104–122). Oxford: Blackwell.
Masson, J. M. (2004). *The pig who sang to the moon: The emotional world of farm animals* London: Jonathan Cape.
Margulis, L., and Sagan, R. (2002). *Acquiring genomes: A theory of the origins of species.* New York: Basic Books.
Marshall, P. (1993). *Demanding the impossible: A history of anarchism.* London: Fontana.
Nibert, D. (2002). *Animal rights/human rights: Entanglements of oppression and liberation.* Lanham, MD: Rowman & Littlefield.
Phoenix, A., and Pattynama, P. (2006). "Editorial: Intersectionality." *European Journal of Women's Studies* 13(3): 187–92.
Plumwood, V. (1993). *Feminism and the mastery of nature.* London: Routledge.
Plumwood, V. (1994). "The ecopolitics debate and the politics of nature" in K. Warren, ed., *Ecological feminism* (pp. 64–87). London: Routledge.

Plumwood, V. (1997) "Androcentrism and anthropocentrism: Parallels and politics," in K. Warren, ed., *Ecofeminism: Women, nature, culture* (pp. 327–355). Philadelphia: New Society.
Rifkin, J. (1994). *Beyond beef: The rise and fall of cattle culture.* London: Thorsons.
Shantu Riley, S. (1993) "Ecology is a sistah's issue too: The politics of emergent Afrocentric ecowomanism," in C. J. Adams, ed., *Ecofeminism and the sacred* (pp. 191–204). New York: Continuum.
Steinfeld, H., et al. (2006). *Livestock's long shadow.* Rome: United Nations FAO.
Torres B. (2007). *Making a killing: The political economy of animal rights.* Oakland: AK Press.
Tuan, Y-F. (1984). *Dominance and affection: The making of pets.* New Haven: Yale University Press.
van Duyn, R. (1969). *Message of a wise kabouter.* London: Duckworth.
Velten, H. (2007). *Cow.* London: Reaktion.
Walby, S. (2007). "Complexity theory, systems theory, and multiple intersecting social inequalities." *Philosophy of the Social Sciences* 37(4): 449–470.
Walby, S. (2009). *Globalization and inequalities: Complexity and contested modernities.* London: Sage.
Young, I. M. (1990). *Justice and the politics of difference.* Princeton: Princeton University Press.

Beyond Suffering
Resisting Patriarchy and Reproductive Control

Nekeisha Alayna Alexis

> [R]ecent research indicates that we may be very close to, if not already at the point where we can genetically engineer factory-farmed livestock with a reduced or completely eliminated capacity to suffer. In as much as animal suffering is the principal concern that motivates the animal welfare movement, this development should be of central interest to its adherents [Shriver, 2013, p. 115].
>
> Tranquility is found also in dungeons, but is that enough to make them desirable places to live in? [Rousseau, 1993, p. 186].

Emphasizing farmed animals' suffering, and more specifically, suffering caused by overt and persistent acts of physical violence and cruelty, has been integral to animal welfare advocates' approach to opposing confined animal feeding operations. Essential to this model of resisting factory farms has been recording and disclosing undercover footage of cows, pigs, chickens and other creatures languishing in appalling conditions; of humans beating, electrocuting, kicking, punching, dragging and using other forms of brute force against the animals; and of animals enduring bloody and excruciating deaths in slaughterhouses. The quote "The question is not, 'Can they reason?' nor 'Can they talk?' but rather, 'Can they suffer?'" (Bentham, 1907) summarizes this strategy for convincing flesh-food eaters to opt out of these systems of terror. But is this focus on suffering—and a very specific kind of suffering at that—enough to promote the freedom these animals deserve?

Building an argument for animal liberation that does not rely on the problems of physical violence and bloodshed as the primary or sole concern is an urgent task facing animal advocates. Today, this suffering narrative is being tested by titans in the factory farming industry, by technological solutions to farmed animal pain and by growing interest in and options for more benign methods of animal agriculture. In light of this reality, animal advocates must continue broadening our discourse to include other compelling narratives as a matter of tactics and as a way to further elucidate the repressive nature of the flesh-food system. One such argument is that controlling the reproductive capacity of farmed female animals is a form of gendered oppression that must be resisted as part of the overall struggle against patriarchy. Said differently, even if physical pain could be entirely eradicated from the system—even if hens were not caged, cows ate grass and sows frolicked in open fields before slaughter—exploiting female bodies against their own best interests and against the best interests of their species is institutionalized domination that should cease.

In this essay, I will outline the possibilities and inherent limitations of using the suffering narrative to make changes on behalf of farmed animals and identify some of the external pressures that challenge this narrative. Following that argument, I will explore the ways patriarchy manifests itself in animal agriculture, particularly in the area of reproductive control, and highlight the connections between animal liberation and female liberation. I will then focus my critique on one reproductive practice that, although used widely across various types of flesh-food production, is usually absent from exposés on animal cruelty. In taking this approach, I aim to show how expanding the farmed animal advocacy narrative to include concerns of resisting patriarchy and reproductive tyranny can undergird a currently beleaguered suffering agenda. In so doing, I hope to help our movement better overcome obstacles threatening our work for liberation.

Before continuing, I want to clarify that my primary audience is not those who use animals for food because of insurmountable geographic and environmental pressures that make it impossible to live healthily on nonanimal alternatives alone. People in those situations need to pursue ethical considerations that elevate farmed animal concerns as much as possible while balancing the needs of the human community. Nevertheless, necessary choices made *in those contexts* do not diminish the call to liberate farmed animals when nonfood human and animal relationships are possible and ecologically speaking, increasingly necessary.

Suffering as Success Story

Exposing the callous treatment of farmed animals generates public discussion and concern about animal welfare in arenas where the issue is usually absent. This strategy alerts consumers to the methods used to bring the majority of flesh-foods to their tables, disrupting the widespread myths associated with present-day animal agriculture and providing catalysts for people to change their perceptions of and relationship to other animals. In March 2014, Mercy for Animals Canada released video documenting conditions at Ontario-based Hybrid Turkeys, a breeding company whose genetic stock accounts for 90 percent of the turkeys eaten in the country. In addition to footage of birds stricken by open wounds, rotting eyes and other gruesome infections, the camera captured violent scenes such as workers beating turkeys to death with a shovel and a metal rod (Griffith-Greene, 2014; Perkel, 2014). Not only did the story reach local and national news outlets, but *Marketplace,* the highest-rated current affairs series on nationally broadcast CBC Television (http://www.cbc.ca/marketplace/about/) aired the entire recording the same day the story broke. This kind of media attention can increase viewers' empathy toward farmed animals and open up conversation on whether and how other animals should be used for food. In some instances, coverage of abuses against farmed animals fosters outrage against specific companies. On other occasions, people respond to what they see by abstaining from particular products, adopting a plant-based diet and/or demanding changes to industry practices through petitions and protest. If it is the case that overturning systems of animal exploitation begins with "the difficult process of ideological delegitimation" (Boggs, 2011, p. 73), then using suffering narratives to raise consciousness about the dominant relationship between humans and farmed animals is a crucial first step in the subversive process.

This method of instigating change through graphic depictions of farmed animals' agony has also produced some benefits for the animals. Companies have suspended and fired workers caught committing abuse, and perpetrators have faced legal penalties for their actions (Hendrick and Hayden, 2013; Hutchinson, 2014, para. 13). Documenting animal cruelty has also forced companies to modify or forgo harsh forms of confinement and slaughter. Ballot initiatives instigated in part by media attention to animal welfare violations have led several states to ban gestation crates for sows (Arizona in 2006, Florida in 2002; and Oregon in 2007); battery cages for hens (California in 2008 and Michigan in 2009); veal crates for calves (Colorado in 2008, Maine in 2011 and Rhode Island in 2012) and a total end to "foie gras" production and sales in California in 2004. Admittedly, exposing worker abuse and tweaking cage sizes is a long way from ending farmed animal exploitation. Yet securing bigger cages for hens and stalls big enough for sows to move around in and socialize are appreciable stopgaps as the larger battle continues.

Undercover investigations into food animal suffering can also devastate targeted companies. In 2008, a landmark action taken by the Humane Society of the United States (HSUS) against Westland/Hallmark Meat Company forced a recall of 143.4 million pounds of "beef"—the largest recall of cattle-flesh in U.S. history—after concerns about animal suffering and food safety arose in response to an HSUS video. The footage of workers kicking and shocking cattle, and using forklifts to drag debilitated cows to their deaths incited anger about animal handling and increased fears about "Mad Cow disease," e-coli and salmonella contamination. The federal government responded by banning the slaughter of severely weakened cows for human consumption (Healey, 2008; Werner, 2008). Shortly after extensive media reporting on the situation, Westland/Hallmark closed its doors. Within six weeks of the recall, the company was besieged by $67.2 million in recall expenses and was bankrupt (Goad, 2008; Schmidt, 2008). Six years later, the case was settled for a mere $3.1 million because of the company's devastating financial fallout (Associated Press, 2013).

In 2009, another HSUS video taken at Bushway Packing Inc. in Grand Isle, Vermont, also forced that plant to shut down. Cameras at the federally monitored, certified organic processor captured workers using similar violence against newborn calves. Footage included workers shocking and hitting calves, many of whom still had their umbilical cords attached, and skinning infants that appeared to be alive and conscious. Not only were plant employees implicated, but an unidentified United States Department of Agriculture inspector was also caught coaching a worker on how to evade penalties for these violations. After the video hit airwaves, Vermont dairy farmers rightly worried that it would "give an enterprise generally viewed as wholesome a black eye" (Gram, 2009, para. 10).

By using undercover surveillance to reveal farmed animal suffering, advocates have forced companies out of business, pushed for alternatives to the cruelest practices, and raised the profile of animal welfare issues in the public sphere. As a result, consumers are changing their choices. Meat and poultry consumption dropped 12.2 percent from 2007 to 2012, thanks in part to "the efforts of a large number of nongovernmental agencies that oppose meat consumption for reasons ranging from the environment to animal rights to social justice" (Meyer & Steiner, 2011). Per capita consumption of cow-derived milk and cream also declined 25 percent between 1975 and 2012, and is expected to fall another 3 percent by 2018 due in part to the growing popularity of soy and almond milk alternatives (Luckerson, 2014, para. 9). A 2010 study on the effects of newspaper and magazine reports about farmed animal handling has also determined that, "media attention to animal welfare has significant negative effects" on flesh-food demand and "triggers consumers to purchase less meat rather than reallocate expenditures across competing meats" (Tonsor & Olynk, 2010, p. 2). Hardest hit by these declines are suppliers of pig-, chicken- and turkey-derived products. However, demand for "beef" is indirectly affected as "consumers make budget adjustments in favor of nonmeat products" and "the aggregate meat market loses the ability to internally compete for those funds" (Tonsor & Olynk, 2010, p. 2). These concrete shifts in consumer habits, industry practices and public discourse are signs that the suffering narrative is a force with which industrial animal agriculture must reckon.

The Trouble with Suffering

Although exposing farmed animal suffering has led to noteworthy successes, it is important not to overstate the narrative's overall impact or underestimate the challenges it faces. One internal dilemma relates to the discourse around factory farm workers who are implicated in abuse. Animal advocates overlook a crucial piece of the puzzle when they celebrate employee layoffs and criminal convictions without attending to the ways racism, sexism, capitalism, and other forms of oppression foster a culture of violence on factory farms. These workers, most of whom are people of color, undocumented immigrants, or part of the white working class are routinely subject to chronic and debilitating injuries and illnesses, physical exhaustion, verbal and emotional abuse by superiors, and severe restrictions on their most basic needs, including sufficient bathroom breaks. Often female workers also endure sexual harassment in addition to the other inhumane treatment they experience (Human Rights Watch, 2004; Nebraska Appleseed, 2009; Southern Poverty Law Center & Alabama Appleseed, 2013). Without meaningful legal protections, employees are compelled to remain silent about these conditions and the aggression used against nonhuman animals. While some people torture animals for sport, it is easy to see how other laborers who are not otherwise prone to sadistic behavior could vent their frustrations on the animals they manage, especially when those animals are defined as property or waste. The likelihood of abuse rapidly increases when some of the most egregious treatment is tacitly approved and expected by plant supervisors. Although cruelty must not be excused, it is crucial to link the trauma factory farm employees undergo to the trauma they inflict on the animals. Without an intersectional approach, animal advocates fail to unmask the full extent of the violence within industrial animal agriculture and miss opportunities to create strategic partnerships with other agitators for justice.

Focusing on individual employees who use official and unofficial-but-tolerated industry violence also provides companies with convenient scapegoats. On the heels of the aforementioned Hybrid Turkeys scandal, company spokesperson Helen Wojcinski quickly painted a picture of rogue workers, saying, "We feel this is an isolated incident.... Employees have been trained. They know what they're supposed to do. There is obviously a lapse. There's been a mistake made here" (Griffith-Greene, 2014, para. 13). In the Westland/Hallmark case, it was worker Rafael Sanchez Herrera and supervisor Daniel Ugarte Navarro who received the U.S.'s first ever felony-abuse charges against slaughterhouse workers. Meanwhile, company president Steve Mendell received no charges for his oversight of the plant, despite Navarro testifying that Mendell condoned the abuse and cattle transporter Rich Sumner, who was fired for complaining about company practices, admitting that the plant routinely purchased the cheapest, sickliest cows at auction (Selzer, Rush & Kinsey, 2010, p. 5). Even though undercover investigations reveal the same kind of violence on factory farms regardless of location, producer or other factors, management's first line of defense is blaming overtaxed laborers who are compelled to follow orders in heinous working environments. Firing low-level employees reassures consumers that, with the exception of a few heartless rule-breakers, all is well on the farm. Animal advocates play into this counter narrative when they praise punitive actions against workers without speaking intersectionally about the industry's injustice.

Even forcing slaughterhouses to close is not always a decisive victory. After the recall dust settled in the Westland/Hallmark saga, Mendell sold the facility to American Beef Packers. Within a year of reopening, the new owners were back to slaughtering 200–300 cattle a day with a goal of returning to the plant's former output of 500 cattle daily (Selzer, Rush & Kinsey, 2010, p. 6, 8). HSUS's win against Bushway Packing was also a temporary one. The doors were closed for less than five months before the USDA allowed two of the three former owners—including an owner who stood by during innumerable acts of cruelty—to resume operation under a new name (Humane Society of the United States, 2010). Although some legislators called for laws like mandatory video surveillance across Vermont slaughterhouses, the state instead opted for tepid reforms such as additional training for workers, self-drafted "humane handling plans" and increased fines for infractions (Abels, 2011). Even if both facilities had remained closed, the overall impact would have been meaningful but modest. Westland/Hallmark and Bushway were tiny operations compared to industry giants like IBP Inc. (formerly Iowa Beef Packers, now Tyson Foods, Inc.) in Garden City, Kansas, and the ConAgra complex in Greeley, Colorado, which each butchers more than 6,400 steers daily (Boggs, 2011, p. 76).

Finally, modifying industry practices regarding farmed animal care does not automatically prevent new abuses in confinement or produce system-wide improvements. Cage-free egg-laying hens may no longer be crammed into spaces the size of filing cabinet drawers. But they are still born in hatcheries where workers mutilate their beaks and grind up fully conscious days-old male chicks. Cage-free operations can also pack hundreds of thousands of hens into giant warehouses with little access to sunlight and no access to the outdoors (LaVeck, 2007, p. 48). Additionally, tweaks in cage and stall sizes does not mean substantially better treatment for farmed animals during transport to slaughter or on the kill-floor. Yet corporations that adopt minimal welfare adjustments still profit from higher priced "cage-free," "free-range" and "organic" fare. These labels suggesting great strides in farmed animal handling lulls consumers into a newfound sense of security while "bolstering the credibility and positive public image of an industry with a long history of betraying public trust" (LaVeck, 2007, p. 48). When animal advocates promote eating industrially raised flesh-foods *so long as* those foods have the right designations, they work against their long-range goals and the long-term interests of farmed animals (Cole, 2011, p. 93)—that is, until new footage from upgraded facilities tells another suffering story.

Suffering Under Siege

In addition to the internal conflicts within the suffering motif, advocates are facing increased external pressure. In recent years, flesh-food producers have locked arms to criminalize undercover investigations, introducing fifteen anti-whistleblower bills in eleven states in 2013 alone. At minimum, these "ag-gag" bills thwart animal advocates from seeking employment at processing plants for surveillance purposes, prohibit people from taking photos or video at factory farms without permission, and require short timelines for reporting abuse in a deliberate attempt to prevent evidence of ongoing systemic cruelty (Humane Society of the United States, 2014). In one extreme example of a model bill, violators of the law would also end up on a "terrorist registry" (Oppel, Jr., 2013, para. 6). Legal threats to the suffering narrative hinder advocates from acquiring the documentation they need and divert resources from educating consumers on farmed animal welfare, encouraging veganism and vegetarianism, and funding ongoing investigations. Thus far, ag-gag laws have only passed in Missouri, Indiana, Iowa and Utah. But if flesh-food consumption continues its unprecedented falloff, companies lose profits, and states depending on industrial animal farming lose substantial revenue, the tide could easily turn toward more legislation, harsher penalties and less evidence to fuel the suffering narrative.

The less industrial or "humane" animal agriculture movement is another obstacle for the suffering narrative. Like animal advocates, proponents of agrarianism, permaculture, homesteading and related movements want to limit farmed animal suffering and openly condemn factory-farming for its cruelty. However, instead of foregoing flesh-foods altogether, these groups redirect their support toward small-scale, local and environmentally friendlier operations that respect their animals' needs and natural tendencies, and use practices that minimize or eliminate suffering. Some "humane" meat sympathizers personally slaughter farmed animals to "take some direct responsibility for the killing on which his meat-eating depends" (Pollan, 2009, p. 231). Engaging this rite of passage is described as another way for participants to be mindful of the individual animals being consumed and to remain sensitized to the way flesh-foods arrive at their tables.

At the surface, there is significant overlap between the concerns of animal advocates and conscious carnists (Joy, 2011, para. 7–13) of varying stripes. However, what is lost in both groups' focus on extreme cruelty of factory farms is the cruelty within less-industrial models. Even a relatively small pasture operation that privileges "letting pigs be pigs" castrates day-old piglets without anesthesia—a medically unnecessary practice carried out to meet consumer tastes—and transports animals long distances to slaughter (Foer, 2009, p. 168–69, 171). And Polyface Farms, a much-celebrated leader in the local, sustainable, organic farming movement that painstakingly strives to mimic natural patterns raises and kills the same genetically modified turkeys as its factory farm counterparts. As one critic remarked, "It's like putting a broken-down Honda on the Autobahn and saying it's a Porsche.... [I]ts genetics are so screwed up" (Foer, 2009, p. 113). Granted the pain that the pasture-raised piglets experience from castration is brief and mitigated, and even industrially bred birds deserve to live free from confinement and abuse. But if the standard is less suffering and not *a total end to unnecessary violence and pain*

Failure to critically examine alternative animal agriculture operations because they are not excessively violent masks and condones the problems that are present. Furthermore, condoning limited animal suffering when plant-based foods that require *no* equivalent pain are readily available works against the argument that *all* cruelty is unacceptable. In praising less-industrial options, animal advocates also overlook the ways adherents to these models remain complicit in the same conventional systems they denounce. Not only are there local, sustainable facilities that breed the same animals as their counterparts, acquire animals from the same hatcheries, and send animals to the same slaughterhouses, anecdotal accounts suggest that it is unusual for humane meat sympathizers to routinely abstain from factory-farmed fare. Even carnists who have killed their own meal will consume flesh-foods from industrial sources, albeit with a self-professed sense of greater awareness (Lam, 2010, para. 14; Kaminer, 2010, para. 17).

In addition to the challenge of humane farming, animal advocates must also contend with technological solutions to the factory farm vs. animal welfare debate. For example, philosopher and neuroscientist Adam Shriver tackles the suffering dilemma with a proposal for genetically engineering animals with a reduced or eliminated capacity to experience pain. He points to current research demonstrating that the brain registers the sensory dimension of pain—its "intensity, localization and quality (whether it is sharp, dull, burning, etc.)"—in a different location than the affective dimension of pain, which is "the unpleasantness of the pain, or 'how much one *minds* the pain'" (Shriver, 2009, p. 117). Scientists have also shown that genetically removing a specific peptide (P311) and two enzymes (AC1 and AC8) in mammals reduces discomfort or suffering, even when test subjects react to the harmful stimuli with actions like moving away. Shriver suggests using these findings to improve the lives of factory-farmed animals by eliminating "the sensitization that occurs as a result of painful or traumatic experiences" (Shriver, 2009, p. 118). Indeed, these animals would be even better suited for life in cages "where they can't do much of anything that would injure or otherwise harm themselves" (Shriver, 2009, p. 119).

Animal advocates open the door to the kind of biological domination Shriver recommends by centering our discourse on extreme suffering. In fact, Shriver cites animal rights architect Peter Singer as an inspiration for this proposal and posits his idea as a direct response to the animal rights movements' inability to prevent the ascendance of factory farming. When ending physical and psychological trauma from overt cruelty monopolizes the conversation, it becomes possible to argue that "genetically engineering livestock will produce a world with better consequences" without introducing "any new 'wrongs' into the world" (Shriver, 2009, p. 116). However, if the goal is elevating other animals from property status and freeing animals from human subjugation, then any solution that furthers the agricultural machine is illegitimate. If liberation is our principle concern, then it is essential to make room for issues beyond suffering. Other aspects of farmed animal oppression must also enter the spotlight.

Broadening the Narrative

One of the first steps toward broadening the advocacy movement's narrative is clearly and consistently acknowledging whose lives are at stake and why. In so doing, we recognize that factory farming is not merely a form of animal cruelty: it is cruelty that disproportionately victimizes *female* bodies because of the distinctively *female* reproductive capacities those bodies possess. As pioneering feminist vegetarian Carol J. Adams reminds us, the majority of the animals brutalized by our flesh-food systems are females and their children. Indeed, "female bodies are doubly exploited: both when they are alive and when they are dead.... Female animals become oppressed by their femaleness, becoming surrogate wetnurses. Then when their (re)productiveness ends, they are butchered and become animalized protein, or protein in the form of flesh" (Adams, 2002, p. 21). Naming the gendered nature of the exploitation—that it is female farmed animals who are forcibly impregnated, continuously bred, and genetically manipulated against their physical, emotional and psychological welfare; that the milk and eggs that are collected and eaten as a result of this arrangement are uniquely "*feminized protein*, that is protein produced by a female body" (Adams, 2002, p. 21); that it is nursing mothers whose offspring are taken away and whose childrearing instincts are constantly frustrated in order to supply feminized products; and that it is female bodies that are slaughtered, dismembered, packaged and sold as objects—demonstrates that flesh-food production is foremost a system of violence against females.

Similarly, identifying where gendered power and privilege lie within animal agriculture makes clear that this method of dominating female bodies is an expression of patriarchy: that is "a political-social system that insists that males are inherently dominating, superior to everything and everyone deemed weak, especially females, and endowed with the right to dominate and rule over the weak and to maintain that dominance through various forms of psychological terrorism and violence" (hooks, undated, p. 1). It was men who created the technologies and techniques used to exploit female bodies in "animal husbandry" and it is predominantly men who continue to improve on its logic and practice. It is male reproductive power, particularly in the form of semen, which is prized in the system. It is also male bodies who usually escape the most persistent forms of exploitation. Within the popular, socially accepted human imagination, it is male bodies who are thought to be dependent on flesh-foods, especially meat. Finally, it is the prototypical male (white, heterosexual, able-bodied, property-holders) who receives financial, legal and social capital as overseers of livestock production operations, and who often escape fallout when cruelty is exposed. In both industrial and more benign forms of farming animals, capitalist understandings of productivity and usefulness dictate when and how female objectification occurs. In both of these systems, the animal herself has little to no intrinsic value and is has worth only when her body is successfully subject to patriarchal control.

That patriarchy is implicit in the human-animal relationship (Adams, 2002, p. 17) and especially in flesh-food production is not accidental. Instead, this situation is reinforced by social structures that grant male-identified persons unconstrained access to power tools like money, land, weapons and scientific exploration; that socialize men to use those tools for self-preservation and elevation; and that legitimize subjugating female and deficient/nonideal male bodies in pursuit of those interests. Consequently, advocacy on behalf of farmed animals is synonymous with the task of female liberation in general and freedom from reproductive tyranny in particular. At times, animal advocates will allude to this overlap between the struggle for females to determine the destinies of their minds and bodies and the struggle to free farmed animals. For example, undercover investigations critique practices such as forced molting whereby hens are shocked into greater egg production through starvation and light deprivation, or breeding female turkeys to have such large breasts that their legs break under their weight. However, advocates usually describe how these manmade technologies are deployed against female bodies when they fit within the suffering narrative. Other reproduction techniques that are not extremely violent or demonstrably painful do not often make the agenda.

When advocates make concessions to limit animals' suffering without simultaneously challenging the social convention that it is acceptable and necessary to dominate female bodies, they remain complicit in patriarchy. On the other hand, drawing connections between freeing farmed animals and female liberation in general makes it possible to condemn all forms of oppression, regardless of whether they result in explicit suffering. Unlike a single focus on factory farming, this intersectional analysis also challenges less industrial flesh-food production and technological solutions to suffering that figuratively and literally thingifies female creatures. Finally, pursuing farmed animal liberation through a narrative of resisting reproductive tyranny and patriarchy has the added advantage of sidestepping "ag-gag" laws because undercover footage, while helpful to the argument, is not essential.

Toward a Narrative Against Reproductive Tyranny

> Given the present power structure, the real question is: Should the machine (the woman) be the one to decide whether, or how often, or with what materials, it goes into production? Obviously not. Machine owners can say this openly when they speak of cows. A cow is "basically a machine" that must "produce this marketable product or unit every year." Few of us feel horror at this view of our sister animals [Corea, 1985, p. 27–28].

Reproductive tyranny over female bodies is the foundation on which animal agriculture relies. It is because of artificial insemination, embryo transfers, forced molting, hormone injections, heat cycle monitoring and other related management practices that cows, hens, turkeys, ewes and other animals become and remain part of the flesh-food system. Given the limited scope of this essay, I cannot give a full account of the multiple reproductive technologies used on farmed female animals and the impact each technology has on their bodies. Instead I will concentrate on the use of artificial insemination in cows as an example of oppression that does not need to fit the common suffering narrative.

Artificial Insemination

Italian priest and physiologist Lazaro Spallanzani conducted research on frogs, fish and dogs to invent the process of collecting live sperm from male nonhuman animals and inserting them into a female's reproductive tract in 1779 (Corea, 1985, p. 35). In approximately 1900, Russian scientists began testing artificial insemination in cattle and sheep and discovered its potential for breeding. In 1914, the first artificial vagina was developed to collect sperm from dogs. Shortly after, Russian scientists adjusted the mechanical vaginas to sexually stimulate stallions, bulls and rams (Corea, 1985, 36). In 1936, Danish cattle breeders created the first cooperative for disseminating the sperm of their prized bulls. Twelve years later, a rectal electrode called the electroejaculator was introduced to compel "reluctant," crippled or old bulls to produce sperm, maximizing the usefulness and longevity of superior animals. By the mid–1960s, "the availability of frozen sperm led to the widespread use of AI" (Corea, 1985, 37). Currently, artificial insemination is used on approximately 60 percent of dairy cows in the United States (University of Wisconsin-Madison, 2000, para. 4).

Artificially inseminating cattle involves handlers immobilizing a cow in her stall, inserting a gloved and lubricated forearm into her rectum, clearing her vulva with paper towels, inserting an inseminating rod (known popularly as a "breeding gun") into her vagina at 30–40 degrees, and pressing the gun forward toward her cervix (DeJarnette & Nebel, undated, p. 2; Corea, 1985, p. 15). At the point where the gun tip contacts the cervix, the handler twists and bends the cervix to guide the tip through her rings of muscle and tissue until it reaches the uterine opening. Then the handler slowly deposits the spermatozoa from the gun into the uterine body where contractions move the sperm toward the cow's oviducts and her uterine horns. Artificial insemination does not involve blood-letting or cruelty. To the contrary, inseminators are cautioned to "be gentle. Don't use too much force," "Take your time" and "Relax" (DeJarnette & Nebel, undated, p. 1). They are also encouraged to use facilities that are "designed for quiet and easy handling" and that minimize "harassment and excitement" (Turner & Raleigh, undated, p. 2). Yet an absence of overt brutality and emphasis on gentle treatment only masks that this calculated act of involuntary vaginal penetration is a form of routine sexual violence.

During artificial insemination, handlers use various pressure tactics to disable the cow's resistance to vaginal intrusion. Luring her into a small stall and/or placing her head in wooden slats limits her movement. Making a fist against her vulva spreads its lips to clear access for the gun. Massaging her rectal constriction rings inhibits her body from expelling the inseminator's arm. If her rectal and abdominal contractions are so strong that her reproductive tract recedes into her pelvic cavity, grabbing the cervix and pushing it forward forces her vagina to straighten son the gun can pass freely. If grabbing and pushing fails, the inseminator can use his wrist to "gently 'milk'" the vaginal folds that are denying entry while sliding the gun forward (DeJarnette & Nebel, undated, p. 2). Watching a heifer undergo artificial insemination, feminist Gena Corea observed, "She jumped and squirmed. She struggled to free herself from the head catch." After the farmhand finished, "the heifer began backing slowly and cautiously out of the pen, returning the way she had been driven in. Her sides were shaking. Her eyes were big. She made no sound. It was if she were tiptoeing away" (Corea, 1985, p. 13).

Using a foreign object to forcefully penetrate the vagina of a trapped individual is rape. Yet, naming it as such when the victim is a some-body who is known as "it," not "she," property not person, is controversial. The circumstances surrounding the first known human artificial insemination with donor sperm in 1884 may make the connection clearer. While conducting infertility treatments for an unnamed woman, Dr. William Pancoast discovered it was her spouse whose low sperm count was hindering a successful pregnancy. Instead of exposing her husband's problem, Pancoast anesthetized the woman with chloroform. Then without her foreknowledge, "he took the receptacle into which one of his students masturbated. With a hard rubber syringe, he inserted the student's semen into her uterus. He then plugged her cervix with gauze" (Corea, 1985, p. 12). He never told her what he did, even after she birthed a son nine months later. Even in that era, one of Dr. Pancoast's peers recognized that such actions constituted rape (Corea, 1985, p. 30, note 1). The similarities between what this patient experienced in her physicians' office and what each cow experiences in her stall, and the fact that the unnamed woman was violated using a technique perfected in the wombs of innumerable unnamed cows makes interspecies rape a fitting descriptor for the aforementioned violations.

Unlike the case with Dr. Pancoasts patient, high failure rates when inseminating cows means that they can experience sexual violence several times before becoming pregnant or being rendered useless. Between 7 and 20 percent of cows are not even "in heat" during the procedure and 10–25 percent of cows are not fertilized afterward. A 2004 survey of 103 herds in 11 states totaling over 600 cows also revealed that managers made at least seven failed artificial insemination attempts before "culling" cows that did not become pregnant (Caraviello et al., 2006, p. 4724). At the same time, human domination is also present in the intensive behind-the-scenes management of female bodies that is required for successful artificial insemination programs. A recurring theme among practitioners is the necessity of accurately detecting each cow's estrus cycle, which is notoriously difficult to pinpoint. Consequently, companies have created a number of bio-surveillance techniques and technologies to monitor each cow, including devices that are attached to her back that change color during mounting, pedometers with microprocessor chips that measure her movement, and tags that "track electronic activity detectors and electronic pressure" (Lima da Costa, de Arujo & Feitosa, 2011, p. 154; Turner & Raleigh, undated, p. 1). In addition to heat detection, a comprehensive system will manage each cow's intervals between birthing and re-impregnation; use hormone treatments to synchronize her and the herd's reproductive cycle; visually assessing and scoring her physiological condition to determine her reproductive potential; and routine gynecological examines. These tedious tasks and extensive investments are made, not for the cow's benefit: but as the means of converting her body into a high-yielding milk and eventually meat machine.

Proponents of artificial insemination praise it for its relatively low financial costs to the farmer and the savings gained by eliminating the costs of maintaining a bull. But "its greatest advantage … is that AI extends the use of service by superior bulls. A sire that's proved capable of transmitting desirable traits to his offspring can thus be mated to thousands of cows" (Kidd, 1981, para. 3). In this way, artificial insemination extends male prowess beyond the bounds of time and space. While natural breeding may only may expose 100–300 cows to a sire in a specific location, AI makes it possible to have as many as 100,000–200,000 exposures throughout the United States and across the globe (Turner & Raleigh, undated, p. 1). The ability to successfully pass on superior male traits long after one has died and across multiple generations through as many hosts as possible fulfills patriarchal fantasies about preserving male power and attaining a kind of genetic immortality. It is men who have determined the desirable qualities in the sire and in the recipient cow. It is also males whose reproductive capacity are safeguarded and deemed valuable, who are not quickly rendered unproductive by routine use and who live on in the system through the hyper-transmission of semen.

In contrast, female bodies are receptacles with temporary value that are primarily acted upon. For high-yielding cows, an unreleting cycle of insemination, impregnation, birthing and milking creates persistent health problems that rapidly destroy their young bodies. "Mastitis and hairy heel warts were noted as the greatest animal health concerns, followed by lameness, abortions, and death losses" (Caraviello et al., 2006, p. 4723). Hormonal imbalances, cystic ovarian disease, placenta insufficiency (damaged or underdeveloped placenta), retained placenta (a portion of the placenta membrane remains in the uterus after birth), metritis (inflammation of the uterus), infected reproductive tracts, stillbirths and infertility are just a few of the other health complications a cow may experience during her tenure in the flesh-food system. (Rodriguez-Martinez et al., 2013). After enduring these afflictions in silence, she pays the ultimate price at slaughter. At this stage, undercover cameras may begin rolling. Yet much of her exploitation has already gone unnoticed.

Conclusion

Using graphic images of workers viciously attacking defenseless farmed animals can shock viewers into a new way of thinking, illicit outrage against specific practices and producers, and mobilize people to take steps away from the flesh-food system. Undercover investigations can also lead to penalties for individual and corporate perpetrators, from bankrupting targeted companies to instigating firings for egregious offenses. Even so, the suffering narrative is plagued by internal contradictions and outside pressures that complicate its effectiveness. Legal challenges to information gathering, alternative farming movements and technological approaches to removing animal suffering are also formidable obstacles.

These tactical weaknesses are further exacerbated by an equally important oversight: that of the animal advocacy movement's failure to consistently and convincingly identify the flesh-food system as an expression of patriarchy. At its core, the animal agriculture machine is a gendered form of oppression that exploits predominantly female bodies and their reproductive capacity in service of male power, imagination and appetite. And artificial insemination in particular is a form of institutionalized sexual violence. Animal advocates must acknowledge and articulate these and other related points to build a case that does not rely on continued access to bloody, violent footage. Drawing connections between farmed animal welfare and resisting patriarchy can move us from calls for more tranquil cages, represented by appreciable but varying adjustments to industrial production and a fascination with "humane" options, to an ethic of total liberation. Expanding the movement's concern to include but not center on suffering provides the tools to not only resist factory farming, but also denounces any and all efforts to control female bodies against their best interests and the best interests of their species. This ideological and strategic shift is crucial to expose all the dungeons in their many forms.

References

Abels, C. (2011, September 1). "Humane Heft." *Vermont's Local Banquet.* Retrieved March 30, 2014, from http://localbanquet.com/stories/on-the-farm/item/humane-heft.

Adams, C. J. (2002). *The Sexual Politics of Meat: A Feminist-Vegetarian Critical Theory,* 10th ed. New York: Continuum.

Associated Press. (2013, November 27). "California: Deal Reached in Suit Over Ani-

mals Abuse." *New York Times.* Retrieved May 12, 2014, from http://www.nytimes.com/2013/11/28/us/california-deal-reached-in-suit-over-animal-abuse.html.
Bentham, J. (1907). *An Introduction to the Principles of Morals and Legislation.* Oxford: Calrendon Press. Library of Economics and Liberty [Online]. Retrieved May 5, 2014 from http://www.econlib.org/library/Bentham/bnthPML.html.
Boggs, C. (2011). "Corporate Power, Ecological Crisis, and Animal Rights." In John Sanbonmatsu ed., *Critical Theory and Animal Liberation* (pp. 71–98). Lanham: Rowman & Littlefield.
Caraviello, D. Z., Weigel, K.A., Fricke, P. M., Wiltbank, M.C., Florent, M. J., Cook, N.B.... Rawson, C. L. (2006). "Survey of Management Practices on Reproductive Performance of Dairy Cattle on Large U.S. Commercial Farms." *Journal of Dairy Science* 89(12). 4723–4735.
Corea, G. (1985). *The Mother Machine: Reproductive Technologies from Artificial Insemination to Artificial Wombs.* New York: Harper and Row.
Cole M. (2011) "'Animal Machines' to 'Happy Meat'? Foucault's Ideas of Disciplinary and Pastoral Power Applied to 'Animal-Centred' Welfare Discourse." *Animals* 1(1), 83–101. doi:*10.3390/ani1010083.* Retrieved July 14, 2014, from http://www.mdpi.com/2076-2615/1/1/83.
DeJarnette, M., & Nebel, R. (undated). "A.I. Technique in Cattle." North Plain City, OH: Select Sires. Retrieved May 13, 2014, from http://www.selectsires.com/resources/fertilitydocs/ai_technique_cattle.pdf.
Foer, J. S. (2009). *Eating Animals.* New York: Little, Brown.
Gram, D. (2009, November 3). "Vermont Slaughterhouse Closed for Inhumane Treatment to Calves." *Huffington Post.* Retrieved March 19, 2014, from http://www.huffingtonpost.com/2009/11/03/vermont-slaughterhouse-cl_n_343934.html.
Griffith-Greene, M. (2014, March 14). "Turkey farm video shows 'gaping hole' in government animal welfare oversight." *CBC News.* Retrieved March 16, 2014, from http://www.cbc.ca/news/turkey-farm-video-shows-gaping-hole-in-government-animal-welfare-oversight-1.2571451.
Goad, B. (2008, April 9). "Beef recall costs reach $67.2 million and rising." *The Press Enterprise.* Retrieved March 16, 2014, from http://www.pe.com/sections/news/reports/beef-recall/beef-recall-headlines/20080409-beef-recall-costs-reach-67.2-million-and-rising.ece.
Healey, J. R. (2008, February 8). "USDA orders largest beef recall: 143.4 million pounds." *USA Today.* Retrieved March 16, 2014, from http://usatoday30.usatoday.com/money/industries/food/2008-02-17-slaughterhouse-recall_N.htm.
Hendrick, T. & Hayden, J. (2013, November 15). "3 workers in alleged animal abuse video fired, cited by Weld deputies." *Fox 31 Denver.* Retrieved June 23, 2014, from http://kdvr.com/2013/11/15/sheriff-cites-3-after-video-of-alleged-animal-cruelty-surfaces/.
hooks, b. (undated). *Understanding Patriarchy.* Louisville: Louisville Anarchist Federation Federation. Retrieved May 8, 2014, from http://imaginenoborders.org/pdf/zines/UnderstandingPatriarchy.pdf.
Human Rights Watch. (2004). *Blood, Sweat, and Fear: Workers' Rights in U.S. Meat and Poultry Plants.* New York. Retrieved May 10, 2014, from http://www.hrw.org/sites/default/files/reports/usa0105.pdf.
Humane Society of the United States. (2010, March 24). "HSUS Statement on the USDA's Decision to Settle its Administrative Complaint Against Bushway Slaughter Plant." Retrieved March 30, 2014, from http://www.humanesociety.org/news/press_releases/2010/03/bushway_032410.html.

Humane Society of the United States. (2014, March 25). "Anti-Whistleblower Bills Hide Factory-Farming Abuses from the Public." Retrieved April 2, 2014, from http://www.humanesociety.org/issues/campaigns/factory_farming/factsheets/ag_gag.html.

Hutchinson, B. (2014, June 20). "Canada's largest dairy farm crippled by abuse allegations from undercover animals rights worker on his first mission." *National Post*. Retrieved June 23, 2014, from http://news.nationalpost.com/2014/06/20/canadas-largest-dairy-farm-crippled-by-abuse-allegations-from-undercover-animal-rights-worker-on-his-first-mission/.

Joy, M. (2011, November 3). "Carnism: Why Eating Animals Is a Social Justice Issue." *One Green Planet*. Retrieved July 13, 201,4 from http://www.onegreenplanet.org/lifestyle/carnism-why-eating-animals-is-a-social-justice-issue/.

Kaminer, A. (2010, November 19). "The Main Course Had an Unhappy Face." *The New York Times*. Retrieved May 18, 2014, from http://www.nytimes.com/2010/11/21/nyregion/21citycritic.html?_r=2&hp&.

Kidd, R. (1981, November/December). "Artificial Insemination in Cattle: An experienced livestock veterinarian offers a primer on artificial insemination in cattle." *Mother Earth News*. Retrieved May 9, 2014, from http://www.motherearthnews.com/homesteading-and-livestock/artificial-insemination-in-cattle-zmaz81ndzraw.aspx.

Lam, F. (2010, August 20). "Killing dinner." *Salon*. Retrieved May 18, 2014, from http://www.salon.com/2010/08/20/first_time_killing_chicken/.

LaVeck, J. (2007, February). "Truthiness is Stranger than Fiction: The Hidden Cost of Selling the Public on 'Cage-Free' Eggs." *Satya Magazine*, 46–48. Retrieved from http://www.tribeofheart.org/pdf/satyaessay3.pdf.

Lima da Costa, A. N., de Arujo, A. A. & Feitosa, J. V. (2011). "Particularities of Bovine Artificial Insemination" in Dr. Milad Manafi, ed., *Artificial Insemination in Farm Animals* (153–166). InTech. doi: 10.5772/17871 Retrieved May 12, 2014, from http://www.intechopen.com/books/artificial-insemination-in-farm-animals/particularities-of-bovine-artificial-insemination.

Luckerson, V. (2014, February 24). "The Dairy Industry is Axing 'Got Milk?" *Time*. Retrieved March 26, 2014, from http://business.time.com/2014/02/24/got-milk-campaign-ends-in-favor-of-milk-life/.

Meyer, S., & Steiner, L. (2011, December 20). "Daily Livestock Report." *CME Group* 9(243). Retrieved from http://www.dailylivestockreport.com/documents/dlr percent2012-20-2011.pdf.

Nebraska Appleseed. (2009). *"The Speed Kills You": The Voice of Nebraska's Meatpacking Workers*. Nebraska. Retrieved May 10, 2014 from http://www.splcenter.org/sites/default/files/downloads/publication/Unsafe_at_These_Speeds_web.pdf.

Oppel, Jr., R. A. (2013, April 6). "Taping of Farm Cruelty is Becoming the Crime." *New York Times*. Retrieved April 2, 2014, from http://www.nytimes.com/2013/04/07/us/taping-of-farm-cruelty-is-becoming-the-crime.html

Perkel, C. (2014, March 14). "Hidden camera captures 'blatant cruelty' at turkey farm." *The Canadian Press*. Retrieved March 16, 2014, from http://www.ctvnews.ca/canada/hidden-camera-captures-blatant-animal-cruelty-at-turkey-farm-1.1729233.

Pollan, M. (2009). *Omnivore's Dilemma: A Natural History of Four Meals*. New York: Penguin.

Rodriguez-Martinez, H., Hultgren, J., Båge, R., Bergqvist, A. S., Svensson, C., Bergsten, C … Gustafsson, H. (2013). "Reproductive Performance in High-producing Dairy

Cows: Can We Sustain it Under Current Practice?—Part III." *Engormix*. Retrieved May 18, 2014, from http://en.engormix.com/MA-dairy-cattle/genetic/articles/reproductive-performance-high-producing-t2593/103-p0.htm.

Rousseau, J.J., Cole, G. D. H., Brumfitt, J. H., Hall, J. C. and Jimack, P. (1993). *The social contract; and, Discourses*. London: J.M. Dent.

Schmidt, J. (2008, April 8). "Impact of meat recall beginning to show." *USA Today*. Retrieved March 16, 2014, from http://usatoday30.usatoday.com/money/industries/food/2008-03-30-meat-recall_N.htm.

Seltzer, J., Rush, J., & Kinsey, J. (2010). "Westland/Hallmark: 2008 Beef Recall. A Case Study by the Food Industry Center." University of Minnesota. Retrieved from http://ageconsearch.umn.edu/bitstream/58145/2/Westland_Hallmark_-_Final.pdf.

Shriver, A. (2009). "Knocking Out Pain in Livestock: Can Technology Succeed Where Morality has Stalled?" *Neuroethics* 2, 115–124. doi: 10.1007/s12152-009-9048-6.

Southern Poverty Law Center and Alabama Appleseed. (2013). "Unsafe at These Speeds: Alabama's Poultry Industry and its Disposable Workers." Alabama. Retrieved May 10, 2014, from http://www.splcenter.org/sites/default/files/downloads/publication/Unsafe_at_These_Speeds_web.pdf.

Tonsor, G. T., & Olynk, N. J. (2010, September). *U.S. Meat Demand: The Influence of Animal Welfare Coverage*. Kansas State University. Retrieved March 15, 2014, from http://www.agmanager.info/livestock/marketing/AnimalWelfare/MF2951.pdf

University of Wisconsin-Madison. (2000, May 5). History of Artificial Insemination. Retrieved May 9, 2014, from http://www.ansci.wisc.edu/jjp1/ansci_repro/lec/handouts/hd8.html.

Werner, E. (2008, May 20). "New ag rule closing downer cow slaughter exception." *USA Today*. Retrieved March 19, 2014, from http://usatoday30.usatoday.com/news/washington/2008-05-20-4234314486_x.htm.

Industrial Society Is Both the Fabrication Department and the Kill Floor
Total Liberation, Green Anarchism and the Violence of Industrialism

MARA J. PFEFFER AND SEAN PARSON

Much is going to be written in this book that connects animal liberation to anarchist critiques of capitalism, hierarchy and the state. Our goal in this short piece is not to reproduce these arguments, but to push them further.

In the short vignettes below we piece together this argument: if we are to be concerned with animal liberation and ending unneeded suffering, then we must go much further than attacking the state and capitalism. It is our assertion that there can be no total liberation: no end to colonization, genocide, or animal exploitation, without addressing the root problem of our era—industrial civilization.

We argue that animal liberationists, anarchists, and all people concerned with exploitation and suffering need to reject the dreams of techno-utopias, worker-run industrial factories, and post-scarcity eco-communism. Industrialism, as David Watson (1998) pointed out in his "We All Live in Bhopal," is an extermination camp and if we wish to live and see life flourish on this planet, there is only one alternative: we must envision a politics centered around burning down the factories, dismantling the energy grid, and liberating all animals, human and nonhuman.

The Hidden Violence of Industrialism: From Sacrifice Zones to Naturalized Violence

Our entire way of life is built on exploitation, emerging after massive social and political shifts during the 15th through 17th century (Federici, 2004; Marx, 1992; Thompson, 1966). Within a century the forests of Europe were transformed into factories and company towns; the peoples of the "new world" were exterminated or forced west in order to provide the colonialists unfettered access to the natural resources of the Americas; and millions of men and women were kidnapped from Africa and forced to work in plantation farms that fed the textile factories of Europe. In Europe and the America's women's bodies where tortured and burned alive during the witch trials, an event that was needed to accumulate and control the social reproductive labor of women (Federici, 2004). In other words, slavery, misogyny and genocide was central to the development of capitalism. For example, the sugars used by wealthy industrialists in England to feed their workers came from the sugar cane plantations in the Caribbean. This means that the sugar needed to spur the industrial revolution was planted on land stolen from native people and watered with the blood of African Slaves (Mintz, 1986).

Although the rise of industrial capitalism was built on the exploitation of labor and genocide, the European powers did not see their actions as "barbaric." That term was reserved for their victims. Spanish conquistadores during their colonization of the Aztec people in the 15th century wrote fantastical stories about savage human sacrifices (Federici, 2014). According to the Spanish accounts, the sacrifices were gifts to the Gods to thank them for the creation of the world and were intended to keep the Aztec society functioning. The validity of such accounts are, understandably, questioned since the "barbarity" of indigenous people, either via human sacrifice or through priests' accounts of cannibalism, was used to justify "civilizing" the native peoples. Regardless, the concept of sacrifice as being central to the maintenance of society has figured prominently in our collective social imagination for centuries.

According to anarcho-primitivist authors like John Zerzan (1998, 1999, 2004, 2008a and 2008b) and David Watson (1998), complex social systems require continual sacrifice. The difference between the modern sacrifices and the ones questionably detailed by Spanish priests is visibility. In the Spanish narratives, those sacrificed were done so publicly, their blood serving as a literal and visual reminder of the power of the gods. In our current world, the "sacrificed" are hidden away, fodder for the modern "gods" of technology, science, and the machine. For instance, the World Health Organization (2014) recently reported that at least 7 million people died in 2012 from direct exposure to airborne pollution. This conservative estimate does not include those who died from indirect exposure or who died from long-term exposure to airborne toxins. Nor does it include the millions who die each year from water, food, and soil toxicity, or those killed in "industrial accidents" such as mining disasters or factory fires. While media accounts refer to these deaths as "accidents," in truth these people have been purposefully killed. These are not accidents, as an accident is an unintended event, and pollution deaths and industrial deaths are designed into the system as "acceptable losses."

If countless millions of human animals are killed each year by the political, economic, and social system that has been created, how many billions of nonhumans are killed? This question seems to be, at its core, unanswerable. Since the majority of those in power have little concern for poor humans who suffer as victims of industrial society, the nonhuman victims are almost completely invisible—except for charismatic megafauna and endangered species that environmental groups use on pamphlets to help raise money. For instance, an estimated 50 billion chickens are killed each year to feed humans and at least 41 million cows are slaughtered each year in the U.S. alone (Purdue University, 2008). While historically these slaughters were visible, in recent decades in the United States the animal industries have been working to hide the suffering and death of these animals, going so far as to make videotaping the conditions in slaughterhouses and Concentrated Animal Feeding Operations (CAFOs) illegal (Potter, 2013). While slaughtering them for food is the most commonly discussed way that our culture "sacrifices" nonhumans, there are countless more who are killed indirectly in order to maintain our civilization.

For instance, the much maligned Tar Sands projects in Northern Alberta have not only poisoned native tribes, they have also killed an untold number of nonhuman animals as well. To extract tar sands, oil companies first must clear-cut the forests, drain the wetlands, and scrape away the vegetation and topsoil from the earth. After the land has been stripped of life the tar sand soil is collected and mixed with chemicals and hot water. This toxic water is then pooled together into "tailing ponds" which invariably leak into aquifers and into rivers. The oil is then sent, via pipelines and trucks, to refining plants. These pipes leak, poisoning the water and soil along its route, and the refining plants further pollute the air and water. As a brief example, in 2010, five hundred and fifty one migratory birds were killed after landing to feed at a tailing pond in Northern Alberta (Roth, 2012). This is not the first times that tailing ponds have killed migratory birds. According to a World Watch Institute Report (Block, 2014), an estimated 1,600 migrating birds die each year due to tailing ponds. Likewise, these tailing ponds have also been responsible for massive fish deaths (Mark, 2012) and there have already been scientific reports linking tar sands mining to the death of caribou and other large arctic mammals (Inkley, Kostyack and Miller, 2012). A similarly destructive fate for nonhumans follows all other forms of resource extraction—from the death of nearly all life with mountain top removal mining in Appalachia (Ward, 2008; 2009) to the death of spotted owls, marbled murrelets and voles with logging in the northwest (Barringer, 2007; Learn, 2012).

Even so called clean forms of energy are not safe for nonhuman animals. According to a Smithsonian report, an estimated 140,000 to 320,000 birds die each year in the United States from windmills (Eveleth, 2013), and birds and other desert life have been found cooked alive at massive industrial solar farms. Likewise, the components needed to make both the solar panels and the industrial windmills require intensive mining operations and are toxic when disposed of (Zehner, 2012). For instance, solar panels require the use of the toxic chemicals "Arsenic, cadmium telluride, hexafluoroethane, lead, and polyvinyl" all of which are known carcinogens (Woody, 2010, para. 2). It is also well documented that dams have had devastating impacts on fish and bird populations (U.S Fish and Wildlife Service). By constructing a social and economic system that systemically leads to the devastation and death of certain species to function, we must conclude that even purveyors of "clean" energy have blood on their hands as well.

Returning our focus to food, we ask: how many animals are killed or displaced in order to produce soy and other massive food plantations? According to the World Wildlife Fund, soy plantations have been instrumental in expanding deforestation in countries like Brazil, endangering the habits of countless rainforest residents (World Wildlife Fund, 2014). In massive industrial farming in the amazon forest, land is converted to soybean plantations or used to graze cattle and in the process nonhumans die and humans are displaced. These expanded plantations take advantage of uneven economic geographies and are connected to colonial practices. In *Sistah Vegan*, A. Breeze Harper (2010) exposes the narrow self-interest of the "civilized" consumer:

> I wonder, has America confused our addictive consumption habits with being "civilized?" The British who sipped their sugary teas considered themselves civilized, despite the torture and slavery it took to get that white sugar into their tea cups, along with the cotton and tobacco they used [p. 24, 28].

The quinoa that currently fills the shelves of natural food stores nationwide is being taken from rural Bolivians who have been eating the "superfood" for centuries. The spike in prices for quinoa has meant, according to the *New York Times*, that "fewer Bolivians can now afford it, hastening their embrace of cheaper, processed foods and raising fears of malnutrition in a country that has long struggled with it" (Romero and Shahriari, 2011). In this sense, the quinoa market has tapped into the long lasting colonial relationship between the U.S. and South America, one where the resources of the global south benefit wealth consumers in the United States to the detriment of local residents.

The same story can be written for nearly any resource, from coal to "beef." The industrial economic system is predicated on such colonial practices, requiring an economically exploited periphery to funnel resources to the elites at the core. In other words, industrialism requires ever-expanding sacrifice zones that now cover the majority of the world, all to allow for the luxury of the few. Under such a system those in power view those that fight back are seen as "primitive," "barbaric" and "uncivilized," all while the "civilized" elites sit on chairs built on top of a mountain of corpses.

Moving Beyond Veganism

> The point is to learn to live in the planetary garden without control or authority. And if life is a voyage, it is necessary to let ourselves be carried along with the river's current without imposing a control to stop it.—Jesús Sepúlveda, *Garden of Peculiarities* [2005].

Veganism is regularly considered to be the moral baseline for animal liberationists. The argument for veganism is clear: since killing and torturing animals for food is unneeded for our survival, it is ethically wrong to do so simply for taste preferences. If one really is concerned with ending animal suffering, the argument goes, it does not make sense to consume a nonhuman animal's flesh or to eat their secretions. Under the rubric and logic of industrial capitalism, this seems to be a reasonable ethical baseline, but it does not go nearly far enough.

In some ways focusing only on the vegan discussion creates a liberal ethical framework that focuses on the individual and their consumer choices and avoids discussing the larger structural components of our lived reality. For instance, the consumer vegan industry is, as all industries are, deeply connected to the global neoliberal economic order—where Amazon tropical forests are clear-cut to create space for palm oil; where large agribusiness dominates the systems of production and distribution; where in the United States and Europe hyper-exploited migrant workers are paid a pittance while being threatened with deportation if they try to organize; where throughout the world people are thrown off the land they and their families have lived on for centuries and forced into cities where they work in industrial factories or scavenge off the waste generated by the affluent; where "food miles," industrial fertilizers, and pesticides are ensuring climate instability. A focus on vegan consumerism does not allow space to address these larger structural issues.

As an example of the limits of a vegan centered politics we can look at the impact of ending native hunting for Inuit communities in Canada. These Inuit communities historically survived through hunting and fishing; this included killing seals for their flesh and fur, much to the horror of many animal rights activists. During the 1980s a well-coordinated and successful campaign was waged to stop indigenous sealing. According to George Wenzel (1991), the ban on seal hunting negatively impacted the Inuit communities he studied. Wenzel argues that by banning an important subsistence practice the activists actually increased the native communities' dependency on the Canadian government and global capitalism. This means that their food—meat, dairy, and vegetables—are now shipped in from long distances and are most likely coming from massive agricultural plantations or from CAFOs that have little to no concern for nonhumans. This means that in stopping seal hunts, animal rights activists have arguably contributed to more nonhuman death since feeding these Inuit communities now means the expansion of roads and CAFOs, more $Co2$ and more processed food. It also means that the activists unintentionally helped the state colonize the native people, working with the colonial state to break up indigenous culture and to make indigenous resistance to capitalism and economic liberalism more difficult.

This does not mean that veganism is inherently wrong and that native hunting is inherently right; it means that the relationship between human and nonhuman animals is much more complex than is commonly assumed by mainstream, western animal rights movements (Anonymous 2014). Additionally, there are animal liberationists who are both native and vegan, whose existence and voices are often overlooked or disregarded while in rooms full of white people debating whether or not veganism is racist. As Claudia Serrato, founder of the blog *Decolonial Food for Thought* states, "Not only has our land been colonized, but so have our bodies. How? Through the imposition of a heavily meat, dairy, and processed food diet coupled with a capitalist, patriarchal food/agricultural paradigm" (Layne, 2012). Of course, this is not to say that indigenous veganism is the same as western veganism, or that all indigenous vegans support western veganism—but instead to recognize that there may be various types of veganism. According to Serrato (2011), indigenous veganism is about rejecting specifically those animal products introduced by colonizers and reclaiming a mainly plant based diet which "kept the land, our bodies, animals and our ecological relations in balance," while non-indigenous veganism "does not carry these ancestral teachings, however, carries a strong weight on the liberation of these confined relatives" (para. 2). About western veganism, Serrato and Rodriguez (2008) also state,

> Capitalism-the colonizer-has, once again, taken away and patented the ancestral knowledge that is our indigenous ways of living-eating. He stole it and keeps it only for his white families on the west side. He calls it "vegan" and "going green" while our gente, east of the river, continue to search for the roots and natural ways–Panche Be–amidst this chaos we call Diabetes (of ALL types), Heart Disease, Obesity, imbalance and the destruction of pachamama [para. 2].

This complexity of oppression demands that animal liberationists "recognize the critical intersections of animal liberation with justice for the earth and humans; and ... find ways to practice groundless solidarity with all those resisting corporatism, patriarchy, racism, colonialism, sexism, classism, ablism, transphobia, homophobia, and ecocide" (Pfeffer, 2014, p. ii). This means moving beyond veganism as a moral baseline, recognizing the entanglements of oppressions discussed above. Cultivating more holistic activisms demands both critical thinking about the implications of vegan consumerism and creative practices in order to develop a moral baseline that directly resists (rather than appeases) the industrialism that rages war on the earth.

To move beyond veganism requires a politics centered around being in solidarity with other oppressed groups. Practicing solidarity means taking responsibility and accountability for your words, promises, and actions. There is a need not only to discuss transforming society and the way we consume its products, but to deeply question industrial civilization and systemic oppression itself—to recognize that becoming "civilized" means dissecting our compassion, standardizing our imaginations, and conforming to institutionalized obedience and sightlessness in order not to feel the heavy pain perpetuated by privileged and "civilized" lifestyles.

Becoming civilized means dismembering ourselves from our deepest emotions, pains, and understandings, from mystery, from the animal world, from one another, and from ourselves as nature. It means taming our wildness, our sensuousness, our longing, our responsiveness. It means resigning to the state of things, adjusting ourselves to our reality by whatever means available rather than changing our reality. It means chopping ourselves and the world to pieces so that everything can be sorted into artificial categories into which nothing actually fits—all for the sake of an efficiency and convenience never to be extended beyond "a narrow yet historically changing group of masters who give themselves the name 'human'" (Kappeler, 1995, p. 334).

Arguments for animal liberation ask us to confront speciesism, and our own dismembering thought processes that are not unlike a slaughterhouse disassembly line (Adams, 1990). It follows that we would also need to recognize that animals are not just resisting being slaughtered, they are literally resisting machines. And not only are these animals resisting machines, they are resisting being treated as such. As Tashee Meadows (2010) articulates, "Unfortunately, unlike car parts on an assembly line, these 'products' are living beings that move, often causing the shooter to miss his mark. They are dismembered while still alive and conscious.... These beings resist at every point of their captivity and torture" (p. 153).

This is the case for the billions of cows who are raped by the dairy industry, whose reproductive systems are exploited, whose calves are ripped from them and given to the veal industry, while they are pumped until "spent" and sent to the slaughterhouse to be killed and bled out, their corpses to be dehided, beheaded, dismembered, carved into standardized slices, wrapped in cellophane, and shipped elsewhere. None of this could be carried out on such a wide scale without the machines, the "technology" of the dairy industry—from rape racks used to force impregnation, to vacuum pumps attached to their breasts, to the electric prods shoved inside of them and the trucks used for their transportation, to the metal walls that hold their shaking bodies still, to the knocking guns that are intended to kill them quickly, to the conveyor belts that move them along even if they are not dead, to the ripping and slicing machines used to turn a living being into a faceless, unrecognizingly swallowable commodity.

The slaughterhouse functions as a complex machine (Pachirat, 2011); the compartmentalization of labor necessary for it to function at such high levels of "efficiency"—killing as many as one animal every 12 seconds—also makes the slaughterhouse one of the most dangerous industries for workers, ranking higher than many other industries in worker injuries even though many injuries go unreported. It is the concept of the machine that allows workers and nonhuman animals to be dismembered on disassembly lines for profit, and workers to be disposed of and replaced like spare parts that make industrial capitalism go.

While many animal welfare and animal rights activists speak out against the conditions of "factory" farmed animals, vegans and animal liberationists decry all exploitation and slaughter of farmed animals, even those which are claimed to be "humanely" and "sustainably" farmed. Yet agriculture as an industry, a machine comprised of more machines, and the use of machines in general, remains largely unexamined by many (but not all) within these movements. While examining agribusiness's "official" slaughterhouses is critical to animal liberation, "as long as the slaughterhouse is understood to be a specific location quarantined off from the rest of society, the rest of us are free to turn our backs, close our eyes, and continue consuming its products while concentrating blame on slaughterhouse workers. In reality, "the slaughterhouse is not a single place at all" (Pachirat, 2011, p. 236). Industrial society is both the fabrication department and the kill floor.

As pattrice jones (2011) argues, a primary way industrialized societies facilitate systemic animal abuse is through forgetting of that which makes us uncomfortable, forgetting our complicity. jones states, "The ease with which we forget facilitates animal abuse and all other atrocities that tend to make us sputter and reach for the word 'unspeakable': child abuse, nukes, poverty in the midst of plenty" (p. 53). Angela Davis argues that this lack of critical thinking about industrialism and human-animal relationships is a symptom of capitalism and colonialism:

The fact that we can sit down and eat a piece of chicken, without thinking about the horrendous conditions under which chickens are industrially bred in this country is a sign of the dangers of capitalism, how capitalism has colonized our minds. The fact that we look no further than the commodity itself, the fact that we refuse to understand the relationships that underlie the commodities that we use on a daily basis. Ask yourself, what is it like to sit down and eat that food that is generated only for the purposes of profit and creates so much suffering? [quoted in Harper, 2012].

When industrial agriculture is examined by consumers and recognized as violent and exploitative for nonhumans, that violence is often not recognized in other industries, and it should. The suffering of killing of animals, and human and none, is important to criticize for any industry. Take the computer industry for example. In order to make a computer, raw materials such as silicon, copper, aluminum, gold, antimony, arsenic, cadmium, cobalt, lead, silver, zinc, iron, and more must be mined from all over the world, then shipped to refineries, factories, and smelters in other parts of the world to be turned into monitors, circuit boards, batteries, plastic cases, and voilà—a computer is born (Natural Resources Defense Center, 2011). Then it is wrapped in Styrofoam, plastic, and cardboard and shipped to stores and suppliers all over the world. Then it is used, and then several years later, it is thrown away. This process is enormously wasteful, exploitative, violence-fueling, and disastrous for peoples and wildlife all over the world. To create just one computer, an estimated "more than 500 pounds of fossil fuels alone are guzzled up— several times the weight of your computer—not to mention nearly 50 pounds of chemicals, and 1.5 tons of water" (Natural Resources Defense Center, 2011, para. 5). Mining for these materials necessitates the destruction of habitats and homes, and as such often met with resistance from the peoples whose lands and ways of life are under threat; their resistance is normalized and frequently dealt with by armed force. We just really need those computers.

In the end the computer is not just a neutral commodity but comes prepackaged with an entire social, political, and economic system; it is a system that requires mining, toxic chemicals, and massive amounts of electricity. For there to be computer and information system there must be economic and political system maintained with coercion since no one goes into the mines voluntarily and no community willing destroys their land base and poison their bodies. This entire structure requires coercion; it requires death. Those in the developed world just pretend those deaths are natural.

In the U.S. alone, people driving hit and kill an estimated one million nonhuman animals per day (Wollan, 2011). This is a kill rate of 11.5 animals every second of every day (*High Country News*, 2005). These statistics do not include animals that don't die immediately after sustaining injuries from vehicles; nor do they include the injuries or deaths of human and nonhuman animals in wars fought over oil; nor the illness, injuries, or deaths of workers in the auto and oil industries. Eleven and a half deaths every second does not include the peoples or wildlife robbed of their homes or poisoned by these industries; nor those already feeling the effects of global warming. These deaths are not, as previously stated, accidents. These statistics are essentially guaranteed. These deaths are necessitated by industrial society's illusion of convenience and need for speed. The moral baseline of veganism, uncritically accepted, is not sufficient to examine these deaths; simply avoiding the consumption of obvious animal products does not challenge an entire system steeped in slaughter. It requires animal liberationists to critically examine capitalism, statism, militarism, and industrialism, which luckily many do.

Critiques of industrialism alone are by no means enough. To move beyond the dismembered, reductionist thinking that labels the programmed slaughter of billions "accidents," "production," "necessary," "for the greater good," and "collateral damage," we need to examine the structures that create these conditions and somehow imagine a way out that moves beyond mechanistic thought and action. Critically examining and challenging industrial civilization does *not* mean echoing the anti-vegan, transphobic, ableist, pro-collapse, noble savage idolizing stance of people like Derrick Jensen and his organization Deep Green Resistance. The anti-industrialism of Jensen is steeped in elitism and is the exact opposite of groundless solidarity practices (*Earth First!* Journal Collective, 2013). The kind of moral baseline that we propose for animal liberationists is one that recognizes and combats the horrors of industrialism, mechanistic thought, and vegan consumerism as well as recognizes the necessity for practicing groundless solidarity, from which more holistic solutions can be explored. "We need to practice fluid, compassionate, creative, spontaneous, and peculiar activisms that transcend single-issue politics and black and white thinking" (Pfeffer, 2014, p. 10–11). We need to de-program. We need to de-mechanize consciousness, action, and politics. We need to re-wild ourselves personally and politically, knowing that true solutions will not be made with machines, but with a vibrant open and feral politics.

Feral Politics: Connecting Total Liberation with Green Anarchism

"Our task is not to rediscover nature but to remake it."
—Raoul Vaneigem, *The Revolution of Everyday Life* [2012]

To move beyond a politics of death, coercion and suffering, we need to embrace total liberation (Best 2011a; Best 2011b; Colling, Parson, Arrigoni,

2013). Central to the idea of total liberation is a belief that human liberation requires animal and earth liberation as well. It is simply the belief that liberation for one group cannot be gained by oppressing another; that whites cannot liberate themselves by stealing the labor of blacks; that humans cannot gain freedom while imprisoning and slaughtering cows and pigs; that no one can live sustainably on this planet while clearcutting forests and damming rivers. Total liberation, because of this, requires a move away from the ideas of "progress." To Steven Best, the idea of economic and technological progress espoused by economists is often morally bankrupt. It is "progress" for only a few—the wealthy elites—and not for the majority of life on this planet. To fight for total liberation means rejecting this colonizing view of progress.

The depth of the struggle, as expressed in Best's work, is repeated in the wonderful work of David Nibert. Nibert argues that agriculture is foundational in the rise of speciesist systems of domination (Nibert, 2002; 2013). To Nibert, the advent of agriculture leads to the creation of hierarchies, the accumulation of capital, and the rise of militaristic, sexist, and speciesist civilization. To Nibert, agriculture was, as Jared Diamond (1987) asserts, "the worst mistake in the history of the human race" (p. 3).

That said, to both Best and Nibert, the struggle for total liberation seems to be disconnected from their historical analysis. For instance, Nibert argues that politically we need to push for world-wide veganism and global socialism in order to end animal exploitation; yet his own critique has shown that the roots go much deeper. If agriculture, industry, and hierarchy are the root causes of animal exploitation and statism, isn't capitalism merely the current iteration of the problem? While the abolition of capitalism is, of course, a good first step, and one we should be fighting for, Nibert is wrong to not dream bigger. We need to rethink mass production and industrialism and move animal liberation away from a politics centered on consumer behavior. Purchasing Gardein (™) meat analogue products is not humane or compassionate, though it might be the most "humane" choice we are giving at the store. By focusing radical activism and politics around consumer choices, we risk being blind to the larger structural systems we need to confront. While there are no easy answers, and we do not have a blueprint for what a green anarchist total liberation politics should look like, we do believe that total liberation requires the end of industrialism; that compassion cannot exist in a system built on sacrifice zones, exploitation, and commodification. A compassionate politics requires fighting against rape racks and slaughterhouses but also against resource extraction, roads, and industrial factories.

Likewise, a primitivist politics needs to be much more critical in examining the way they understand animality. It is not good enough to call for a politics of "rewilding," where humans reconnect to their "natural" animality because colonialism, classism, racism, and sexism have worked in tandem to construct what the term means. To uncritically "become animal" means potentially reinforcing sexism, colonialism, and white supremacy. Likewise, it means turning ones back on the responsibility we, as humans, have to dismantle the economic and social systems that are killing this planet. What is needed is a primitivist politics centered on love, compassion, and solidarity where the goal is to dismantle the social and economic system that are killing this planet. In addition, we need a politics to create real and lasting communities, not only between humans but also between humans and the more-than-human world. To get there we need to not only throw wrenches into industrial machines, or burn down mink farms, but to hold out our hands and be willing to fight beside all peoples on this planet fighting against oppression, suffering, and ecocide.

REFERENCES

Adams, C. J. (1990). *The Sexual Politics of Meat: A Feminist-vegetarian Critical Theory.* New York: Continuum.
Barringer, F. (2007, October 18). "New Battle of Logging vs. Spotted Owl Looms in West." *New York Times.*
Best, S. (2005). "The New Abolitionism: Capitalism, Slavery and Animal Liberation." Retrieved May 2014, from http://drstevebest.wordpress.com/2011/07/20/the-new-abolitionism-capitalism-slavery-and-animal-liberation–2005/.
Best, S. (2011a). "Manifesto for Radical Liberationism: Total Liberation by Any Means Necessary." Retrieved May 2014, from http://drstevebest.wordpress.com/2011/07/14/manifesto-for-radical-liberationism-total-liberation-by-any-means-necessary/.
Best, S. (2011b). "Total Liberation and Moral Progress: The Struggle for Human Evolution." Retrieved May 2014, from http://drstevebest.wordpress.com/2011/06/22/total-liberation-and-moral-progress-the-struggle-for-human-evolution–3/.
Best, S. (2011c). "Rethinking revolution: total liberation, alliance politics, and prolegemna to resistance movements in the twenty-first century." In Amster, R., et al., eds, *Contemporary Anarchist Studies.* New York: Routledge.
Block, B. (2013). "Oil Sands Could Threaten Millions of Migratory Birds." *World Watch Institute.* Retrieved May 2014, from http://www.worldwatch.org/node/6052.
Colling, S., Parson, S., and Arrigoni, A. (2013). "Until All Are Free: Total Liberation Through Revolutionary Decolonization, Groundless Solidarity, and a Relationship Framework." In Nocella II, A., Sorenson, J., Matsuoka, A., eds., *Defining Critical Animal Studies: An Intersectional Social Justice Approach for Liberation.* New York: Peter Lang International.
Diamond, J. (1987). "The Worst Mistake in the History of the Human Race." *Discover Magazine.* Retrieved May 2014, from http://discovermagazine.com/1987/may/02-the-worst-mistake-in-the-history-of-the-human-race.
The *Earth First! Journal* Collective. (2013, May 15). "Deep Green Transphobia: A statement from the *Earth First! Journal* Collective." *Earth First! Newswire.* Retrieved February 26, 2014 from http://earthfirstjournal.org/newswire/2013/05/15/deep-green-transphobia/.
Eveleth, R. (2013). "How Many Birds Do Wind Turbines Really Kill?" Retrieved June

27, 2014, from http://www.smithsonianmag.com/smart-news/how-many-birds-do-wind-turbines-really-kill–180948154.
Federici, S. (2004). *Caliban and the Witch: Woman, the Body and Primitive Accumulation.* New York: Autonomedia.
Harper, A. B. (2010). "Social justice beliefs and addiction to uncompassionate consumption." In A. Breeze Harper, ed., *Sistah Vegan: Black female vegans speak on food, identity, health* and *society* (pp. 20–41). New York: Lantern Books.
Harper, A. B. (2012, February 23). Angela Davis on eating chickens, Occupy, and including animals in social justice initiative of the 99 percent. *The Sistah Vegan Project.* Retrieved November 15, 2013, from http://sistahvegan.com/2012/02/23/angela-davis-on-eating-chickens-occupy-and-including-animals-in-social-justice-initiative-of-the–99/.
High Country News. (2005, February 7). "The Asphalt Graveyard: Road Kill Statistics." Retrieved May 2014, from http://www.hcn.org/issues/291/15268.
Inkley, D., Kostyack, J., and Miller, S. (2012, February 6). "Tar Sands Development to Lead to Poisoning of Wolves: Canada's Minister of Environment said that thousands of Alberta wolves will need to be killed to rescue caribou impacted by tar sands development." *National Wildlife Federation Report.* Retrieved May 2014, from http://www.nwf.org/News-and-Magazines/Media-Center/News-by-Topic/Wildlife/2012/02–06–12-Tar-Sands-Development-to-Lead-to-Poisoning-of-Wolves.aspx.
jones, p. (2011). In Kemmerer, Lisa, ed., *Sister Species: Women, Animals, and Social Justice* (pp. 45–56). Urbana: University of Illinois Press.
Kappeler, S. (1995). "Speciesism, racism, nationalism or the power of scientific subjectivity." In Adams, Carol J., and Donovan, Josephine, ed., *Animals and Women: Feminist Theoretical Explorations* (pp. 320–352). Durham: Duke University Press.
Layne, J. (2012, December 3). "Decolonizing our Diets." *The Manitoban.* Retrieved February 26, 2014, from http://www.themanitoban.com/2012/12/decolonizing-our-diets/13040/.
Learn, S. (2012, November 21). "Obama Administration Increases 'Critical Habitat' for Northern Spotted Owl." *Oregonian.* Retrieved June 27, 2014, from http://www.conservationnw.org/news/pressroom/press-clips/obama-administration-increases-critical-habitat-for-northern-spotted-owl.
Mark, J. (2012, June 13). "Deformed Fish Found Downstream of Tar Sands Mines." *Earth Island Journal.* Retrieved May 2014, from http://www.earthisland.org/journal/index.php/elist/eListRead/deformed_fish_found_downstream_of_tar_sands_mines/.
Marx, K. (1992). *Capital: Vol. 1: A Critique of Political Economy.* New York: Penguin.
Meadows, T. (2010). "Because they Matter." In A. Breeze Harper, ed., *Sistah Vegan: Black female vegans speak on food, identity, health, and society* (pp. 150–154). New York: Lantern Books.
Mintz, S. (1986). *Sweetness and Power: The Place of Sugar in Modern History.* New York: Penguin.
Nibert, D. (2002). *Animal Rights/Human Rights: Entanglements of Oppression and Liberation.* New York: Rowman & Littlefield.
Nibert, D. (2013). *Animal Oppression and Human Violence: Domesecration, Capitalism, and Global Conflict.* Columbia: Columbia University Press.
Natural Resources Defense Center. (2011, November 30). "Your Computer's Lifetime Journey." Retrieved May 2014, from http://www.nrdc.org/living/stuff/your-computers-lifetime-journey.asp.

Pachirat, T. (2011). *Every Twelve Seconds: Industrial Slaughter and the Politics of Sight.* New Haven: Yale University Press.

Pfeffer, M. (2014). *Total Liberation Action Research Team: Re-membering Practices of Holistic, Creative, and Compassionate Justice.* M.A., Northern Arizona University.

Potter, W. (2013). "Big Ag Wants to Rewrite the Law So That You'll Never See This." Retrieved June 29, 2014, from http://www.greenisthenewred.com/blog/new-ag-gag-bills-targets-whistleblowers-investigators-journalists/6736/.

Purdue University. (2008). "Poultry Facts." *Purdue Animal Education Network.* Retrieved June 2014, from http://www.ansc.purdue.edu/faen/poultry%20facts.html.

RedPleb. (2013, May 16). "Wither Derrick Jensen: Transphobia within Deep Green Resistance." *The Red Plebeian.* Retrieved June 2014, from http://theredplebeian.wordpress.com/2013/05/16/wither-derrick-jensen-the-transphobia-of-deep-green-resistance/.

Rodriguez, C. (2013, February 28). "Black Panther Party-Zapatista Foodways: Lessons from Home." *Decolonial Food for Thought.* Retrieved February 26, 2014, from *http://www.decolonialfoodforthought.com/2013/02/an-excerpt-from-another-way-of-doing.html.*

Romero, S., & Shahriari, S. (2011, March 9). "Quinoa's Global Success Creates Quandary at Home." *New York Times.* Retrieved May 2014, from http://www.nytimes.com/2011/03/20/world/americas/20bolivia.html.

Roth, P. (2012, October 4). "Bird deaths at oilsands tailings ponds in northern Alberta net no charges." *Edmonton Sun.* Retrieved May 2014, from http://www.edmontonsun.com/2012/10/04/tailings-ponds-bird-deaths-in-northern-alberta-net-no-charges.

Sepúlveda, J. (2005). *The Garden of Peculiarities.* Los Angeles: Feral House.

Serrato, C., & Rodriguez, C. (2008, November). "Reclaiming 'Veganism' and Healing Aztlan." Retrieved June 2014, from http://claudiaserrato.tumblr.com/post/63904340136/palabra-on-indigenous-veganism.

Serrato, C. (2011, March). "Palabra on Indigenous Veganism: What is the difference between indigenous veganism and veganism?" Retrieved June 2014, from http://claudiaserrato.tumblr.com/post/63904340136/palabra-on-indigenous-veganism.

Thompson, E. P. (1966). *The Making of the English Working Class.* New York: Vintage.

U.S. Fish and Wildlife Service Report. (n.d.) Salmon of the West. Retrieved May 2014, from www.fws.gov/salmonofthewest/dams.htm.

Vaneigem, R. (2012). *Revolution of Everyday.* London: PM Press.

Ward, Jr., K. (2008, April). "Mine's selenium deforms fish, expert says." *The Charleston-Gazette.*

Ward, Jr., K (2009, February). "Admitting the Cost of Coal." *The Charleston-Gazette.*

Watson, D. (1998). *Against the Megamachine: Essays on Empire & Its Enemies.* New York: Autonomedia.

Wenzel, G. (1991). *Animal Rights, Human Rights: Ecology, Economy, and Ideology in the Canadian Arctic.* Toronto: University of Toronto Press.

Wollan, M. (2010, September 12). "Mapping Traffic's Toll on Wildlife." *The New York Times.*

Woody, T. (2010). "Solar Energy's Dirty Little Secret." *Grist: A Beacon in the Fog.* Retrieved May 2014, from http://grist.org/article/2010-01-06/solars-dirty-little-secret/.

World Health Organization. (2014). "7 million premature deaths annually linked to air pollution." Retrieved May 2014, from http://www.who.int/mediacentre/news/releases/2014/air-pollution/en/.

Zehner, O. (2012). *Green Illusions: The Dirty Secrets of Clean Energy and the Future of Environmentalism*. Lincoln: University of Nebraska Press.
Zerzan, J. (2008a). *Running on Emptiness: The Pathology of Civilization*. Los Angeles: Feral House.
Zerzan, J. (2008b). *Twilight of the Machines*. Los Angeles: Feral House.
Zerzan, J. (2012). *Future Primitive Revisited*. Los Angeles: Feral House.

"A wider vision"
Coercion, Solidarity and Animal Liberation

Will Boisseau

This essay considers the relationship between animal rights groups who pursue allegedly coercive or violent tactics and the contemporary anarchist movement in Britain. The Animal Liberation Front (ALF) was founded in Britain in 1976, and at the time was seen as a peculiarly British phenomenon. Even in 2008 the North American anarchist journal *Rolling Thunder* felt able to praise the distinctly British character of animal rights militancy following the internationalization of Stop Huntingdon Animal Cruelty (SHAC). The essay begins by considering the broad ways that anarchist and animal liberation tactics might coincide, for instance both may be organized as affinity groups or under "banners." In an affinity group a small, tightly-knit set of activists are able to plan and carry out actions, these actions are often claimed under a "banner," which is the larger context in which an affinity group works and allows numerous autonomous groups to work towards the same goal.

Following this, the essay concentrates on the use of allegedly coercive or violent tactics by some animal rights groups, and how this may or may not coincide with contemporary anarchist conceptions of legitimate tactics. Animal liberationists have been mislabeled as "terrorists" by politically motivated opponents, even though ALF guidelines ensure that no human or non-human animals are harmed by their actions (Potter, 2011). While ensuring that labels such as "terrorist" are rejected, one must acknowledge that there have been groups, such as the Justice Department, who act outside of the ALF's non-violent guidelines and use tactics including "razor blade letters, bomb threats or bomb attacks, arson, harassment, death threats, and physical assaults" (Best & Nocella II, 2004, p. 36). It is actions such as these that are referred to when discussing violent or coercive tactics in this chapter. Property damage is not understood to constitute violence unless it implies or is experienced as a psychological threat or deliberate endangerment (Nocella II, 2011, p. 156).

The focus on tactics in this essay acknowledges that animal liberation has often acted as the site of discourse between anarchist groups and the wider British left without concern for animal liberation (or even animal welfare) being of principle importance. This is arguably the case for the class struggle anarchist group Class War who became perhaps the most recognizable anarchist presence in Britain after their formation in 1983. Some Class War supporters actively embraced animal liberation, while others admitted that they cynically harnessed the idea that animal rights was a stepping stone towards anarchism. As Class War founder Ian Bone (2006) later wrote, the group "weren't particularly committed to animal liberation at the time but we knew that … future recruits were going to come from activists in that broad movement" (p. 143). By the end of the 1980s a tactical dispute occurred between the ALF and Class War. It is fitting that this split was caused by a tactical divergence rather than a debate directly relating to nonhuman animals, because Class War were not principally motivated by animal concern. After considering this disagreement the chapter concludes by looking at examples in which anarchist animal liberationists have either succeeded or failed to successfully combine with other social justice issues involving class, race and gender.

This essay is underpinned by the demonstration of Critical Animal Studies scholar-activists that different forms of oppression are connected and must be simultaneously opposed (Nocella II, Sorenson, Socha & Matsuoka, 2014). The chapter relies on new primary information collected from interviews by the author between April 2013 and April 2014 with animal advocates, including former political prisoners. Magazines such as *Class War* and *Arkangel* are also utilized. *Arkangel*, which was founded in 1989 by Ronnie Lee and Vivian Smith, is a particularly valuable source because of its non-censorship policy. This means that the magazine carried a series of lively debates about controversial topics, including the use of violence and the legitimacy of far right activists joining the animal rights movement. Two former *Arkangel* editors are interviewed, which enables one to consider the development of the views of key figures within the movement over a number of decades.

"The politicos are ashamed": Connections Between Animal Liberation and Anarchist Tactics

As the present volume illustrates, there is a historical and contemporary connection between anarchism and animal liberation. The concern for nonhuman animals among some early anarchists did not necessarily guarantee that self-identified anarchists in the twenty first century would embrace animal liberation; nonetheless there is a clear lineage in the development of anarchistic concern for nonhuman animals. This ancestry starts with Peter Kropotkin (1998/1901) and his work *Mutual Aid*, which many subsequent libertarians took as their starting point when considering the relationship of humans to nonhuman animals and the natural world. Élisée Reclus, the French geographer and anarchist, framed his conception of equality with non-human animals in terms of his understanding of *Mutual Aid*. Reclus (1901) believed that the animal world was "our tutor in the art of existence," and therefore humans could join the species who "work in common." Writing almost a hundred years after Reclus, Brian Dominick argued that animal liberation and social revolution were inseparable. Dominick (1995) framed his argument around Kropotkin's theory; arguing against vivisection he wrote that "the only thing we can learn from animals is how to live in a sane and sound relationship with our environment" (p. 8). Continuing this tradition, Bob Torres expanded on Dominick's idea that animal oppression is linked to that of race, class and gender. Therefore, according to Torres (2007), one needs "to fight the heart of the economic order that drives these oppressions … capitalism" (p. 11). As well as these thinkers, there has also been an international history of practical activism with regards to the protection of non-human animals. Such activism includes anarchistic communes that embraced vegetarianism, such as the Brotherhood Workshop which formed in 1897 in Britain and the anarchist intentional community in Stelton, New Jersey (Bevir, 2011, pp. 275–276). Since the mid–1970s animal liberation groups have shared tactics and ideals with certain sections of the anarchist movement in Britain and America.

Present day activist movements such as the Earth Liberation Front (ELF), Earth First!, the ALF and SHAC all share ideals and personnel with anarchist groups. The ALF and ELF engage in direct action tactics whereby they confront "oppressors on their own high-pressure terms through actions ranging from blockades to sabotage" (Best & Nocella II, 2006, p. 16). The ALF emerged from the Hunt Saboteurs' Association in 1976 after a group of determined activists had broken off to form the Band of Mercy. The ALF have been described as "anarchistic in both aims and means" (jones, 2004, p. 143). The ALF represent an emergence of radicalism within the animal rights movement and beyond since the 1970s. Kim Stallwood (2004), former campaigns officer of the British Union for the Abolition of Vivisection (BUAV), characterized this new group of activists as "younger, unemployed, and anarchist" (p. 83). David Henshaw (1989), in his sensationalized and often factually inaccurate depiction of the ALF, describes the group as operating as an anarchistic military squadron: "there was to be no central high command or 'army council,' or in fact any precisely defined hierarchy" to select which site of abuse to target next (p. 50). Certainly, activist Keith Mann's (2007) description of the ALF's structure seems entirely anarchistic:

> The Animal Liberation Front in reality isn't so much an organisation, more like a banner—a title ... or a state of mind if you like—under which individuals and groups of people claim responsibility for illegal actions, which are designed to either directly or indirectly help the cause of animals. Anyone can be an ALF activist: there is no membership form to fill in [p. 55].

However, a decentralized structure is not enough to label a group as anarchistic. Instead, a group's structure must reflect their ideological commitment to decentralization and autonomy as linked to a rejection of social hierarchies. Certainly, direct action can be considered more than just a tactic, it is a process "whereby activists develop decentralized and egalitarian politics based on cells, affinity groups, and consensus decision-making models" (Best & Nocella II, 2006, p. 16). Nonetheless, ALF founder Ronnie Lee believes that although "there were certainly people in the ALF who were anarchists as well as being animal liberationists" most were "primarily concerned with protecting animals" (interview, April 2013). If this is the case, the non-hierarchical structure can be regarded merely as an organizational tool. As Ronnie Lee explains, many activists

> recognised that that way of operating was the most effective in terms of doing the most action and also avoiding [arrest] ... I think that people understood that it meant that the authorities couldn't destroy what was going on just by arresting one or two people, so people realised what the thinking behind that way of doing things was, even if they might not have been anarchists or had a wider vision of anything apart from wanting to protect animals [interview, April 2013].

Anarchist ALF activists do aim to challenge social hierarchy. In America the ALF's Western Wildlife Unit (n.d) believed that their actions "reflect the frustration and oppression felt by various members of America's citizens who like the animals were victimized by big business" (p. 11). As a result of this, the ALF moved away from being "simply just an 'animal' group" and became an organization that also opposed "the entire [capitalist] system" including "institutions that thrived on human abuse" (Western Wildlife Unit, p. 11). Indeed, all ALF actions challenge "the systemic violence which structures the modern capitalist society" by challenging the system that turns living creatures into property and makes them commodities (Colling & Nocella II, 2012, pp. 25–27). Ryan Gunderson (2011) argues that it is the willingness of animal liberationists to contest the property status of nonhuman animals and to challenge the means of production that makes animal advocacy a radical antisystemic movement, because they challenge the prevailing productive forces and are able to connect with other social justice movements. Similarly, Lawrence Wilde (2000) states that "the furious response of corporations and the state" to pressure from animal liberation groups indicates the "extent to which the economic and political elites recognize that what is being questioned here are the rights of the owners of the means of production" (p. 50). Moreover, challenging the property status of nonhuman animals may help animal liberationists develop connections with other social justice movements, because other oppressed groups have been labeled as property "for the purpose of economic exploitation or simply domination" (Nocella II, 2011, p. 157).

Even if the non-hierarchical structure was only an organizational tool, it is still relevant to consider the tactical significance of the ALF's actions, and particularly the conflicts between the ALF and class struggle anarchist groups. Part of this significance is that ALF tactics had an effect on both animal rights advocates and the wider anarchist movement. Larry Law (1982), writing for *Spectacular Times*, argued that a supposed split between animal advocates and the left was not due to a genuine theoretical disagreement, but was because "the politicos are ashamed" that "the animal liberation activists have undertaken more direct action and caused more physical and financial damage than the entire British revolutionary left put together" (p. 23). In this context it would be understandable if the anarchist movement looked to animal liberationists for tactical guidance. In fact, animal liberation and anarchist organizational practices often evolved simultaneously.

The ALF's successful use of the affinity group structure was influenced by anarchist practice, and also influenced the organizational approach of subsequent anarchistic groups. For instance, the ELF, which emerged in the early 1990s, "wanted to become an eco–ALF that will do whatever is necessary to save the planet and it's inhabitants" (Molland, 2006, p. 50). The affinity group has become one established anarchist approach, through which activists can "avoid the necessity of coordinating action, relying instead on a small, tightly-knit group in which consensus is most readily available" (Cohn, 2006, p. 205). The affinity group is regarded by many as "better suited to carrying off daring and decisive actions" which it would not be possible for "the masses" to "accomplish spontaneously" (Skirda, 2001, p. 83). More recently there has been an increased use in operation under "banners," which are often the wider context in which an affinity group works. Uri Gordon (2008) describes these banners as "even more fluid than networks" with different activists able to operate "a free vegan street-kitchen today under the Food Not Bombs banner, [and] meet to design a leaflet against the G8 under the Dissent! banner tomorrow" (p. 15).

Although ALF tactics may have emerged from a process of trial and error while individuals and groups built up confidence and trust, Ronnie Lee and the ALF founders also possessed "a good knowledge of the tactics of other revolutionary groups," Lee was particularly inspired by the Angry Brigade (Mann, 2007, p. 51). The Angry Brigade were an urban guerrilla group responsible for a series of politically motivated bombings between 1970 and 1972. Lee describes his interest in Angry Brigade activity which was

> outside of the normal left wing parameters that you had at the time ... most left wing stuff was to do with the workplace ... but they did things outside of that.... And that made me think that ... direct action against property could be extended to the animal liberation struggle [interview, April 2013].

The Angry Brigade "held a mish-mash of libertarian and militant beliefs strongly influenced by anarchism and the situationists" (Mansfield & Vanson, 2009, p. 32). Like the Situationists, the Angry Brigade hoped that provocation would draw repression from the state, which in turn would rally mass support. Lee may have been particularly drawn to this "youthful, vaguely anarchistic circle" because they refused to "accept the confines of legality set by the state." The ALF, like the Situationists before them, wanted to offer young people "brought up in the affluence of Western societies an attractive cause and an opportunity to get out and do something about it" (Carr, 1975, pp. 17–27). Animal liberationists were also influenced by Guy Debord's theory of the spectacle. As Larry Law (1982) writes: "in the Society of the Spectacle the world we see is not the real world—it is the world we have been conditioned to see" (p. 4). This "conditioning," underpinned by mass media, allows "well-conditioned people" to engage in practices as consumers that are harmful to their fellow beings (Law, 1982, pp. 6–7). Ronnie Lee and the ALF believed in disrupting the Spectacle, which incorporated "speciesism," by "taking action to wake people up" and making people question their relationship to nonhuman animals (interview, April 2013).

"Part of our tradition": The Use of Coercive Tactics

Although the ALF guidelines state that an action can only be claimed on behalf of the ALF if it takes "all necessary precautions against harming any animal, human and non-human" there are those—operating outside these guidelines and therefore outside of the ALF—who do aim to impose psychological harm on perceived animal abusers (Best & Nocella II, 2004, pp. 7–8). Both animal and environmental liberationists have resorted to "name-calling, threats, and harassment tactics, not to mention damage to personal property," however it is believed that "such actions are justified, even required, in order to counter the real violence which they see as the abuse and murder of nonhumans" (Laws, 2006, p. 147). A tiny group of British campaigners have gone further by engaging in violent tactics that could potentially cause injury to the general public. In December 1993 the Justice Department, an animal rights group who rejected the ALF's non-violent stance, began a "postal device campaign" in which the group, who allegedly threatened to spread the AIDS virus, sent "poster tubes said to contain needles packed in explosive material" (Lane, 1994, p. 39). As Robin Lane, who worked for the ALF Supporters' Group and press office, noted, "surely postal workers ... and secretaries ... would be most at risk" (p. 39). The Justice Department's campaign continued throughout the mid–1990s; one device disguised as a video "detonated in a Coventry sorting office"; in 1994 rat traps "primed with razor blades" were sent to Prince Charles and then Home Secretary Michael Howard in protest against the Criminal Justice Act, and ALF press officer Robin Webb seemed delighted with the ominous warning that accompanied a device sent to the owner of Wickham Research Laboratories that the package contained "a little bit extra"—a reference to the previous contamination threats the group had made (Webb, n.d.a, p. 26, Webb, n.d.b, p. 6). Of course not all of the media scare stories regarding the animal rights movement were true, but reports such as the *Daily Mirror*'s claim that the ALF had "threatened to bomb libraries unless they stop stocking field sports magazines" must have had an impact on the ALF's relationship with other anarchist groups and wider social justice movements (Arkangel, n.d.a, p. 22).

The relationship between anarchists and animal rights groups who pursue aggressive tactics is particularly complex. Firstly, anarchists could see violent actions as isolating and authoritarian, especially when the actions are combined with an absence of consensus or horizontal discussion. As will be discussed, this attitude caused the split between the ALF and Class War. A seemingly cavalier attitude towards violent actions is linked to a lack of concern for other oppressed groups, and as such distances these animal advocates from the wider anarchist movement. While anarchists have emphasized solidarity, a minority of animal advocates have focused solely on their single issue. For instance, David Olivier (n.d) wrote that he "felt only annoyance or hostility, or at best indifference towards ... exploited workers, deported immigrants and raped women ... I saw [them] only as part of the globally privileged category to which the human species belongs" (p. 30). In 1990 a bomb exploded under the car of a vivisector in Bristol, injuring a thirteen-month-old baby. No claim of responsibility was made, but both the national media and those writing in *Arkangel* accepted that the action was part of series of incendiary devices planted by an animal rights group acting outside the ALF's guidelines. Writing after the incident, ALF activist and later hunger striker Barry Horne (n.d) believed that he would have "to rack my brains to think of any [action by animal rights groups] that could reasonably be called violent." More problematically for anarchists, Horne also believed that "condemning alleged Animal Liberation violence is speciesist" because "if an action is carried out with the intention of helping the animals, then that action should always be above criticism" (p. 35). To anarchists who have placed emphasis on freedom, autonomy and non-coercion, such a ban on criticism is troubling—although, of course, debates did continue within the pages of the animal liberation magazine *Arkangel*, and, as Uri Gordon (2008) explores, anarchist attitudes to coercion are not so simplistic (chapter 4). Some anarchists might also place emphasis on prefigurative politics, believing that a society free of hierarchical domination and oppression will never be achieved if the means by which such a society is brought about involve coercion and intimidation. This is particularly the case for animal advocates whose position already states that one cannot cause suffering to end more suffering in the long term—for instance by causing suffering to animals to bring about benefits to human health—and as such animal advocates should not cause short term suffering through coercive tactics even if this would mean long term benefits for nonhuman animals (Ryder, 2000, p. 241). Although some anarchists would argue that the morality of causing "suffering" will depend on whether it was perpetrated by those in power, or with the intention of removing power. For instance, violent resistance against a despotic dictator would not be regarded as equally worthy of condemnation as the tyrant's use of police repression (Richards, 1993).

Other activists, while pointing out that "there are many autonomous and incognito groups," who do not represent the larger campaigns such as SHAC, believe that anarchism is in no way contradicted by the use of aggressive tactics. Max Gastone, SHAC's legal representative and adviser, argues that "if anything, the history of anarchism shows a strand that is willing to use assassination as a political tool. Direct action took many forms from violence to property damage over the 150 years or so of anarchism" (interview, conducted via e-mail, November 2013). In such an interpretation, "it is one of the stronger points of anarchism that it never elevated the tactic of (non-) violence ... into a strategy or identity, refusing to be forced by hegemonic liberalism to conform to a set of norms it never chose" (interview, November 2013). Anarchists and animal advocates may share the opinion that it is the corporations engaging in industries which harm nonhuman animals, as well as the state that supports and protects them, who are the real perpetrators of violent and coercive tactics. One must distinguish between different types of tactics and definitions of violence, which could range from intimidating phone calls to planting explosives. Certainly, there were few members of the ALF who "agreed with the proposition that property can be harmed" (Roger Yates interview, conducted via e-mail, December 2013). If property cannot be harmed this could make planting a car bomb a non-violent action. Nicole Vosper, an anarchist who was jailed for three and a half years for her involvement in SHAC, believes that "people have been very naive in the movement if they thought that our tactics hadn't involved coercion, we should be more proud of that" and rather than claiming that all ALF actions are non-violent, the movement should "own" the term (interview, January 2014). For Vosper, these tactics are linked to and supported by her anarchism, because "political violence has been a huge part of anarchist tradition." Although community and workplace organization is a larger component of anarchism, and "the direct action end of the spectrum in terms of violence and coercion is very small," this has still been "a part of anarchist history and tradition that people have felt proud of—that we've got a right to resist oppression by any means necessary." For Vosper the right of the victim is more significant than the right of the oppressor, and therefore there is no contradiction between anarchism and coercive tactics: "we can still be committed to working for the eradication of domination but still using violence as a tactic" (interview, January 2014). It is clear from animal rights literature that this view would be shared by numerous animal liberation anarchists.

From the literature and actions of the animal advocacy movement it is clear that non-violence is accepted by a majority of activists, however this is not necessarily the case with the anarchist strand of the movement. Anarchists are more likely to agree with Derrick Jensen's (2007) assertion that "anybody's freedom from being exploited will *always* come at the expense of the oppressor's ability to exploit" (p. 22). Jensen stipulates that the "freedom" of animals "to survive will come at the expense of those who profit" from their destruction; but he does not account for the possibility that an individual may start as an oppressor and in turn become oppressed by more powerful groups, or that someone can simultaneously exploit and be exploited. One SHAC activist suggested that reading Ward Churchill's work would enable one to understand anarchist conceptions of violence. Churchill (2007) believes that non-violence is a privileged position because it is held by people living in a "comfort zone," whereas he contends that the lives of most people are already "violent" because of oppressive state action (p. 77). Uri Gordon (2008), who defines a violent act as one in which a recipient "experiences [the action] as an attack or as deliberate endangerment," highlights a number of reasons why anarchists may adopt violent tactics (p. 93). Firstly, Gordon believes that it is "simply untrue that anarchists desire a 'non-violent society' and nothing else," instead anarchists are principally concerned with abolishing institutional violence or violent enforcement (p. 98). Gordon argues that anarchists seek a model of non-violence that is achieved through universal consent, and since the state is currently prepared "to resort to violence" then "the anarchist model of non-violence by mutual consent simply cannot be enacted" (p. 98). It has been argued that anarchists should not use violent or coercive tactics because of their stress on prefigurative politics; however, Gordon believes that such prefigurative methods can justify violence: in an "anarchist society" people would be expected to defend themselves against the imposition of a hierarchical social order, by violent resistance if necessary, and therefore anarchists could prefiguratively use those tactics today. Moreover, Gordon contends that in choosing legal methods activists are not ruling out the use of violent coercion, they are hoping that state legislation will be introduced and this in turn may be implemented by coercive or violent methods: "we only entrust the decision on whether this will happen to the state" (p. 101). Even if anarchists have justified violence in some circumstances, others may believe that it remains contradictory in the case of animal advocacy, which is above all about ending suffering and violence. Different stands of anarchism may be split on this issue, with anarcho-pacifists more likely to reject the use of seemingly violent tactics in favor of civil disobedience and non-violent direct action. Many eco-feminist groups have adopted an anarchistic belief in the power of non-violent civil disobedience which "for many women has come to symbolise the living enactment of feminist principles" in that it "invokes opposition to violence and exploitation and yet it does not employ the violent tactics of those that exploit" (Huffman, 1984, p. 2).

Coercive Tactics and the Far Right

Some writers and activists have suggested that the use of violence by animal rights groups is dangerous because of the potential for "disaffected and potentially violent young men to use the ALF as an excuse to vent their anger in inappropriate ways" (jones, 2004, p. 149). Val Graham reacted to news of a car bomb planted by an unidentified animal rights group, by asking, "What kind of psychos, gun-fanatics and violent misfits will now be drawn to animal liberation?" (1990, p. 37). One must consider whether far right activists will be drawn to the animal rights movement because of the use of violent tactics.

The Save the Newchurch Guinea Pigs campaign was a six year operation by British animal rights advocates that began in 1999 and was partly orchestrated by a self-identified anarchist, Jonny Ablewhite. Ablewhite (2009) was influenced by Murray Bookchin's "readings on hierarchy and oppression" and believed

> it is so important to gain an understanding of what Bookchin called "social ecology." Loosely speaking, it is "anarchy"; but you must ditch immediately any stereotypical preconceptions and notions about that word—they are negative and deliberate connotations that have been purposefully bound in the propaganda of capitalist dialogue [p. 8].

Despite this, the strategies allegedly used by the group more accurately resemble what one might presume to be fascist tactics rather than those that would be associated with anarchists. Alongside the peaceful vigils, the campaign against Christopher and John Hill's "farm":

[S]pread out against the whole village, and involved abusive graffiti, bricks thrown through windows, cars paint-stripped, phone lines cut off, and explosives let off at night. Effigies were burned. May Hudson, a cleaner, was warned that her dead husband would be disinterred unless she stopped working [Hall, 2006, p. 116].

One worker had "his name spelled out with shotgun cartridges on his lawn" and eventually quit when death threats were made against his grandmother, another business associate was publically accused of pedophilia, and most famously the bones of Gladys Hammond, Christopher Hill's mother-in-law, were stolen in October 2004 (Hall, p. 116).

With such tactics of coercion and intimidation in operation, perhaps it is unsurprising that fascist elements would be attracted to the animal rights movement. The Hunt Saboteurs' Association (HSA), for instance, has suffered persistent attempts at right wing infiltration and has recently "affiliated to the Anti-Fascist Network because there has been moves from nationalist organisations to move into animal rights through hunt sabbing" (interview, April 2014; Gee, 1994, p. 46). This is not to say that the HSA have engaged in any activity which could be regarded as coercive, but that right wing elements see hunt sabbing as a convenient entry point and "an easy way to get involved and get support" (interview, April 2014). Simon Russell (1990), a correspondent to *Arkangel* asked, "Why is it OK to march against Fascists alongside speciesists but [we] shouldn't march against speciesists alongside Fascists? It's inconsistent, illogical, bizarre and speciesist?" (p. 39). Another correspondent was "saddened" and "disturbed" that "fascists are not welcome in the animal rights movement" given that "animals do not care whether someone is a fascist or a communist, only that someone is friendly towards them" (Paul, 1990, p. 40). The fact that these correspondents were complaining about the exclusion of fascists shows that far right politics were rejected by the majority of those in the animal rights movement. Writing in the summer 1990 issue of *Arkangel*, Sonja Morris argued that "if we ultimately seek the breakdown of speciesism ... then fascism, through its attempt to create barriers within a single species, must be a contradiction to our aims" (p. 46). The sporadic accusation of racism or cooperation with far right groups by certain animal rights activists weakens the ability of animal liberationists to attract support from potentially fraternal social justice movements. As Nicole Vosper argues, animal rights groups are "full of people with white privilege" and as such many activists feel isolated (interview, January 2014). Robin Lane explains that this isolation was exacerbated by the willingness of some animal rights groups to work alongside far right organizations if they are opposing speciesism, something Lane consistently challenged (interview, March 2014).

Moreover, coercive tactics, whether supported by self-identified anarchists or fascists could also be regarded as a contradiction to the aims of the animal rights movement—especially if it diminishes opportunities to build links with other social justice movements. Anarchistic animal advocates discuss creating a society free of oppression and hierarchy, indeed it is the current hierarchical society which allows for animal abuse; and as such surely it is illogical to use might-makes-right tactics which mirror current social hierarchies and power relations. If the real coercive tactics come from the State which has a monopoly on violence, then animal advocates eventually seeking a non-hierarchical society must not resort to these tactics.

The Tactical Divergence of the ALF and Class War

It was not just this alleged use of coercive tactics, particularly the posting of incendiary devices, which led to the disagreement between Class War and the ALF, it was also linked to the condescending attitude of some animal advocates towards the general public. Although Ronnie Lee now focuses on vegan outreach, encouraging the public to adopt a meat-free diet, he could once seem dismissive of "ordinary" people; in one *Arkangel* article Lee asked, "What reason for living do ordinary unenlightened people have, dragging out their meaningless lives, changing nothing, achieving nothing, merely taking up space in an already grossly overcrowded world?" (1991, p. 40). Indeed, it was this perceived "arrogance of terrorist vanguard groups" with their "thinly veiled contempt for the working class" that caused a divergence between Class War (1989) and the ALF (p. 2). This was not mere name calling, some ALF activists genuinely did wish to "represent the vanguard of the revolution" (Mann, 2007, p. 60).

Perhaps Class War were never genuinely interested in animal rights, but used the cause as a cynical attempt to recruit new followers. Certainly, Class War regarded the fact that "you can often find yourself face to face with a bunch of human vermin" to be the "major advantage of being on a hunt sab" (*Class War*, n.d.a, p. 3). The paper, in its typical hyper-violent manner, threatened to "screw up" the gentry's "silly games," "just as you've screwed up our lives … watch out! … we will be hunting you" (*Class War*, n.d.b, p. 7). The fact that animal protection is not of principle concern is made clear with the warning that "you'll be bricked off your horses," a threat that, if carried out, would be traumatic and distressing for the animals involved (p. 7).

Bone (2006) again writes that Class War supported the ALF because they wanted "to establish a common base of direct action militancy with them," however there does not seem to be an underlying commitment to the issue (p. 146). Moreover, the class struggle group intimidated and disrupted BUAV meetings, not to make a statement about animal welfare, but because BUAV "were a reformist Labour Party–like group and we thought it might be possible to deepen the divide between them and the ALF" (Bone, p. 146). BUAV campaigner Kim Stallwood has even come to believe that certain anarchist groups were infiltrated by agent provocateurs with the intention of disrupting the animal rights movement (interview, October 2013). Whether BUAV really were the stagnant group that Class War seemed to think is debatable, but it is interesting here that animal issues act as a site of discourse between anarchists and the wider left, even when the actual status of nonhuman animals are not of primary concern. Although the connection between animal liberation and these class struggle groups never disappeared, Class War (1989) came to believe that the ALF regarded the working class as too "stupid and 'wicked' to care about animal rights so the ALF ... has decided to abandon 'public opinion' and do the job for us" (p. 2). If the connection between the two groups was more about the shared use of militant tactics than the underlying moral issue then it is fitting that the fracture should be framed in terms of tactics, for Class War: "there's a vital difference between a fight that's based in our communities and workplaces and the hare-brained schemes of the balaclava brigade" (p. 2).

Learning from This Criticism

Anarchist animal liberationists must learn from this criticism if they desire to build alliances and solidarity across social justice movements, not simply to gain additional support but because from an intersectional perspective it is impossible to challenge one form of hierarchical oppression while leaving others intact. This form of alliance politics will "come from a place of respect that carries out listening projects and healing and transformative actions" (Nocella II, 2010, p. 183). Animal liberationists must combine with other social justice issues involving class, race and gender; if coercive tactics are likely to alienate other social justice campaigners rather than advancing solidarity then they must be avoided. As Steven Best explains, the "human/animal liberation movements have much to learn from one another. Just as those in the Left and social justice movements have much to teach many in the animal advocacy movement ... so they have much to learn" (Best, 2009, p. 199).

In terms of class, animal liberationists can acknowledge Class War's criticism by highlighting the health benefits and better use of resources that veganism would bring. Anarchist animal liberationists can also campaign against the animal industrial complex that exploits both workers and nonhuman animals. As Catharine Grant (2006) highlights, there are numerous reasons to regard workers in fur, leather and meat industries as an exploited group. Slaughterhouse workers are habitually paid minimum wages, they are exposed to dangerous chemicals and high levels of ammonia from livestock manure, in America the injury rate in the meat packing industry is three times the national average (Grant, 2006, pp. 104–105). A recent study reported that 70 percent of chicken farm workers suffered from chronic sore eyes, 30 percent suffered from regular coughing and 15 percent have chronic bronchitis and asthma (Grant, 2006, pp. 104–105).

One of the most significant actions by an anarchist group against animal industries was the McLibel trial, in which two activists from London Greenpeace were taken to court by McDonald's for distributing an allegedly libelous pamphlet. London Greenpeace—an anarchist environmentalist collective with no affiliation to the larger Greenpeace organization—ran an anti–McDonald's campaign between 1987 and 1990 in which the leaflet "What's Wrong With McDonald's?" was distributed at selected London stores. Following the trial—in which Helen Steel and Dave Morris defended themselves against the corporate giants—the pamphlet was read by thousands of activists across the globe (Morris & Steel, 2003). What is significant here is that the pamphlet did not solely focus on the "murder of millions of animals," but gave equal consideration to the devastating environmental impact of McDonald's, the dispossession of land "for cash crops or for cattle ranching" and the exploitation of fast food workers. The pamphlet stated that

> workers in the fast food industry are paid low wages. McDonald's do not pay overtime rates even when employees work very long hours. Pressure to keep profits high and wage costs low results in understaffing ... accidents (particularly burns) are common. The majority of employees are people who have few job options and so are forced to accept this exploitation, and they're compelled to "smile" too! Not surprisingly staff turnover at McDonald's is high, making it virtually impossible to unionise and fight for a better deal, which suits McDonald's who have always been opposed to Unions ["What's wrong with McDonald's?"].

At the trial Morris and Steel called as witnesses up to 30 ex-employees of McDonald's, including employees who had promoted trade unionism within the workplace. Among the evidence considered was the case of a McDonald's manager from France who was arrested in July 1994 for "trying to rig union elections," and the case of Hassen Lamit who was "harassed for union activity": "an attempt was made to frame him for armed robbery, and McDonald's offered him a bribe if he renounced the union" (Arkangel, n.d.b, n.d.c). The "McLibel Two" proved that an anarchist campaign could gain mass support if it focused on interlocking oppressions rather than concentrating on single issue politics.

The animal rights movement has been charged with racism on numerous occasions (Nocella II, 2012, p. 119). Delicia Dunham (2010) believes that "the world can be even lonelier for a vegan when you're Black" as not only can activists feel isolated from the animal rights movement—"injecting myself into a subculture where Black women are rare"—but, as many of the authors in *Sistah Vegan* argue, "our culture, if not cultures, are typically unsupportive of the life we have been called to lead" (p. 42). This is significant for animal advocates who aim to link animal abuse to other forms of oppression, as potentially supportive social justice campaigners could be alienated due to the lack of inclusion and perhaps the dogmatic image of some animal advocates. To confront this, anarchist animal advocates must never engage in campaigns which alienate other groups who may be the victims of an interrelated form of hierarchical oppression, such as the Makah nation (Nocella II & Kahn, 2004). Animal advocates must listen to and learn from other groups, responding to calls for solidarity and engaging in activities that challenge multiple forms of oppression, such as opposing the prison industrial complex (Nocella II, 2012, p. 124).

The case of gender may be different because the majority of animal advocates are female. Nonetheless, the animal rights movement have been guilty of orchestrating sexist campaigns which do nothing to highlight the intersectionality of oppression uncovered by Critical Animal Studies. The spring 1990 issue of *Arkangel* rounded up recent acts of "Direct Action," including

> in Surrey a woman had her £3,000 silver fox fur coat ripped from her in Guildford when she stopped to ask for directions. The attackers ordered her back into her car without it and told her to leave town immediately [Lee & Smith, 1990, p. 28].

One could take issue with all intimidation tactics, but it is particularly disturbing that the report of violence against a woman by unknown attackers is included in the list of praiseworthy actions without comment. The mention of a prosperous home counties town, and the presumed price tag, is seemingly enough to elevate this incident to a positive action with a legitimate upper-class target. This unusual example of intimidation should be set in the context of the everyday sexism promoted by strands of the animal rights movement, particularly by the largest animal rights group People for the Ethical Treatment of Animals (PETA) which uses sexualized images of women for titillation, and as such contributes to the oppression of women and leaves hierarchical structures unchallenged. As "discourses supporting injustices against women are intimately connected ... to injustices against animals," and PETA's campaign forgets "other oppressions and hierarchies," then the group's campaign does nothing to challenge the system of society that allows animal abuse to continue (Deckha, 2008, p. 59). To challenge this, anarcha-feminist animal rights groups should promote the solidarity between women and other oppressed groups; such a campaign would: "gesture towards the subversive potential of cross-species identification" (Deckha, p. 59) while challenging all forms of patriarchal and hierarchical oppression, perhaps by embracing a feminist ethic of care.

Conclusion

Anarchist animal liberationists, supported by Critical Animal Studies scholar-activists, must listen to and learn from participants in other social justice movements, building bonds with other campaigns against oppression and—as Class War's criticism suggested—working within communities and workplaces to develop solidarity and mutual support. In this way, and by challenging interrelated forms of oppression and social hierarchies under capitalism, animal liberationists can demonstrate that they are "for the freedom of prisoners, immigrants, children, people with disabilities, feminists, LGBTQ, and all oppressed groups across the globe" (Colling & Nocella II, 2012, p. 24). Animal liberationists must be aware that focusing on single issue politics or using coercive tactics can be detrimental towards this task, particularly because coercive tactics have been directed towards groups who are themselves resisting interrelated forms of oppression. Just as in the 1970s animal advocates were inspired by Ronnie Lee and the ALF, today we can once again learn from Lee (2014), whose experience has caused him to amend his views towards the wider public, and make sure that animal advocates unite with other groups seeking to end all forms of oppression:

> My early years in the struggle for animal liberation were spent with a movement that did not engage with the public, but sought to bypass them in its direct war against animal abusers. I now recognize ... engagement with ordinary people counts for everything if we are to radically change their attitudes towards other animals. And engagement with ordinary people also means engagement in the struggle for a fair and just society for human beings, as well as for other animals [p. xiv].

REFERENCES

Ablewhite, J. (2009). "Updates." *Animal Liberation Front Supporters Group*, April, 7–8.
Arkangel. (n.d.a). "What the papers say." *Arkangel: For Animal Liberation* 18, 19–26.
Arkangel. (n.d.b). "Big mac: Still on the grill." *Arkangel: For Animal Liberation* 14, 54–57.
Arkangel. (n.d.c). "Big mac: Faces the facts." *Arkangel: For Animal Liberation* 15, 51–56.
Best, S., & Nocella II, A. J., eds. (2004). *Terrorists or freedom fighters? Reflections on the liberation of animals*. New York: Lantern Books.
Best, S., & Nocella II, A. J. (2006). "Introduction: A fire in the belly of the beast: The emergence of revolutionary environmentalism." In Best, S., & Nocella II, A. J., eds., *Igniting a revolution: Voices in defence of the Earth* (pp. 8–29). Oakland: AK Press.
Best, S. (2009). "Rethinking revolution: Total liberation, alliance politics, and a pro-

legomena toresistance movements in the twenty-first century." In Amster, R., DeLeon, A., Fernandez, L. A., Nocella II, A. J., & Shannon, D., eds., *Contemporary anarchist studies: An introductory anthology of anarchy in the academy.* London: Routledge.
Bevir, M. (2011). *The Making of British Socialism.* Princeton: Princeton University Press.
Bone, I. (2006). *Bash the rich: True-life confessions of an anarchist in the UK.* Bath: Tangent.
Carr, G. (1975). *The Angry Brigade: The cause and the case.* London: Victor Gollancz.
Class War. (1989). Bombs. *Class War* 32, 2.
Class War. (n.d.a). The best cut of all. *Class War*, Unnumbered, 3.
Class War. (n.d.b). Bash the rich. *Class War*, Unnumbered, 7.
Churchill, W., & Ryan, M. (2007). *Pacifism as pathology: Reflections on the role of armed struggle in North America.* Edinburgh: AK Press.
Cohn, J. S. (2006). *Anarchism and the crisis of representation: Hermeneutics, aesthetics, politics.* Selinsgrove: Susquehanna University Press.
Colling, S., & Nocella II, A. J. (2012). *Love and liberation: An animal liberation front story.* Williamstown, MA: Piraeus.
Deckha, M. (2008). "Disturbing images: Peta and the feminist ethics of animal advocacy." *Ethics and the Environment* 13, no. 2, 35–76.
Dominick, B. A. (1995). *Animal Liberation and Social Revolution: A Vegan Perspective on Anarchism or an Anarchist Perspective on Veganism.* London: Active Distribution.
Dunham, D. (2010). "On being black and vegan." In A. Breeze Harper, Ed., *Sistah vegan: Black female vegans speak on food, identity, health, and society* (pp. 42–46). New York: Lantern Books.
Franks, B. (2006). *Rebel alliances: The means and ends of contemporary British anarchism.* Edinburgh: AK Press and Dark Star.
Gee, G. (1994). "Hunt saboteurs and the police: Sleeping with the enemy." *Arkangel: For Animal Liberation* 11, 45–46.
Gordon, U. (2008). *Anarchy alive! Anti-authoritarian politics from practice to theory.* London: Pluto Press.
Graham, V. (1990). "Beyond the pale." *Arkangel: For Animal Liberation* 3, 37.
Grant, C. (2006). *The no-nonsense guide to animal rights.* Oxford: New Internationalist.
Gunderson, R. (2011). "From cattle to capital: Exchange value, animal commodification, and barbarism." *Critical Sociology* 39, no.2, 259–275.
Hall, L. (2006). *Capers in the churchyard: Animal rights advocacy in the age of terror.* Darien, CT: Nectar Bat Press.
Henshaw, D. (1989). *Animal warfare: The story of the animal liberation front.* London: Fontana.
Horne, B. (n.d.). "Another question of violence." *Arkangel: For Animal Liberation* 18, 35–36.
Huffman, L. (1984). "Convict." *Feminists for Animal Rights Newsletter* 1. no. 3, 2–4.
Jensen, D. (2007). Preface. In Churchill, W., & Ryan, M., *Pacifism as pathology: Reflections on the role of armed struggle in North America* (pp. 3–30). Edinburgh: AK Press.
jones, p. (2004). "Mothers with monkeywrenches: Feminist imperatives and the ALF." In Best, S., & Nocella II, A. J., eds., *Terrorists or freedom fighters? Reflections on the liberation of animals* (pp. 137–156). New York: Lantern Books.

Kropotkin, P. (1998/1901). *Mutual aid: A factor of evolution*. London: Freedom.
Lane, R. (1994). "The justice department: A point of view." *Arkangel: For Animal Liberation* 11, 39.
Law, L. (1982). *Spectacular times: Animals*. London: Spectacular Times.
Laws, C. (2006). "Jains, the Alf, and the Elf: Antagonists or allies?" In Best, S., & Nocella II, A. J., eds., *Igniting a revolution: Voices in defence of the Earth* (pp. 143–155). Oakland: AK Press.
Lee, R., & Smith, V. (1990). "Direct action." *Arkangel: For Animal Liberation* 3, 28.
Lee, R. (1991). "Some lessons from our loss." *Arkangel: For Animal Liberation* 5, 40–41.
Lee, R. (2014). Preface. In Nocella II, A. J., Sorenson, J., Socha, K., & Matsuoka, A., eds., *Defining Critical Animal Studies* (pp. xiiv-xv). New York: Peter Lang.
London Greenpeace. (2003). "What's wrong with McDonalds?" *The Raven: Anarchist Quarterly* 11, no. 3, 217–220.
Mann, K. (2007). *From dusk 'til dawn: An insider's view of the growth of the animal liberation movement*. London: Puppy Pincher Press.
Mansfield, M., & Vanson, Y. (2009). *Memoirs of a radical lawyer*. London: Bloomsbury.
Molland, N. (2006). "A spark that ignited a flame: The evolution of the earth liberation front." In Best, S., & Nocella II, A. J., eds., *Igniting a revolution: Voices in defence of the Earth* (pp. 47–58). Oakland: AK Press.
Morris, D., & Steel, H. (2003). "McWorld on trial." *The Raven: Anarchist Quarterly* 11, no. 3, 193–216.
Morris. S. (1990). "Fascism and animal rights." *Arkangel: For Animal Liberation* 3, 46.
Nocella II, A. J., & Kahn, R. (2004). "Listen to us! A dialogue for solidarity with Lawrence Sampson, American Indian Movement spokesperson." *Animal Liberation Philosophy and Policy Journal* 2, no. 1, 1–8.
Nocella II, A. J. (2010). "Abolition a multi-tactical movement strategy." *Journal for Critical Animal Studies* 8, no. 1-2, 176–183.
Nocella II, A. J. (2011). "A dis-ability perspective on the stigmatization of dissent: Critical pedagogy, critical criminology, and Critical Animal Studies." *Social Science—Dissertations*. Paper 178.
Nocella II, A. J. (2012). "Animal advocates for prison and slave abolition: a transformative justice approach to movement politics for an end to racism." *Journal for Critical Animal Studies* 10, no. 2, 119–126.
Nocella II, A. J., Sorenson, J., Socha, K., & Matsuoka, A., eds. (2014). *Defining Critical Animal Studies*. New York: Peter Lang.
Olivier, D. (n.d.). "Humans are animals too." *Arkangel: For Animal Liberation* 16, 27–31.
Paul. (1990). "Leave out the political comment." *Arkangel: For Animal Liberation* 4, 40.
Potter, W. (2011). *Green is the new red: An insider's account of a social movement under siege*. San Francisco: City Lights Books.
Reclus, É. (1901). "On vegetarianism." Retrieved from http://theanarchistlibrary.org/library/elisee-reclus-on-vegetarianism.pdf.
Richards, V., ed. (1993). *Violence and anarchism: A polemic*. London: Freedom Press.
Rolling Thunder. (2008). "The SHAC story." *Rolling thunder: an anarchist journal of dangerous living* 6, 11–28.
Russell, S. (1990). "Censorship." *Arkangel: For Animal Liberation* 4, 39.
Ryder, R. D. (2000). *Animal revolution: Changing attitudes towards speciesism*. Oxford: Berg.

Skirda, A. (2001). *Facing the enemy: A history of anarchist organisation from Proudhon to May 1968*. Edinburgh: AK Press.
Stallwood, K. (2004). "A personal overview of direct action in the United Kingdom and the United States." In Best, S., & Nocella II, A. J., eds., *Terrorists or freedom fighters? Reflections on the liberation of animals* (pp. 81–90). New York: Lantern Books.
Torres, B. (2007). *Making a Killing: The Political Economy of Animal Rights*. Edinburgh: AK Press.
Webb, R. (n.d.a). "News from the ALF press office." *Arkangel: For Animal Liberation* 12, 25–27.
Webb, R. (n.d.b). "News from the ALF press office." *Arkangel: For Animal Liberation* 13, 30–34.
Western Wildlife Unit of the Animal Liberation Front. (n.d). *Memories of freedom*. The Anarchist Library, retrieved on May 21st 2012, http://theanarchistlibrary.org/library/western-wildlife-unit-of-the-animal-liberation-front-memories-of-freedom.
Wilde, L. (2000). "'The creatures, too, must become free': Marx and the animal/human distinction." *Capital & Class* 72, 37–53.

Part III
Strategies

"Give us what belongs to us in peace, and if you don't
give it to us in peace, we will take it by force."
—Emma Goldman

"That last moment belongs to us—
that agony is our triumph."
—Bartolomeo Vanzetti

"If you build it, we will burn it."
—Earth Liberation Front

Anarchy for Educational Praxis in the Animal Liberation Movement in an Era of Capitalist Triumphalism

LARA DREW AND KIM SOCHA

Animal liberation activists are *de facto* educators. No matter the activist, no matter the context, the activist's work innately involves teaching others about human (mis)use of other species. This form of teaching may be overt, such as holding a workshop or lecture that people voluntarily attend. Teaching comes in less traditional forms as well, such as leafleting, flyering, protesting, etc.; in these cases, people are introduced to messages about animal liberation by happenstance such as walking by a bulletin board or driving by a protest.

Anarchist theory has a history in politics, sociology, philosophy, economics, and more recently education, and has been used as a platform for radical social movements. Radical learning and education in activist communities are more urgent now given the dire concerns facing human animals, nonhuman animals, and the Earth. This urgency is further highlighted by the animal activist movement's (AAM) growing reliance on destructive, counterproductive capitalist methods for change, some of which will be discussed below.

In response to these AAM realities, we herein explore the inclusion of anarchist theory and praxis as an informal pedagogical application for activists involved in animal liberation. Some fundamental anarchist pedagogical practices include autonomy, choice, critical thinking, and deconstructing hierarchy to facilitate diverse models of learning. Bringing together anarchist studies, Critical Animal Studies, and adult education literature, we offer ideas for how such theories can inform activists to resist oppressive practices, particularly in an era of capitalist triumphalism.

Through our experiences, we have independently fostered similar intersectional approaches to activism, with both of us experiencing radicalization toward anarchism by way of the AAM. Therefore, along with broad application of anarchist concepts, we offer personalized accounts to demonstrate the ways in which we have developed critical consciousness and have come to see activism as a learning process. As activists and educators, we have developed new knowledge and new ways of knowing and seeing the world. This knowledge has enabled us to think more critically and become self-directed learners, which is what we most hope to impart to our readers.

We also want to convince activists and the general public that these radical processes work. Most educational establishments and research tend to ignore informal spaces of learning. There is a privileging of institutionalized erudition that results in the silencing of other important learning that takes place outside educational institutions in activist places and spaces. Institutional learning is privileged because it maintains political, economic, and social capital that reproduces inequitable power relations. Informal and incidental learning is tellingly absent from this model, particularly in a social action setting, because it provides an ongoing threat to capitalist and statist structures. The creation of radical informal learning spaces that implement liberatory pedagogies is vital for the AAM. However, *learning* and *pedagogy* as a dimension of *political action* are often ignored or unrecognized by mainstream political activists, particularly given their foremost concerns are usually strategy and campaigns (Foley, 1999). Our goal as activists, therefore, should be to mirror strains of the radical anti-colonialism and feminist movements that integrated pedagogy within their political identities and practices. For example, in the 1980s, feminist John Stoltenberg (1994) held workshops in which men re-enacted women's uncomfortable poses from conventional pornography, thereby teaching them that female sexuality as determined by the mass media is unnatural and inauthentic.

Education is a challenging subject for many anarchists. This is particularly so given that education is never neutral and always has some political or ideological agenda giving legitimacy to economic and social structures (Freire & Shor, 1987). As Althusser (1971) argues, education is an ideological state apparatus. As such, education traditionally functions to benefit those who control the processes of production and power disparities (see Apple, 2013; Gillborn, 2008; Kahn, 2010; McLaren and Kincheloe, 2007). Institutional education is also a challenging subject for both of us given our shared histories of being excluded by teachers and labeled as "slow learners," as opposed to being children who learned differently than teachers expected. Unsurprisingly, we internalized this negative labeling as "stupidity," resulting in poor self-concepts. As adults, we recognize forms of education that work against the inclusion of certain "Others." But even though Kim has obtained her

Ph.D. and Lara experiences relationships of nurture and care in her current Ph.D. studies, we both still cringe at the authoritarian and hierarchical structures entrenched in education. As such, we see anarchist pedagogy as a process that can build upon activists' present knowledge bases and inform better practice, particularly at an intersectional level, although our particular focus in this chapter is on the AAM.

Capitalism and Animal Liberation Activism

Before providing details of anarchist pedagogy and its application to activism, we must first appraise the AAM as a whole. The field of Critical Animal Studies (CAS) offers an excellent contribution to understanding social change tactics and education within the AAM and at a broader level. CAS is rooted in animal liberation and underpinned by critical theory, radical education, anarchism, and holistic social justice advocating a multi-movement approach for total liberty (Nocella, Sorenson, Socha, & Matsuoka, 2014). CAS seeks to abolish all systems of domination for humans, nonhuman animals and the Earth by drawing attention to the interlocking systems of power and domination (Nocella, Sorenson, Socha, & Matsuoka, 2014).

Like many other social movements, while there is a vast array of philosophical and strategic positions, some components of the AAM are still largely reliant on statist and capitalist methods for change through the use of law, government, or consumer based methods. Most predominately, the animal welfare and rights strands generally promote strictly legal forms of change through education and legislation (Best, 2006). A recent example of using capitalism and welfare to promote animal liberation arose when the Humane Society of the United States (HSUS) and United Egg Producers came to an agreement to phase out battery cages in their egg production in favor of supposedly more natural confinement units (cages). In effect, the average consumer will feel more comfortable eating eggs because of the HSUS stamp of approval, with few realizing that the "maceration and suffocation of male chicks is not addressed. Debeaking is not addressed.... Reduction of food and manipulation of light and dark cycles, presumably, are still allowable" (Swanson, 2013, p. 218).

In sum, the welfare and rights traditions of the AAM generally assume institutions remain central to the system and we can modify and control corporations and the legislature to make them more socially just. Consequently, institutions underpinned by the status quo structure become essential to the production of reform based change. This reliance on destructive institutions is also seen in the work of activists using an animal rights "pragmatist focus" or "new welfarist" strategies (Sztybel, 2007). Pragmatist or welfarist strategies include problem solving methods using the basic institutional structures of the liberal capitalist "democracy." So rather than ultimately acting for principals such as rights or liberation, reformists will mostly act to reduce suffering. Reform may have its uses by advocating animals to be acknowledged in legislation and government to cultivate a kinder culture of compassion (Sztybel, 2007). However, these reform methods with reliance on government are still far reaching from radical and anarchist perspectives. Strategies in the grips of a social structure legitimizing the existing order of unjust power relations are problematic. As an alternative, a radical challenge to the existing social order is paramount if we wish to achieve liberatory based change for humans and animals.

Within each philosophical and strategic position, capitalist methods dominate the AAM landscape. A common example of capitalist activist methods include vegan outreach media that use images of young, white, thin, and/or muscular vegans, thereby subjecting pressure on viewers to conform to the Western ideal of beauty. Harper (2010) confirms this, arguing that vegetarian, vegan, and organic advertisements have mostly white and thin bodies, thereby showing an underlying theme of veganism equals a thin white body. This approach merely reinforces and amplifies oppressive tactics of body policing. For example, the shaming of overweight women masked under the guise of health advice is used to sell veganism as an attractive "product." Failing to present a diverse range of body types suggests any deviation from this ideal is abnormal. Socha (2013) argues that activists who engage in strategies used by the diet-industrial complex are playing upon people's inadequacies if they do not fit the Western ideal; this approach perpetuates the commodity cultural mindset that one must be a certain way (skinny or muscular) to be attractive. Compassion is the foundation of the AAM, and exploitation through methods of body shaming is an "unethical and callous way to market animal liberation" (Socha, 2013, p. 58). These tactics are tools of social control entrenched in the capitalist system that reinforces oppression, objectification, and vegan lifestyle-ism.

Of course, veganism is a necessary step within the goal of animal liberation; however, on its own, it is hardly sufficient. As it stands, global meat consumption is growing at steady rates despite increased media focus on animal welfare issues (Food and Agriculture Organization, 2008). For anarchist vegans, there are certainly ethical implications when consuming anything within an economic cultural system that encourages unlimited growth. There is no guarantee that humans and nonhuman animals are free from violence under a system that needs to expand and profit at all costs (Dominick, 1997). Vegan outreach as we have observed it in both Australia and the U.S. is largely consumer focused and removed from the liberationist values that are the essence of radical social change. There is a presumption that merely buying products marked as "vegan" is the end game of the AAM, as opposed to challenging the political and institutional structures that promote capitalism and other forms of oppression. Using the argument that "to change the world we must begin with ourselves" can at times be too simplistic because it risks seeing individual choice as the only solution to global problems. While personal choice is a fundamental aspect of change, this approach alone inherently accepts dominant discourses of power and ignores important structural factors of exploitation. As Dean (2009) states, "the individualization of politics into commodifiable 'lifestyles' and opinions subsumes politics into consumption" (p. 23). Instead, a radical, social, and political model of activism and veganism is needed; otherwise, veganism becomes relegated to an elitist bourgeois lifestyle practice.

Single issue activism does not necessarily challenge political, economic, and social systems as a whole. These AAM approaches tend to hold a narrow focus, and activists may find it difficult (or too time consuming) to see how their work fits into larger social, political, and economic contexts. A radical position holds that regulating industry though welfare or legal reform is as limited as are the law and government themselves—the very institutions protecting and profiting from exploitative practices. Also, single issue and reformist methods tend to ignore alliance politics and solidarity with other struggles against oppression and hierarchy (Nocella, Sorenson, Socha, & Matsuoka, 2014). Thus, the dominant structures need to be challenged to assist/enable long term change. Otherwise, activists are simply perpetuating parts of the institutional apparatus creating the problem to begin with (Socha, 2011).

In the introduction to Haworth's (2012) collection *Anarchist Pedagogies*, he states the following:

> Historically, anarchists have steadily criticized the state and public schools and have considered them mundane institutions that uniformly reinforce capitalism and hierarchical models of control. However, over the last century, anarchists have made numerous attempts to create educational processes that transgress authoritative factory models and deterministic curriculum of the state and corporate entities [p. 2].

In kind, progressive animal activists critique the rise of animal advocacy groups with paid employees, "mundane" institutional procedures, top-down hierarchical models (president, vice president, treasurer, secretary, voting members, non-voting members, volunteers), and reinforcement of commodity culture. Coterminously, once radical individuals and groups have softened their messages to win the public's attention and affection, fearing if we, as animal voices by proxy, ask for too much we will wind up with nothing (Torres, 2007).

One of the most flagrant examples of commercial culture's infiltration of the animal rights and liberation movements is found in the work of Mercy for Animals' (MFA) Director of Education Nick Cooney. Although MFA promotes veganism and Cooney himself is vegan, his latest book is titled *Veganomics: The Surprising Science on What Motivates Vegetarians, from the Breakfast Table to the Bedroom* (2013). The focus on vegetarianism in the title, as opposed to veganism, is a prime example of disingenuously asking for less lest we get nothing. In his earlier *Changes of Heart* (2010), he advises organizations to use more attractive volunteers to engage in outreach. When considering the commercial landscape from which Cooney likely draws his ideas of what constitutes attractiveness, one can assume he means young, thin, and/or white (as noted above). The conclusions one might draw from this circumscribed criteria are alarming but also unsurprising in a capitalist culture and from an activist seemingly disinterested in social ills such as ableism, ageism, racism, fatism, lookism, etc. But this is what happens when liberation movements start acting like capitalist corporations.

Also arising from the commercial model of animal advocacy is the idea that one can buy animal liberation through books, glossy magazines, and equal trades of the bad commodities (meat, cheese, leather, fur) for the good ones (meat analogs, cheeze, pleather, faux fur). Vegan outreach often looks just like this. Typical leaflets and booklets, under the guise of "vegetarian starter kits," list ways one can veganize goods and services. The underlying assumption is if you purchase only products labeled "vegan," you will have done all that is expected to make the world a better place; the underlying message is that vegan capitalism will save animals. Torres (2007) observes that this sole focus on vegan commodities draws attention away from "other negative production practices that exploit people or harm the ecosystem" (p. 136), which are the basis of the capitalist structure. It is the rare piece of vegan literature alerting readers to issues associated with industrial vegetable and grain agriculture (monoculture) leading to severe ecological dilemmas such as topsoil erosion. Again in fear of asking for too much, emphasis is put on being vegan, but not on buying locally, organically, and non-exploitatively whenever possible.

In the animal rights movement, there is a tacit refusal to critique capitalism that also occurs in mainstream America. As Foster and Chesney (2010) explain,

> This prohibition on critically assessing capitalism begins in the economics departments and business schools of our universities where, with but a few exceptions, it is easier to find an advocate of the immediate colonization of Mars than it is to find a scholar engaged in genuine radical criticism of capitalism. This critical dearth extends to our news media, which have a documented track record of promoting the profit system, and a keen distaste for those that advocate radical change [para. 4].

Foster and Chesney (2010) conclude that this problem exists because to attack capitalism is to seemingly attack one's country and the democratic system.

For animal advocates who are part of an initially fringe movement that is slowly gaining wider acceptance (which doesn't mean animals are being killed at lower rates, ironically), there is even more tendency to ignore the metaphorical elephant in the room for fear of looking too radical, too weird, and too demanding. Consequently, not only is a major reason (capitalism) for animal cruelty tolerated, but it is paradoxically seen as a means by which animal cruelty will cease! To be effective, we must be willing to dig more deeply into social issues even if that means challenging those in our communities to consider the systematic structures that foster nonhuman animal and other types of exploitation. Anarchist pedagogy can direct us to that goal.

Anarchy as Educational Praxis in Activist Communities

In regards to social change, any sort of emancipatory transformation of social relations at the macro-level must start with a transformation of power relations at a micro-level (White & Cudworth, 2014). In an educational context, the learning and pedagogical approaches used in activist circles could be argued as highly relevant to transform these everyday micro-level relations to lead to macro-level change. In fact, the education of activists is a situated activity in which they learn largely through doing and by participating in communities of practice (Lave & Wenger, 1991). The educational methods used in activist circles influence learning and often determine how effective activists are in practice. In other words, it is the learning and education of activists that support and develop effective actions for social change.

In particular, Haworth (2012) writes about anarchist pedagogy by drawing on the areas of deschooling, unschooling, informal learning, and radical critical pedagogy. Haworth (2012) predominantly addresses the importance of teaching and learning environments outside of authoritarian structures and through examining informal learning spaces. As Shantz (2012) argues, "for anarchists, educational alternatives are situated as part of overall attempts, within collective movements, to change broader structures and systems of power, including but not limited to those of education" (p. 134). Non-hierarchical, antiauthoritarian, mutual, and voluntary educational spaces are at the core of anarchist pedagogical processes. If our aim is to contest capitalist and hierarchical politics, particularly if we want to challenge trans-species domination, anarchist pedagogical processes are fundamental for holistic and wider social change.

Activist communities have the opportunity to create alternative learning spaces which are guided by the principles of anarchism: "When contemplating strategies of resistance, a local setting should be sought, one which places particular emphasis on the roles and responsibilities of the individual and the community as having the potential to be(come) meaningful sites of resistance that can effectively challenge inter-species domination" (White & Cudworth, 2014, p. 203). If we are to challenge this dominance, activist communities must interrogate their interactions amongst those they work with, as these actions tend to subversively reproduce authoritarian structures. Goldman (2011) criticizes approaches to learning that emphasize actions dominated by rules, elites, and governments. Activists must work within the discourse of liberatory and resistant pedagogical processes in practice to work against the reproduction of statist structures.

Anarchism, as a theory and practice, provides ideas and practices for activist groups who are looking to challenge hegemonic dynamics in hierarchical systems (DeLeon, 2008). Anarchism can inform activist communities to advance an anti-capitalist stance and anti-hierarchical politics in a pedagogical context. Some fundamental anarchist pedagogical principles include leveling hierarchy, championing autonomy and choice, and consensus decision making. These processes reflect the recommendations of many critical scholars of education, including Freire (1975), Brookfield (1993), and McLaren (1995).

Although these guiding practices and philosophies exist in some activist circles already, they are often glaringly absent from the AAM. In response to this void, the next section asks us to think about anarchist pedagogical frameworks that can be applied to AAM activist communities with the following question in mind: How can we creatively construct non-hierarchical and anti-authoritarian educational spaces for animal activists?

Deconstructing Hierarchy and Traditional Educational Models in Animal Liberation Communities

Many mainstream animal rights organizations are run with hierarchical, top-down leadership that creates an ongoing reliance on "experts" to act on issues rather than autonomously acting on issues ourselves. Most animal liberation organizations in Australia and the U.S. are run in this customary way with a board of directors and formal committee with defined and structured roles. Indeed, Kim reports experiences within such organizations that beg for anarchist critique, as when a fellow board member yelled, "This organization *is* hierarchical" in response to another member's comment that she didn't want to endorse hierarchy within their animal advocacy organization. There is also ongoing reliance from activists on corporatized and professionalized others to engage in the most important advocacy for change (Torres,

2007). This reliance fosters dependence and passivity within the AAM. For example, volunteers of organizations have relatively little power and autonomy and generally work under the direction of those in charge. These externally imposed structures or rigid rules tend to foster manipulation and passivity and are the most precarious forms activism can take for they reinforce stratified thinking. Therefore, a critical pedagogical anarchist principle that can influence activist groups is they should be organized not on the basis of hierarchical, centralist, top-down structures, but on a foundation of mutual, voluntary agreements in which participants unlearn passivity and deconstruct hierarchy within their activist roles. Admittedly, as Freeman famously notes in "The Tyranny of Structurelessness" (1970), attempting to foster a complete lack of structure is an exercise in futility. What we propose, in contrast, are *less* rigid structures, more flexibility, and an acceptance that group dynamics can (and likely should) change from time to time.

As educators, activists, and anarchists, we feel it our duty to cultivate vigilant critique of social norms and challenge conventional pedagogical models while also destabilizing the authoritarianism of the traditional schoolhouse setting. Following the principles of Critical Animal Pedagogy (CAP), we wish to draw attention to largely ignored and oppressive cultural norms that continue for financial and traditional reasons (Corman & Vandrovcová, 2014). Activist forums are likely better, or at least easier, places to integrate anarchist pedagogies than classrooms because although there are leaders and heroes in the AAM, activists are more often on an even plane and there is no promise of knowledge in exchange for money (barring those instances where an admission fee is required). In contrast, the traditional classroom is still built around the model of the practiced teacher and neophyte student who looks up to the instructor even if that teacher is conscious of classroom geography and situates all in a circle or some such ostensibly power-leveling design.

We are not saying those new to animal advocacy have nothing to learn from activists with long histories in the movement. Rather, this dynamic can be better acted out with attention to the function of anarchist theory and pedagogy within intra-movement settings. This outcome can be achieved in simple ways, with leaders and long-time activists remaining ever conscious of and being willing to subvert their roles as authority figures even if they do not see themselves as such. From a CAP perspective, as Corman and Vandrovcová (2014) state, this means "[s]elf-righteousness and shaming" should be put aside for the sake of "[s]elf-reflection of our own biases" as educators (p. 153).

A more complex task is for activists to consider how their methodologies may in fact lead to "imitating their own masters in State, commercial, social and moral affairs, by forcibly suppressing every independent attempt to analyze the ills of society and every sincere effort toward the abolition of these ills" (Goldman, 1906, para. 20). We borrow these words from Goldman's critique of the educational system in "The Child and Its Enemies" to usher in the vast importance of, but regularly ignored, critique of hierarchy within the animal rights and liberation movements. One way to deconstruct hierarchy within activist spaces is to facilitate and promote the role of collectives. Activist groups could be run as collectives balanced with both individual and group initiatives.

An exemplar of this strategy in action is Lara's involvement with a local animal rights group in Australia. When first joining, the organization was run in a traditional format with formal positions of a hierarchical nature ranging from president to vice president and other traditionalized committee roles. Lara and another member began advocating for and proposing to erase these stratified positions. A collective format was implemented instead. With time, the non-hierarchical format of the group promoted an atmosphere where activists became more self-directed and less reliant on leaders in charge at the time. This alteration created a sense of collective responsibility empowering everyone to become involved in various activist tasks.

Lara's experience aligns with the objectives of an anarchist pedagogical process where a group atmosphere transformed into a collective format promoting autonomy and self-directed learning. It facilitated an environment of self-reliance where activists engaged in more active roles based on their own skill base, with individuals determining the best ways they could be of service to the *cause*, not to a board of directors. Brown and Pickerill (2009) confirm that one of the strengths of autonomous activism is it facilitates autonomy for groups in their choice of actions, strategies, and directions. Anarchists argue that creating an environment of sovereignty actually encourages collective responsibility. Indeed, this process Lara experienced facilitated the unlearning of compliance and encouraged a deeper learning process that motivated activists towards understanding the nature of hierarchy and the promise of liberatory based change.

However, ultimately, committee members began clinging to traditional organizational arrangements. One committee member proposed to re-develop a hierarchical set-up, suggesting a president and vice president were necessary. Although this proposal was not officially passed, people became increasingly dependent upon a few committed, active individuals, thus obstructing the self-direction and autonomy that had briefly blossomed. In the end, Lara made the decision to step off the committee and engage in other types of activism. This outcome aligns with Shantz's (2012) argument that the majority of people are passive and expect group leaders to direct events. In Kropotkin's (1902/2006) *Mutual Aid*, he notes that the "individual is a result of both [his/her] inherited instincts and [his/her] education" (p. 228). Frequently, however, education can stifle instincts toward inquiry and rebellion. In "The Social Importance of the Modern School" (1911), Goldman bemoans the commonly accepted "notion that knowledge can be obtained only in school through systematic drilling, and that school time is the only period during which knowledge may be acquired" (para. 5). Most individuals new to social movements take this customary educational paradigm and apply it to the activist community of which they want to be part, making them passive receivers of information as opposed to active participants with equal say and the ability to act independently. This reliance and hierarchical set-up fundamentally conflicts with anarchist, educational, and liberationist values.

Reflecting upon those values, Lara began to see ways to put them into practice. At present, she engages in hunt sabotage (hunt sab) methodology against kangaroo culls and duck hunting. Through hunt sab methods, activist bodies are used as political tools of resistance. In fact, some hunt saboteurs are self-consciously anarchist (Doherty, Paterson, & Seel, 2000). Direct action hunt sab methods build alternative learning spaces to engage in particular pedagogical practices that represent horizontal and shared learning spaces. As Conway (2006) describes, social movement knowledge is largely tacit when learning is produced through organizational or action processes. Hunt sab work provides an informal organizational avenue to break dependency and inhibition within activist work, providing an opportunity to inspire anarchist pedagogical learning.

Further, the bottom-up nature of hunt sab offsets passivity and facilitates self-direction and empowerment. Hunt sab is grounded in a bottom-up style using grassroots methods, which includes active collaboration. This is conducted through informal chats to bring forth ideas and tactics on equal grounding, rather than relying on dogmatic structures where ideas must be run past or approved by a specific leader. The hunt sub method generally encourages ideas from all participants, facilitating creativity and self-direction, ultimately fostering enhanced self-esteem and independence. Shantz (2012) says educational practices and relations need to contribute to the nurturance of non-authoritarian people demanding greater personal control and choice. One activist new to hunt sab methods said to Lara: "I feel like I've grown a lot in confidence through the experience." As Shantz (2012) explains, learning should contribute to independence of thought and action, contributing to self-determination. If we want to facilitate deeper and more critical forms of activist learning, then anarchist pedagogical processes through autonomy with limited externally imposed structures are fundamental.

Lara's experience with hunt sab methods enabled her to reflect on her own internalized authority and previous inherent reliance on external forms of organization. Through direct action, Lara came to face and reflect on this internalized authority and ways in which to overcome it. As Shantz (2012) urges, "rather than learning how to act one should determine themselves how to act" (p. 137). In this same way, Drew (2014) talks of the importance of self-directed acts of rebellion and resistance. This process changes and reshapes one's political identity, contributing to deeper learning processes (Drew, 2014). Best and Nocella (2006) contend that direct action tactics empower activists against corporate based structures that are impossible to achieve through pre-approved legal and political channels.

Kim's experiences within traditional AAM organizational structures mirror Lara's, as do her attempts to confront those traditions. At the time of this writing, Kim sat on a board as vice president of an animal advocacy group. As a representative of a 501(c)3 organization (meaning tax-exempt non-profit) reliant on members' financial donations, it is ill advised for her to engage in activities that could bring bad press to her group and/or result in their liability for any legal infractions. Even if she were to engage in a borderline (or over-the-line) illegal activity on her own time, her association with the organization would likely arise in the case of legal fallout. For these reasons, she has stifled some activist impulses so as not to set a bad example for those she is "leading" in a campaign or protest. Yet recent experiences have led her to rethink the top-down model of liberatory action.

In an analysis of anarchist schooling, Shantz (2012) asserts that *events*, not courses, are often the best ways to practice liberatory pedagogy. Sometimes these events are spontaneous. For instance, at a recent protest Kim organized against animal research at the University of Minnesota, her fellow activists expressed interest in taking their demonstration from off the public street and into the private space of a particular researcher's office building. Her initial reaction was "What will the board think?" thereby putting the plan of the majority into the hands of a select few board members, only two of whom were actually at the event (Kim being one of them). But rather than assert her authority as a board member of a hierarchical organization, she followed her instincts and moved with her fellow activists into the private space. What started as a traditional protest with participants arranged in a line, holding signs, and chanting, became a lively action allowing participants to be creative, active, and inspired. According to Shantz (2012), "learning should help people to free themselves and encourage them to change the world in which they live" (p. 126), and it "should contribute to independence of thought and action and contribute to capacities for self-determination" (p. 131). This unplanned event, as small as it was, demonstrates the value of anarchist learning principles within the course of social change.

More importantly, this deviation from the norm brought Kim closer to those in her activist community, leading them to form a separate band who wanted to take action removed from the aegis of a sponsoring organization. Twice since that initial protest, Kim and her cohort joined together again and took part in cooperative events divorced from the approval (or disapproval) of an overseer. With the assistance of a seasoned organizer and activist dedicated to teaching direct action strategies, they came up with plans to educate the public and send a message to the University through subversive methodologies. These deeds epitomize de Cleyre's (1912/2004) definition of direct action:

> Every person who ever had a plan to do anything, and went and did it, or who laid his (sic) plans before others, and won their co-operation to do it with him, without going to external authorities to please do the thing for them, was a direct actionist. All co-operative experiments are essentially direct action [p. 48].

In truth, Kim *did* first go to "external authorities" in an attempt to obtain sanction of the plan. She approached the person "above" her in her organization's ranked schema—the board president. Yet this approval was not to be found due to (somewhat farfetched) concerns about possible legal ramifications. The lesson here was not to bother going to those authorities in the first place. Ultimately, Kim is pleased to have ignored the president's feedback because for brief moments she and her cohort saw through the "anarchist ideal" of liberated critical thinking demonstrated in non-hierarchical cooperative organizing (Mueller, 2012, p. 14). Most importantly, they made a statement on behalf of nonhuman animals silenced in research labs.

Having alternative learning spaces in social and political contexts helps challenge inter-species domination for not only the animals we seek to liberate but for the people we seek to work with. Meaningful change and liberation are not obtainable by a reliance on "experts" or the political and cultural elite. Rather, effective sites of resistance operate through bottom-up strategies of resistance (White & Cudworth, 2014). If these hierarchical interactions and dynamics are not examined in activist communities, they remain a detriment for liberatory forms of resistance in political action for both humans and nonhuman animals. If we can start to look at our interactions in a community setting and see activists as learners, we can begin to solve the relations of human domination that serve to reproduce our domination of nature. Anarchist pedagogies should be viewed as pedagogies of freedom embodied in activist practice that directly and indirectly defy hierarchy, passivity, and dependence.

As radical justice advocates, we must explore avenues, both narrow and broad, for upending the governing structure of animal rights and liberation movements in the West. We must find ways to take back power from the nonprofit industrial complex as manifest in organizations such as the Humane Society of the United States, People for the Ethical Treatment of Animals, Mercy for Animals, Farm Sanctuary, Animals Australia, and some Animal Liberation organizations within Australia, all of which have an ideological stranglehold on what animal rights and liberation should look like, which is far from anarchist liberatory ideals. There are alternatives.

Working independently, either by oneself or with a small collective, is the most promising way to start. Elise (2013) argues for the importance of moving away from both the corporate and "democratic, grassroots" models for social change (p. 35). Rather than the traditional board structure with authority over members and volunteers, *all* should be seen as equal participants who can decide on campaign issues, fund allocation, rhetoric for Web sites and literature, etc. And as Elise further advises in "Anti-Capitalism and Abolitionism" (2013): "In addition to animal liberation, such an organization should place anti-capitalism and human struggles on its agenda as well" (p. 36). Organizations should also remain relatively small, lest we lose our focus on animal liberation as we fixate on the capitalist compunction to gain ever more funding and open up satellite offices across the country and beyond. Being an activist-educator requires critical and creative thinking, as explored previously, but it also includes honest assessment of ourselves. If we speak and act based upon others' expectations, as opposed to our own truths, we will remain forever bound to a system of "change" that propagates the very ills it superficially claims to cure.

Conclusion

As our principles influence practice, they must always drive us in our actions. To overturn the world, this "transformation begins with us, in the spaces and places of our communities" (White & Cudworth, 2014, p. 216). The goal of overcoming domination and hierarchy must remain in our sights at all times, and this can be done in a pedagogical-activist context. Understanding these knowledge practices is politically crucial given that activist learning is by nature concrete and embodied in practice, making pedagogy intrinsically paramount for activists. As Freire (1971) famously remarked, "we take the role of agents, makers and remakers of our world in a permanent, critical approach to reality" (p. 24). Anarchist praxis confronts the interlocking nature of systems of abuse and domination that underpin humans and animals in society. Given the escalation of exploitation, it is an imperative to act. Change must begin now, every second counts, just as every life counts. Anarchist principles could be used for activist communities to address the dire concerns facing humans, nonhuman animals, and the environment in the age of global neoliberalism and uninhibited capitalism.

REFERENCES

Althusser, L. (1971). Ideology and ideological state apparatuses. In L. Althusser, Ed., *Lenin and philosophy and other essays* (pp. 127–188). London: New Left Books.
Apple, M. (2013). *Can education change society?* New York: Routledge.
Best, S. (2006). "Rethinking revolution: Animal liberation, human liberation, and the future of the left." *International Journal of Inclusive Democracy* 2 (3), 1–31.

Best, S., & Nocella II, A.J. (2006). Introduction. In S. Best & A.J. Nocella II, eds., *Igniting a revolution: Voices in defence of the Earth* (pp. 8–29). Oakland: AK Press.
Brookfield, S. (1987). *Developing critical thinkers: Challenging adults to explore alternative ways of thinking and action.* Milton Keynes: Open University Press.
Brown, G., & Pickerill, J. (2009). "Space for emotions in spaces of activism." *Emotion, Space and Society* 2, 24–35.
Conway, J. (2006). *Praxis and politics: Knowledge production in social movements.* New York: Routledge.
Cooney, N. (2010). *Change of heart: What psychology can teach us about spreading social change* [Kindle edition]. Retrieved from Amazon.com.
Cooney, N. (2013). *Veganomics: The surprising science on what motivates vegetarians, from the breakfast table to the bedroom.* New York: Lantern Books.
Corman, L., & Vandrovcová, T. (2014). "Radical humility: Toward a more holistic Critical Animal Studies pedagogy." In A.J. Nocella II, J. Sorenson, K. Socha, & A. Matsuoka, eds., *Defining Critical Animal Studies: An intersectional social justice approach to liberation* (pp. 135–157). New York: Peter Lang.
De Cleyre, V. (1912/2004). "Direct action." In A.J. Brigati Ed., *The Voltairine de Cleyre reader* (pp. 47–61). Oakland, CA: AK Press.
Dean, J. (2009). *Democracy and other neoliberal fantasies: Communicative capitalism and left politics.* Durham: Duke University Press.
DeLeon, A. (2008). "Oh no, not the 'A' word! Proposing an 'anarchism' for education." *Educational Studies* 44 (2), 122–141.
Doherty, B., Paterson, M., & Seel, B. (2000). *Direct action in British environmentalism.* London: Routledge.
Dominick, B. (1997). *Animal liberation and social revolution: A Vegan perspective on anarchism or an anarchist perspective on veganism,* 2d ed. Syracuse: Critical Mess Media.
Drew, L. (2014). "Embodied learning processes in social action." Paper presented at the 33rd Annual Conference of the Canadian Association for the Study of Adult Education (CASAE). Ontario, Canada.
Elise, T. (2013). "Anti-capitalism and abolitionism." In K. Socha & S. Blum, eds., *Confronting animal exploitation: Grassroots essays on liberation and veganism* (pp. 22–43). Jefferson, NC: McFarland.
Food and Agriculture Organization of the United Nations: Economic and Social Development Department (2008). "World agriculture: Towards 2015/2013: An FAO perspective." J. Bruinsma, Ed. Retrieved from http://www.fao.org/docrep/005/y4252e/y4252e05b.htm.
Foley, G. (1999). *Learning in social action: A contribution to understanding informal education.* London: Zed Books.
Foster, J.B., & Chesney, R.W. (2010). "Capitalism, the absurd system: A view from the United States." *Monthly Review* 62(2). Retrieved from http://monthlyreview.org/2010/06/01/capitalism-the-absurd-system-a-view-from-the-united-states.
Freeman, J. (1970). "The tyranny of structurelessness." Retrieved from http://www.jofreeman.com/joreen/tyranny.htm.
Freire, P. (1971). "A few notions about the word conscientization." *Hard Cheese* 1, 23–28.
Freire, P. (1975). *Pedagogy of the oppressed.* London: Penguin.
Freire, P. & Shor, I. (1987). *A pedagogy for liberation: Dialogues on transforming education.* New York: Bergin & Garvey.
Gillborn, D. (2008). *Racism and education. Coincidence or conspiracy.* Oxon: Routledge.
Goldman, E. (1906). "The child and its enemies." Retrieved from http://theanarchistlibrary.org/library/emma-goldman-the-child-and-its-enemies.

Goldman, E. (1911). "The social importance of the Modern School." Retrieved from http://theanarchistlibrary.org/library/emma-goldman-the-social-importance-of-the-modern-school.

Goldman, E. (2011). *Anarchism and other essays*. London: Martino Publishing Association.

Harper, B. (2010). *Sistah vegan: food, identity, health, and society: Black female vegans speak*. New York: Lantern Books.

Haworth, R. H. (2012). Introduction. In R.H. Haworth, Ed., *Anarchist pedagogies: Collective Actions, theories, and critical reflections on education* (pp. 1–10). Oakland: PM Press.

Kahn, R. (2010). *Critical pedagogy, ecoliteracy, & planetary crisis: the ecopedagogy movement*. New York: Peter Lang.

Kropotkin, P. (1902/2006). *Mutual aid: A factor of evolution*. Chelmsford, MA: Courier Dover.

Lave, J., & Wenger, E. (1991). *Situated learning, legitimate peripheral participation*. Cambridge: Cambridge University Press.

McLaren, P. (1995). *Critical pedagogy and predatory culture: Oppositional politics in a postmodern era*. New York: Routledge.

McLaren, P. & Kincheloe, J. (2007). *Critical pedagogy: where are we now?* New York: Peter Lang.

Mueller, J. (2012). "Anarchism, the State, and role of education." In R.H. Howarth, Ed., *Anarchist pedagogies: Collective actions, theories, and critical reflections on education* (pp. 14–31). Oakland: PM Press.

Nocella, A., Sorenson, J., Socha, K., & Matsuoka, A. (2014). Introduction:" The emergence of Critical Animal Studies: The rise of intersectional animal liberation." In A.J. Nocella II, J. Sorenson, K. Socha, & A. Matsuoka, eds., *Defining Critical Animal Studies: An intersectional social justice approach to liberation*. (pp. xix-xxxvi). New York: Peter Lang.

Shantz, J. (2012)." Spaces of learning: The anarchist free skool." In R.H. Howarth, Ed., *Anarchist pedagogies: Collective actions, theories, and critical reflections on education* (pp. 124–144). Oakland: PM Press.

Socha, K. (2011). *Women, destruction, and the avant-garde: A paradigm for animal liberation*. Amsterdam: Rodopi.

Socha, K. (2013). "'Just tell the truth': A polemic on the value of radical activism." In K. Socha & S. Blum, eds., *Confronting animal exploitation: Grassroots essays on liberation and veganism* (pp. 44–65). Jefferson, NC: McFarland.

Stoltenberg, J. (1994). *What makes pornography "sexy"?* Minneapolis: Milkweed.

Swanson, M. (2013). "How 'humane' labels harm chickens: Why our focus should be egg-free diets, not cage-free eggs." In K. Socha & S. Blum, eds., *Confronting animal exploitation: Grassroots essays on liberation and veganism* (pp. 204–222). Jefferson, NC: McFarland.

Sztybel, D. (2007). "Animal rights law: fundamentalism versus pragmatism." *Journal for Critical Animal Studies* V(1), 1–35.

Torres, B. (2007). *Making a killing: The political economy of animal rights*. Oakland: AK Press.

White, R., & Cudworth, E. (2014). "Taking it to the streets: Challenging systems of domination from below." In A.J. Nocella II, J. Sorenson, K. Socha, & A. Matsuoka, eds., *Defining Critical Animal Studies: An intersectional social justice approach to liberation* (pp. 202–219). New York: Peter Lang.

Recognizing Human-Supremacy
Interrupt, Inspire and Expose

John Lupinacci

"Human freedom, animal rights. It's one struggle, one fight"—Conflict, 1986

"Speak up. Act out. Silence is complicity.... Wake up the world's on fire"—Ferlinghetti, 2007, p. 31

As an urban educator and an activist-scholar, I have found the interruptive and inspiring acts of anarchism to have a powerful impact on exposing the authoritarian practices of Western dominant culture. Furthermore, direct action organizations like the Animal Liberation Front (ALF), the Earth Liberation Front (ELF), and their diverse support networks call attention to the importance of anarchist projects. Specifically, these organizations question how it is we identify as human beings in relationship to addressing social suffering and environmental degradation—or to our commitment to alleviating and eliminating injustice for all living beings from the ills of authoritarianism masquerading as democracy. I am not alone in this line of inquiry as evidenced by the growing body of scholarship—like critical animal studies, critical disability studies, queer theory, ecofeminist projects, ecojustice, ecopedagogy, and anarchist scholarship—in connection with a multitude of direct action organizations and the efforts of the many activists who dedicate, and have dedicated, their life work to the liberation of all living beings. When addressing the injustices perpetuated by human supremacy on the planet it is important to recognize the important role that direct action organizations play. Direct action organizations interrupt, inspire, and expose stories that influence and call to action scholarship that recognizes, respects, and represents projects to rethink the dominant discourses and discursive practices influencing power in relation to current regimes of oppressive ideologies.

A primary premise guiding this essay is that the manifestation of a human-supremacist worldview is cultural. In other words, this essay asserts that we as humans, specifically those of us constituted by—and constituting—dominant Western industrial culture, have learned to think and behave according to a culturally constructed set of maps we use to interpret relationships and thus shape meaning. Since meaning is constructed culturally then it can be assumed that the process can be interrupted and shifted if we learn to think differently about our relationships to each other and to the natural world. As an anarchist educator, I present in this essay the importance of rethinking human supremacy and the role of direct action organizations and anarchism to interrupting and inspiring projects that further expose the injustice and pervasive violence of Western industrial culture.

As activist-scholar educators, it is essential to recognize and value those among us who do not explicitly perpetuate human-supremacy and in doing so work to identify and revalue the critical practices of mutual aid and interdependence that still exist in communities all over the world. While anarchic activist projects are occurring all over the planet, in many Western industrial communities there is a need to bring attention to rethinking how we conceive culturally constructed concepts like property and ownership in connection with the legacy of Eurocentric human-supremacy. In this essay it is my assertion that there is a key role anarchist scholar-activists ought to play to support educational spaces that work toward bringing this diverse work together in solidarity, through what I am calling pedagogies of solidarity.

The concept of pedagogies of solidarity is a direct nod and tribute to Freire's *Pedagogy of the Oppressed* (1993) and *Pedagogy of Freedom: Ethics, Democracy, and Civic Courage* (2000), as well as other critical and ethical contributions to a diversity of approaches to the cultural aspects of education. Richard Kahn (2010a, 2010b), growing the work of Freire and critical pedagogy, advocates for solidarity on activism and critical education conceptualizing what he calls an ecopedagogy. An ecopedagogy movement in education applies the basic principles of critical pedagogy to the interrelated nature of social and ecological issues. Kahn (2010a) explaining ecopedagogy, illuminates how such pedagogical projects in the movement recognize "ecological ideas such as the intrinsic value of all species, the need to care for and live in harmony with the planet, as well as the emancipatory potential contained in human aesthetic experiences of nature" (Kahn, 2010a, p. 19). Pedagogies of solidarity refer to educational projects—like the pedagogical efforts described by Kahn as ecopedagogy—that resist claims of a single solution for stopping injustice. Such pedagogical projects facilitate the potential of critical and ethical education to empower local members of any community to not only respond and reframe learning but also to do so in any such way that contributes to the collective battle to break the will of their oppressors. Specifically the phrase, pedagogies of solidarity, intentionally draws attention to the multitude of pedagogical possibilities and the value of the diverse experimentation of teaching and learning toward diverse, decentralized, sovereign communities for all beings. Critical dimensions of these pedagogies of solidarity are in reference to a diversity of public pedagogical approaches that can be understood in relation to other deformations of public life under neoliberalism.

Among these deformations that rationalize the exploitation of each other and our animal kin include, but are not limited to, intensified and expanded processes of criminalization (Giroux, 2009); the rapid transfer of wealth and opportunity upwards; the erosion of social identities and bonds (Bauman, 2007); and the emptying of public space and redefinition of public discourses under neoliberalism (Couldry, 2010). In this essay, I am drawing from and simultaneously critiquing the role of radical social justice efforts that commit to fighting racism, sexism, classism, ableism, and other aspects of human struggle but in doing so reinforce the subjugation and exploitation of otherized living beings. As an anarchist educator navigating the authoritarian constraints of neoliberalized institutions of higher education, this chapter outlines efforts to educate, organize, and support eco-anarchic direct action through pedagogical projects that call attention to particular relationships, practices, and discourses at work in conjunction with a common enemy— the dominant discourses and discursive practices of Western industrial culture. Such anarchic pedagogical projects take place in a variety of locally situated learning initiatives that organize in support of living systems. These local and diverse pedagogies operate concurrently, sometimes separately, and in conversation with each other. Through pedagogies of solidarity these projects stem from the recognition that there are powerful phenomena occurring within schools and in our society that are profoundly abusive and are violently reproducing relationships that make racism, sexism, classism, and speciesism to name a few—seem inevitable and inescapable. However, anarchism reminds and encourages us to imagine possibilities beyond current constraints of culturally constructed regimes of cruelty.

We perceive that to be in school, by situation of its location in society, means learning to function within, accept, and submit to the authority of a tremendously exploitive culture. This so-called reality is preparing young people for their fate in a very unhealthy and in many ways broken society. Despite this raw exposure to life for so many of us, and our children, there are existing relationships that offer not only an alternative, but also a plethora of alternatives. In life, or in the living systems within which humans exist, there are counternarratives to the abuse—there are stories about how living together ought to be, about what it could be, and about who and what belongs. This all revels together in what Dr. Cornell West refers to as the complexity, or messiness of living relationships—the funk and stank of life (Mendieta, 2011). These are the stories, smells, tastes, joys, and pains that explore the potential of community and the power of a decentralized locally sovereign existence. There are voices of activism whispering, chatting, talking, rapping, dancing, singing, and sharing stories that offer alternatives to what is and unapologetically welcomes the reimagining of a very different society—which for many students and educators is a call to action to identify the role education both plays and ought to play in transitioning toward socially just and sustainable communities: to confront and overcome human supremacy—to recognize how we make meaning through fundamentally different worldviews and the potential for constructing meaning in non-anthropocentric ways.

When thinking about the diverse work among scholars and activists challenging human supremacy, it is through recognizing, respecting, and representing our solidarity in a growing movement that I consider how human-supremacy functions—not only in our day-to-day lives, but also how it simultaneously works to dominate our perceptions of self, one another, and who is constituted as a member of an often romanticized, but important concept: community. In this essay I address these stories, goals, admissions, confessions, and dreams in ways that complement, inspire, and challenge current perceptions of our roles as part of institutions in Western industrial culture--especially within schools, colleges, and universities. The phrase "more-than-human" introduced by David Abram (1996), in *The Spell of the Sensuous: Perception and Language in a More-Than-Human World*, draws attention to the larger set of living relationships within which human-human relationships are a very small number in comparison. This phrase is a nice alternative to the marginalizing, commonly used phrase of non-human.

Specifically, this esssay calls attention to eco-anarchist scholarship that addresses and examines dominant discourses and discursive practices of human-supremacy and its impact on all of the members, both human and more-than-human, in the community to whom we are ethically responsible. With the shared goals of social justice and sustainability in the form of truly decentralized communities, when we listen to the voices of the members who are silenced in our day-to-day lives we become more aware of the injustices experienced by so many. These are voices, and often cries, that we might wonder how we could have ignored, and often continue to struggle with ignoring—voices that tell the stories of atrocities which we grow to know too much about and to which in life we simply owe too much to let continue (Callaway, 2004). In listening to the voices of each other and the life systems to which we all belong we can begin to heal. These are the systems we as humans are in debt to for both our existence and for the pain and suffering some of us have inflicted—and in many ways continue to inflict—out of ignorance, selfishness, and abuse. This violence is predicated on the dominant assumption that our understanding of the world is culturally constructed and dependent upon the notion of a human-being as an individual separate and superior to all other beings.

Critical Animal Studies & Anarchism

Critical Animal Studies (CAS) as a scholar-activist project focuses on the atrocities that stem from and include the rationalization of cruelty to animals in modern society—the systematic discrimination and domination by humans against other humans and all other species. Defining CAS, the Institute for Critical Animal Studies (ICAS) explains:

> Rooted in animal liberation, CAS is an interdisciplinary field dedicated to establishing a holistic total liberation movement for humans, nonhuman animals, and the Earth. CAS is engaged in an intersectional, theory-to-action politics, in solidarity with movements to abolish all systems of domination [retrieved from http://www.criticalanimalstudies.org/about/].

While several critical, social justice projects and frameworks take a broad view of injustice and even focus on the cultural roots of forms of domination and violence, CAS offers a deeper critique than many other perspectives. CAS is a fast growing field inspired by and supportive of direct action of organizations like the ALF and ELF as well as the diverse networks of activist-scholarship taken in direct response to the audacious authorities of Western industrial culture (Nocella II, 2007, 2012; Twine, 2012). Critical Animal Studies scholars interrogate the ideological manifestation of anthropocentrism in relationship to humanist discourses that emerge in relationship to an ontology of being rooted in Western philosophy and science (Nocella et al., 2014).

Anarchism, as presented by Judith Sussia (2010), contributes a concise overview of anarchist philosophy's inherent, yet often overlooked, role in activist and educational discourses. What is clear from contemporary anarchist relationships with education is that they are complex and diverse in how they describe the role that education both plays and ought to play (Amster et al., 2009; Haworth, 2012). The social anarchist view that emerges from nineteenth century anarchists to offer insight into how anarchist perspectives of freedom and equality interrupt authoritarianism and fits very well with the eco-anarchic projects of a CAS framework. The work of nineteenth century anarchists like Proudhon, Bakunin, Kropotkin, and more contemporary anarchists like Chomsky and Bookchin, offer an important voice from anarchist theory in educational efforts to rethink dominant assumptions in Western industrial culture and engage in actions of resistance to support the liberation of all those suffering unjustly.

Anarchist literature, like the writing of Mikhail Bakunin, Peter Kropotkin, Emma Goldman, and situalitionalists, like Guy Debord, presents strong scholarship that connects us to philosophical discussions that take opposition to any centralized authority exerting and abusing power. Such anarchist voices are essential to understanding anarchic experiments as they work to expose the often silenced or ignored history of anarchist engagement with learning to resist and why it is some choose to engage in direct action against the violence of the State. Abraham Deleon in *Against the Grain of the Status Quo: Anarchism behind Enemy Lines* (2012) explains, "Anarchism is embedded in a politics that seeks to resist hierarchies, coercive experiences, and official and unofficial State politics" (p. 317). Anarchism emerged as resistance to unjust authorities governing how we relate to each other and the more-than-human world. Anarchic dissent has always worked in diverse ways to reclaim how we imagine the world. Therefor it becomes difficult to ignore the contributions of anarchism when engaging in eco-anarchic scholarship and activist projects like the ALF, ELF, and all other movements in support of total liberation.

While CAS and networks of direct action organizations working to liberate animals may not necessarily identify as anarchist, these movements are not exactly something meaningfully distinct or separate from anarchism. In fact, one might argue that the ALF, ELF, and the supporting scholarship of CAS are a direct form of anarchic action. DeLeon (2012) explains that anarchism includes and "has integrated work that questions rigid boundaries of sexuality, class, racism, gendered oppression, and other political projects" (p. 317). Drawing from Amster et al. (2009), DeLeon (2012) explains how "because it [anarchism] has been infused with a variety of different perspectives and positionalities, it lends itself to being easily adaptable to a variety of situations, critiques, and approaches" (p. 317). It is through this conceptualization of eco-anarchist activist-scholarship that I situate CAS and the work of the ALF as direct anarchic action—diverse projects that are local, situational, and in support of decentralized living systems (Lupinacci, 2011).

Eco-anarchism—together with activists dedicated to earth and animal liberation—can be understood as a movement of analysis and action. Describing such a movement Derrick Jensen (2009) makes the statement that "the role of an activist is not to navigate systems of oppressive power with as much integrity as possible, but rather to confront and take down those systems" (para. 12). For many activists battling regimes of human supremacy, the heart of their commitment to direct action lies in the strong belief that the current dominant human-centered culture will not likely undergo a voluntary transformation in which power and privilege is relinquished and an intrinsic worth of all members of the planet recognized and respected. This sort of movement is informed activism that moves from ethical inquiry about why things are the way they are, to action aimed at changing the dominant culture. Such anarchic movements can be understood as interrupting dominant regimes of power and reminding us that there is a place for those who simply refuse to stand by and bear witness to the associated atrocities of an ecocide. While some members of this shared interest take action by pulling up asphalt, sitting in trees, interrupting deforestation, freeing animals tortured in research labs, and dismantling dams—to name a few from a long list—it is important that those activists are supported by activist-educators taking direct action to interrupt and destroy dominant discourses that rationalize the atrocities against which anarchic dissent in the form of direct action is necessary. In other words, this a battle fought on multiple fronts in efforts to overcome human supremacy both immediately and for future generations.

Confronting human-supremacy through direct action includes an understanding of how anarchists and anarchist theory contribute to ever-evolving and adapting perspectives through which we can learn to support and value concepts like community, mutual aid, diversity, and solidarity. In today's neoliberal institutions an agenda to enclose the last vestiges of public space works through educational institutions that reproduce a limited set of practices disciplined by modern discourses that support the illusion that we, as humans, are separate from and superior to everything else, which manufactures a sense of insecurity, instability, and erodes solidarity. The impacts of authoritarian, top down policy often result in resistance, especially in the form of anarchist dissent, which creates the opportunity to commit to reclaiming power from a centralized authority and redistributing power in decentralized communities that are situational, local, and in support of living systems. Anarchists educate and organize in ways that engage participants in addressing the assumptions that have led to an erosion of solidarity. Learning that anarchism isn't "anything goes," but that it is a way of living through critical and ethical decentralized decision-making, helps us to stand firmly and in solidarity with others. Anarchism, which I assert is at the heart of an earth and animal liberation framework, reaffirms that imagination and interruptions to authority are necessary in order to understand and change the social and economic conditions that create the illusions of individualism, and rationalize the exploitation and torture associated with the commodification of living things. It is my assertion that scholar-activist educators supportive of the diverse projects eco-anarchism and CAS work on two interrelated fronts. They work to critically and ethically examine Western industrial culture and the impacts on social and environmental systems while examining and identifying how to rethink the assumptions that shape how we organize and share skills and strategies that directly support just and sustainable communities for all living beings. As a part of that process they directly confront systems of domination that share the same human-supremacist assumptions rationalizing authoritarianism and the illusion of being dependent on the State.

Anthropocentrism

While there are several dominant discourses contributing to what is shaping and shaped by a Eurocentric human supremacist culture, in this chapter I focus on one of these modernist discourses—anthropocentrism or human-centered thinking as it contributes to the gangland of human supremacy. I choose anthropocentrism with the conviction and belief that in most cases when examining social justice and sustainability human-supremacy exists unchecked as it works to provide a foundation for injustices directly experienced by other modernist discourses. However, I am not trying to argue that it supersedes other dominant, modernist discourses—like patriarchy, racism, ableism, classism, and so forth—as they all exist in a complex relationship to constitute modernity, or what might be considered by Polish-British sociologist Zygmunt Bauman as a late modernity culture (Martusewicz, et al. 2015; Bauman, 2000). I will also take some liberty here and discuss my general observations of anthropocentric influences on daily life as they are often the impetus and inspiration for direct actions taken by the ALF and ELF (Colling & Nocella II, 2012; Nocella II & Best, 2004; Rosebraugh, 2004). The following is an open letter I share with my friends, colleagues, students, future friends, and of course to any of those who may position themselves as adversaries (although they may resist such a label). In the spirit of diversity and the anarchist tradition, it's important to admit we don't all agree and that in fact it is in recognizing those differences that we can talk authentically about solidarity—essentially we can commit to learning why it is some activists have dedicated their lives and freedom to actions in defense of the right of all living beings to belong and exist in peace on the planet.

The focus here is not to educate those activists in the movement, but to extend the call to action to educators and scholars who stand to play a vital role in bringing awareness and preparing more citizens who both understand the purpose and potential in direct action in support of just lives for all those diverse species claimed by and claiming community. My intention in the following sections of this essay is to voice something too often silenced in critical dialogues among educators and scholars that claim to be radical but don't support the radical stances of the efforts of so many activists. Disciplined by dominant discourses of Western industrial constructions of research, it is the stories of anarchic actions to break oppression that foster the potential to remind such educators and scholars to find the will to say it out loud more often and to challenge anthropocentrism in our institutions carefully and sensitively. In addition to addressing anthropocentrism, this essay is intended to foster the fire of an anti-human supremacist charge in solidarity with the fire of social justice and sustainability. In other words, this work explores the ways in which we recognize and value difference to educate, organize, and take action in solidarity.

An Open Letter to Teachers, Scholars, and Activists in Western Industrial Culture:

> I see anthropocentrism enacted every day, all of the time, and I needn't venture far to be reminded of its broad acceptance—even among some of the most socially conscious and environmentally concerned advocates of change. Anthropocentrism is an unspoken taboo among those who fancy themselves as advocates of justice. To name the ways in which this deeply embedded discourse of modernity plays out requires that I speak outside of the frameworks of what is conventionally recognized among my peers as reasonable. When I bring specific attention to the injustices done to our more-than-human kin, I often hear that I can't be serious. I am.
>
> It has gotten to the point that I have come to terms with the fact that for some of my human pals this particular discourse will be one of heated contention and that in their eyes it is a measure of my rationality that I am willing to sacrifice my social standing in the name of the billions murdered. The graves of so many nameless kin, some of whom are humans, reduced to objects as their torture and death are rationalized and justified because they are likened to animals—and therefore expendable and exploitable as resources of human supremacy. We are so quick to dismiss the value of another species as inferior to our existence because we are told they don't feel pain or they are without a soul. When we disregard the value of a non-human life, we are vulnerable to extending that condition of value onto one another.
>
> I am not ashamed, nor shy, to say that this so-called *logic* or *reasoning* is often a "conscience eased by lies" (Hannah, 1996). Anthropocentrism justifies the unjust in the name of holding up the status of human as a supreme being. It cannot be ethically denied that the preservation of humans as superior beings is a justification for suffering in the form of domination, exploitation, and murder. Yet this is often the case. And any resistance to this position is all too often dismissed as unrealistic or irrational.
>
> I myself am not ashamed to say that I too slip into, and live daily in hypocrisy, as I find myself deeply entrenched in anthropocentric discursive practices. But as a committed eco-ethical anarchic educator—and more importantly as a member of an ecological system to which we are akin as living members—I am forced to confront the vast sea of indifference to the suffering and slaughtering of our kin with all my heart, mind, and body.
>
> As a person drawn toward standing up to social injustices, I came into the field of education with an activist with a burning desire to work toward confronting and challenging the unjust suffering perpetuated by schools and society. I worked, and continue to work, ardently to recognize how the privileges of race, class, gender, sexual orientation, and ability contribute to oppression. I recognize how these forms of social injustices exploit and marginalize, but when I fail to consider *other* species, I neglect to recognize the source of all the aforemen-

tioned injustices. I miss the root of these inequalities because all around me, including within my own frame of reference, we are under the influence of the discourse of anthropocentrism. So to take this discourse into account, simply put, life is too short to unjustly cause another's to be shorter. If I believe that humans are superior beings, then in order to cast others as inferior I need only to liken them to non-human species. This is the position from which many of my friends and adversaries argue and sharply informs the following question:

To my very *brilliant* and *productive* friends, why do you ignore the issue and deny the clear relationship between anthropocentrism, consumerism, and brutality? When I speak of our responsibility to all members of our community, you roll your eyes and, intentionally or unintentionally, your dismissal marginalizes, socially isolates, and preys on the shame of those who would otherwise be willing to respond to the suffering of those in pain. While in the grasps of anthropocentrism, you cringe at the idea of being equal in worth to another species, yet you speak that you live toward equality for all humans. This is an issue of acting out of selfishness and superiority, and before you even listen you find yourself enslaved by your impulse to reject the worth of any other species as equivocal to that of your own.

I thought that I shared common ground with advocates of social justice, and I do as long as together we challenge and confront the conventions fed to us by a past and present language that interprets living, breathing, feeling beings as mechanized objects. While among company who don't challenge anthropocentrism, it's only a matter of time until it is any one of us, including I, who is served as your commodity. The institutionalized violence and oppression of racism, slavery, the subjugation and objectification of women, the genocide on Native Americans, the prison industrial complex, the slaughter of so many of our animal kin in factory farming, and razing of lush forests—to name only a few—all hinge on reasoning that the other is less in value and is not fully human. Do you still feign indignant to injustice? Because without addressing anthropocentrism—or conversely, your willingness to uphold your human superiority—you are in fact making way for the rape, slavery, and murder of the human and the more-than-human family: the animals, the land, each other, and the oceans to which we all belong.

Points of Action: Pedagogies of Solidarity

Indigenous scholar Jack Forbes (2008), describing today's dominant culture, wrote:

This is a no holds-barred modern society in which college graduates are expected to be willing to "give their all" to developing or selling a product, even if the product is harmful or worthless, where technicians are expected to kill and torture captive animals because they are ordered to do so by some government experimenter or paper-producing professor, and where the opportunities for being "one's own boss" in a non-exploitive, non-crooked, or non-demeaning role are precious and few indeed [p. xxi].

This captures the condition in which diverse anarchist projects put to use a wide range of strategies and tactics that not only call into question Western industrial culture but also resist it. Subcomandante Marcos, turning our attention away from how we think and reminding us that equally and arguably more important in matters of justice is how we feel, states: "Abajo y a la Izquierda está el Corazón!" (Day, 1998). Roughly translated into English this statement reminds us that, "Below and to the Left is the Heart." The matters of injustice to which Forbes is calling our attention are the atrocities of earth and animal suffering that the activists of the ALF and ELF are taking direct action to stop. It is these matters and the resistance movements that inspire and inform the role activist-scholar educators ought to play in working to educate in solidarity toward ending the isolating dictatorship of human-supremacy. All of which are matters of the heart.

The more scholar-activist educators address anthropocentrism among social justice advocates, the more potential there is to recognize the tendency of the privileged to dismiss what they would rather not confront. While on one hand I admire, value, and am a firm supporter of a shared commitment to respond to the undeniable atrocities that we—as humans—enact on one another, none of these atrocities occur in isolation. It is paramount that scholar-activist educators work as allies to those suffering while challenging and confronting the systemic roots of oppression on our respective fronts. In other words, we all have a responsibility—many of us as privileged members of society—to support the oppressed in whatever capacity we can. Together our goal is to break the will of the oppressor.

This is something that is an ongoing effort and that calls for diverse strategies. In some ways it calls for some subversive work but also direct action. In all cases, the goal is not victory as though this is a personal conquest, but rather equal respect and consideration for all. In such instances we listen, despite the fact that many, or perhaps most, are too often not listening to all of the silenced voices of the suffering.

In conclusion, it is in the spirit of anarchism I turn attention toward the difficult necessity for cultural change. I truly believe that if we, enactors of dominant Western industrial culture, do not rethink the framework by which meaning is constructed then we are destined to recreate the very predicament that we set out to change. Inspired by movements to liberate our human and more-than-human kin, I would like to employ the guiding principles of solidarity and action to the following practical steps toward cultural change and activist scholarship aimed toward supporting a paradigm shift from rational, mechanized, and human-centered thinking to discourses that are local, situational, and supportive of living systems (Lupinacci, 2011, 2013). It is hard for me to suggest or outline an action plan without including rethinking our cultural traditions. That being made clear, I conclude by suggesting a few steps that pertain to my local community, and how scholar-activist educators in that local community continually engage in the necessary healing from, and reimagining of, dominant culture. The principal action in the following steps is building networks of solidarity which translate to recognizing, respecting, and representing diversity among a multitude of movements to educate, organize, and take action together in diverse ways to break the will of the oppressor and seek liberation from Eurocentric, anthropocentric domination. Drawing from the anarchic spirit in projects of EcoJustice and Ecopedagogy, CAS, and a transformative justice framework (Nocella, 2011), defined here are steps towards engaging in the valuing of pedagogies of solidarity that ensure and support the importance resisting the State in favor of local governance in the most decentralized form—decisions made by those directly impacted by the decision.

- Engage in dialogical teaching and learning that explores in solidarity rethinking the assumptions influencing how we, as humans, construct meaning and thus how we learn to relate to each other and the more-than-human world. Further, make the commitment to critically and ethically examine how we understand educating, organizing, and taking action towards supporting healthy communities that include all beings and the intrinsic value of recognizing, respecting, and representing the right of all beings to belong to and live in peace within an ecological system.
- Engage in critical and ethical examinations of community. As notions of community are all too often defined in terms of human-centered exclusion, it is important to work to reclaim community in terms of who and what is included in our definitions of this construct—and how those definitions contribute to the either supporting or undermining the right of all beings to coexist in peace.
- Engage in examining community in terms of inclusion and the diverse ways in which our living relationships can be recognized, respected, and represented through teaching and learning among all members. Specifically, engage in recognizing the role activist networks play in alleviating and eliminating unjust suffering in our communities. Build networks of solidarity with these organizations.
- Engage in supporting the diverse approaches to healing from Western industrial culture and in solidarity show respect for epistemologies that differ from the current dominant discourses of Empire (Hardt, & Negri, 2001) and support the ways in which diverse forms of resistance work to break the will of their oppressors.
- Engage in strong alliance with all those suffering and support the oppressed in solidarity while simultaneously working to shift and

challenge the dominant systems that often govern the alleviation of the suffering of all marginalized and subjugated beings. In all cases stand up, speak out, and take action to stop the systemic domination of one another, ourselves, and our more-than-human kin.

So one place to start is to simplify all of that and to make friends, engage with our adversaries, and share stories. Challenge dominant perceptions of what is legal or acceptable and imagine what could be possible. Resist the State and reject the illusion that as humans we are separate from and superior to each other and all other things on the planet. Make friends with other humans and especially make friends with more-than-humans—be it some animals, some trees, a river, the songbirds that wake us up in the morning, the food that we grow, or the soil that gives us life. The point is that we learn compassion and dependency when we understand in an ecological sense what it means to be friends. We learn what it means to belong without framing that understanding as human-centered. We learn to join the fight to overcome the isolating ills of Western industrial culture when we take action with our diverse sisters and brothers to interrupt, inspire, and expose!

REFERENCES

Abram, D. (1996). *The spell of the sensuous: perception and language in a more-than-human world.* New York: Vintage.
Amster, R., DeLeon, A. P., Fernandez, L. A., Nocella II, A. J., & Shannon, D., eds. (2009). *Contemporary anarchist studies: An introductory anthology of anarchy in the academy.* New York, NY: Routledge.
Arnold, P. (2008, May 19). "Cee-Lo Green: What A Long, Strange Trip It's Been." [Web log post]. Retrieved from http://www.hiphopdx.com/index/interviews/id.1124/title.cee-lo-green-what-a-long-strange-trip-its-been.
Bauman, Z. (2000). *Liquid modernity.* Malden, MA: Polity Press.
Bauman, Z. (2007). *Consuming life.* Cambridge, MA: Polity Press.
Callaway, T. (2004). "Die Trying" [Recorded by CeeLo Green]. *On Cee-Lo Green ... Is the Soul Machine.* [MP3]. Los Angeles: Artista.
Colling, S., & Nocella II, A. J. (2012). *Love and liberation: An animal liberation front story.* Williamstown, MA: Piraeus Books.
Conflict. (1986). "This is the A.L.F." [Recorded by Conflict]. *The Ungovernable Force.* [MP3]. London: Morterhate.
Couldry, N. (2010). *Why voice matters: culture and politics after neoliberalism.* London: Sage.
Day, C. (1998). *Ezln comminques. Navigating the seas, Dec. 22, 1997-Jan. 29, 1998.* Berkeley: Regent Press.
DeLeon, A. P. (2012). "Against the grain of the status quo: Anarchism behind enemy lines." In R. H. Haworth, Ed., *Anarchist pedagogies: Collective actions, theories, and critical reflections on education.* Oakland: PM Press.
Ferlinghetti, L. (2007). *Poetry as insurgent art.* New York: New Directions.
Forbes, J. D. (2008). *Columbus and other cannibals: The wétiko disease of exploitation, imperialism, and terrorism.* New York: Seven Stories Press.

Freire, P. (1993). *Pedagogy of the oppressed.* M. B. Ramos, trans. Rev. 20th Anniv. ed. New York: Continuum.
Freire, P. (1998). *Pedagogy of freedom: Ethics, democracy, and civic courage.* P. Clarke, trans. Lanham, MD: Roman & Littlefield.
Giroux, H. A. (2009). *Youth in a suspect society: democracy or disposability.* New York: Palgrave Macmillan.
Hannah, C. (1996). "Nailing Descartes to the Wall/(Liquid) Meat Is Still Murder" [Recorded by Propagandhi]. *Less Talk, More Rock* [Audio cassette]. San Francisco: Fat Wreck Chords.
Hardt, M., & Negri, A. (2001). *Empire.* Cambridge: Harvard University Press.
Haworth, R. H., Ed. (2012). *Anarchist pedagogies: Collective actions, theories, and critical reflections on education.* Oakland: PM Press.
Jensen, D. (2009). "Forget shorter showers: Why personal change does not equal political change." *Orion Magazine, July/August.* Retrieved from http://www.orionmagazine.org/index.php/articles/article/4801/.
Kahn, R. (2010a). *Critical pedagogy, ecoliteracy and planetary crisis: The ecopedagogy movement.* New York: Peter Lang.
Kahn, R. (2010b). "Love hurts: Ecopedagogy between avatars and elegies." *Teacher Education Quarterly* 37(4), 55–70.
Lupinacci, J. (2011). "Educating for commons sense: Learning that is situational, local, and supportive of living systems." *PowerPlay: A Journal of Educational Justice* 3(1), 97–104.
Lupinacci, J. (2012). "Anarchism and education: A philosophical perspective." *Educational Studies* 48(1), 108–111.
Lupinacci, J. (2013). "Eco-ethical environmental education: Critically and ethically examining our existence as humans." In A. Kulnieks, D. R. Longboat & K. Young, eds., *Contemporary studies in environmental and indigenous pedagogies: A curricula of stories and place.* Rotterdam: Sense.
Martusewicz, R., Edmundson, J., & Lupinacci, J. (2015). *EcoJustice education: Toward diverse, democratic, and sustainable communities,* 2d ed. New York: Routledge.
Mendieta, E. (2011, October 11). Focus on the funk: An interview with Cornel West [Web log post]. Retrieved from http://blogs.ssrc.org/tif/2011/10/06/focus-on-the-funk-an-interview-with-cornel-west/.
Nocella II, A. J. (2004). "Understanding the ALF: From critical analysis to critical pedagogy." In A. J. Nocella II & S. Best, eds., *Terrorists or freedom fighter? Reflections on the liberation of animals* (pp. 195–201). New York: Lantern Books.
Nocella II, A. J. (2007). "Unmasking the animal liberation front using critical pedagogy: Seeing the ALF for who they really are." *Journal for Critical Animal Studies* 5(1), 1–10.
Nocella II, A. J. (2011). "An overview of the history and theory of transformative justice." *Peace & Conflict Review* 6(1), 1–10.
Nocella II, A. J. (2012). "Challenging whiteness in the animal advocacy movement." *Journal for Critical Animal Studies* 10(1), 142–154.
Nocella II, A. J., Sorensen, J., Socha, K., & Matsuoka, A., eds. (2014). *Defining Critical Animal Studies: An Intersectional Social Justice Approach for Liberation.* New York: Peter Lang.
Nocella II, A. J., & Best, S. (2004). *Terrorists or freedom fighter? Reflections on the liberation of animals.* New York: Lantern Books.
Rosebraugh, C. (2004). *Burning rage of a dying planet: Speaking for the Earth Liberation Front.* New York: Lantern Books.

Suissa, J. (2010). *Anarchism and education: A philosophical perspective.* Oakland: PM Press.
Twine, R. (2012). "Revealing the 'animal-industrial complex': A concept & method for Critical Animal Studies?" *Journal for Critical Animal Studies* 10(1), 12–39.

Do Anarchists Dream of Emancipated Sheep?
Contemporary Anarchism, Animal Liberation and the Implications of New Philosophy

ARAGORN ELOFF

> *Everything fits together, from the bird whose brood is crushed to the humans whose nest is destroyed by war.*—Louise Michel

In this essay I explore the relations between contemporary anarchism and animal rights/liberation through the lens of Deleuze/Guattari-inflected complex systems theory. Specifically, I look at the liberalism and normative practices endemic to the mainstream animal rights movement, engaging with some of the more salient critiques that have emerged from Leftist and radical (anti-)political milieus and exploring the ways in which the theory and practice of anarchism—including its post- and nihilist strains—suggests an alternative, possibly more effective way of conceiving of animal liberation.

In mid-2010 a friend and I conducted an informal online survey of anarchists (Knoll S. and A. Eloff 2010). The survey took the form of an extended questionnaire containing around 60 questions. We were hoping that the results would provide us with a cursory sense of the composition and internal dynamics of the contemporary anarchist milieu. While the results of the survey, which was completed by around 2,500 people, were inevitably slanted due to its English language bias, mode of promotion and delivery (Anglophone anarchist internet channels) and structure (neither of us were experienced in this form of research), they are also highly suggestive; in many instances our key findings were strengthened by our subsequent meetings with anarchists from around the globe, including many from South America and various non-Anglophone European countries.

One of the most striking findings, although to some extent anticipated, was the number of vegans in the anarchist milieu. While general surveys of the U.S., UK and so on usually put the number of vegans at around 0.2–1.4 percent of the general population, over 11 percent of those taking our survey described their diet/lifestyle as vegan. While to some extent this can be explained as the result of subcultural practices—rites of inclusion and exclusion forming in and out groups—the correlations between veganism and various strains within anarchism, as well as the reasons given for practicing veganism, suggests something slightly more interesting.

Nineteen point six percent of self-identified anarcha-feminists, for instance, also identified as vegan, as did 19.4 percent of green anarchists. So-called 'anarcho'-capitalists on the other hand, were only vegan 1.8 percent of the time, a percentage roughly in line with the general population. Given the intersectional work done by feminists exploring the parallels between the oppression of other animals and the oppression of women under patriarchy, the first figure is unsurprising. The negative correlations between animal agriculture and ecological destruction, as well as the way in which the subjugation of other animals within industrial society is antithetical to the free, thriving, dis-alienated life sought by green anarchists, also suggests why veganism would feature as strongly as it does for this group. The gender distribution of vegans within the anarchist milieu paints a similar picture: 7 percent of male-identi-fied participants described themselves as vegan, compared to 16.7 percent of female-identified participants and 25.7 percent of those identified as genderqueer/other (the survey had a free form gender box that we awkwardly summarized with this tentative descriptor).

Finally, 76 percent of vegans surveyed saw a connection between their diet and anarchism, whereas only 24 percent of non-vegans did. Reasons given by vegans for their practice of a vegan diet/lifestyle included: "animal liberation," "total liberation," "respect for all beings," "no one is free while others are oppressed," "compassion establishing why we should care about equality in the first place," "veganism is an expression of anti-authoritarianism and personal empowerment through dietary choices; it directly divests from (and actively promotes an alternative to) a particularly barbarous and destructive sector of our society," "eating meat and other animal products is bad for the environment and represents another form of oppression," "extend the same ethics to non-human animals: no hierarchy, solidarity etc.," "speciesism is another oppressive institution that we should consider and address as anarchists" and "opposition to all forms of domination requires a willingness to refuse oppression animals."

Reasons given by non-vegans for their diet are equally illuminating: "I eat what I want," "anarchy is a life without structure or authority, therefore my diet follows neither of these," "I believe all things are equal and therefore anything goes," "I get sick if I don't eat animal protein, how can I smash the state if I'm too tired to get out of bed?," "anarchism is about people; we eat what we want to eat; dictating that is fascist," "a restrictive diet makes it very difficult to organize with community outside of the anarchist scene," "all forms of consumption are related to the oppression of workers," "meat eating is natural and right for humans—naturalism and anarchism go hand in hand" and, notably, "I see that my diet stands in contradiction to my anarchist beliefs, and while I'm not willing to stop eating meat, I do wish to find ways to raise animals in a far more humane way than is the norm now."

It seems reasonably clear that in both cases, anarchists applied the basic principles of the anarchist ethos—a critique of relations of hierarchy and domination and the pursuit of a life of free equals—to their diet/lifestyle, reaching vastly different conclusions in the process. It is also clear, however, that the case for veganism as a part of anarchist practice appears substantially more coherent and well-reasoned. While we will not debate the merits of each application of anarchism to diet here, it is worth considering the historical scope of the relation between anarchism and a critique of animal exploitation.

Early Anarchists and Radicals and Animal Liberation

In her memoirs, French anarchist and radical schoolteacher Louise Michel, famous for her role in the Paris Commune of 1871, wrote that she could trace her anarchist politics back to her early experiences of animal exploitation: "As far back as I can remember, the origin of my revolt against the powerful was my horror at the tortures inflicted on animals.... I used to wish animals could get revenge, that the dog could bite the man who was mercilessly beating him, that the horse bleeding under the whip could throw off the man tormenting him" (Michel 1981, p. 24).

From an early age, Michel rescued animals, even finding time during the height of the Commune to rescue a cat: "I was accused of allowing my concern for animals to outweigh the problems of humans at the Perronnnet barricade ... during the Commune, when I ran to help a cat in peril.... The unfortunate beast was crouched in a corner that was being scoured by shells, and it was crying out" (Michel 1981, p. 28).

She also appears to have been one of the very first people to recognize the link between animal exploitation and human subjugation and was opposed to vivisection, arguing that "this useless suffering perpetrated in the name of science must end" (Michel 1981, p. 29).

Renowned geographer and anarchist Élisée Reclus, a contemporary of Michel's, came out even more strongly against the oppression of other animals, presaging many contemporary views around the objectification of these others in arguing that

> the animals sacrificed to man's appetite have been systematically and methodically made hideous, shapeless, and debased in intelligence and moral worth.... The name even of the animal into which the boar has been transformed is used as the grossest of insults; the mass of flesh we see wallowing in noisome pools is so loathsome to look at that we agree to avoid all similarity of name between the beast and the dishes we make out of it [Reclus 1901].

Like Michel, Reclus also saw the connection between the subjugation of humans and that of other animals, asking whether there was indeed "so much difference between the dead body of a bullock and that of a man," and, in an early comparison of speciesism with racism, questioning the morality that imposed two laws for mankind, one that applied "to the yellow races and the other ... the privilege of the white," observing that "to assassinate or torture the first named is, it seems, henceforth permissible, while it is wrong to do so to the second," and seeing "our morality, as applied to animals, [as] equally elastic" (Reclus 1901).

Michel and Reclus were far from the only historical anarchists concerned with the subjugation of other animals; their views reflect a perennial strand of anti-speciesism weaving its way through the last 160-odd years of anarchist theory and practice. French anarchists in the 1920s, for example, ran a number of vegetarian restaurants and social centers and even in some cases argued against the inconsistencies of vegetarianism and for a more rigorous végétalienism (roughly equivalent to contemporary veganism). The anarchist G. Butaud, for instance, distinguished strongly between the two and opened a restaurant called the Foyer Végétalien in 1923.

Elsewhere, the notorious Bonnot Gang—a group of French illegalist anarchists that operated in France and Belgium in 1911–12—were also strict vegetarians and végétaliens, practising what was then termed *la vie naturelle* and arguing for the cognitive and physical benefits of a plant-based diet for revolutionaries (Parry 1987).

Vegetarianism was also a notable trend amongst Spanish anarcho-syndicalists (including those of the CNT-FAI) from the late 19th century onwards, especially among the poor peasants of the south. As Daniel Guérin argues in *Anarchism: From Theory to Practice* (Guérin 1970), vegetarian/végétalien living were sometimes viewed as an integral part of the prefigurative practices of those preparing for life in an anarchist society, even if this sometimes also drifted towards the proscriptive and moralistic (some anarchists also *a priori* eschewed all intoxicating substances and even, in some cases, sex before marriage). As late as 1936, the CNT devoted an entire discussion at its national congress to "vegetarians, nudists, naturists and 'opponents of industrial technology' within a libertarian communist [anarchist] society."

It would be fascinating, albeit beyond the scope of this piece, to trace the trajectory of these early moves towards radical veganism, animal liberation and anti-speciesism through the decades to the current time. In the interest of brevity, however, we will move straight ahead to the early 80s and the emergence of "veganarchism."

No Meat, No Milk, No Masters!

The sudden growth of veganism and animal liberation theory and practice within the anarchist milieu post–80s can probably be traced back to the influence of anarcho-punk and specifically the band Crass, who loudly endorsed anti-speciesism from the late 70s onwards and influenced an entire generation of European anarchists to mobilize against the exploitation of other animals not just through their lifestyle practices but also through the development of a direct action approach to animal liberation typified by the ALF, an organizational practice and philosophy created by anarchists.

These practices remained, for the most part and with some notable exceptions, under-theorized until the early '90s, at which time anarchists began to analyze them in more depth in order to provide a stronger philosophical foundation—in line with anarchism—for a vegan/animal liberation position that had by then veered towards a partly unconsidered subculturalism. These early analyses are perhaps best typified by Brian A. Dominick's *Animal Liberation and Social Revolution* (Dominick 1997), an essay wherein the term "veganarchism" appears to have been first coined. In this essay, which has been widely distributed throughout the milieu and is still found in zine form on the shelves of many infoshops around the world, Dominick explores the intersections between economic oppression, statism, sexism, homophobia, patriarchy, racism, speciesism and environmental destruction. He argues that these hierarchical and oppressive social relations and their myriad interconnections need to be engaged in a comprehensive way without arbitrarily reducing them to one or two solely relevant factors (e.g., the class reductionism of some Marxisms).

Anarchist and animal liberation philosopher Dr. Steve Best encapsulates this position well in his promotion of what he terms "total liberation":

> The global capitalist world system is inherently destructive to people, animals, and nature. It is unsustainable and the bills for three centuries of industrialization are now due. It cannot be humanized, civilized, or made green-friendly, but rather must be transcended through revolution at all levels—economic, political, legal, cultural, technological, moral, and conceptual [Best, 2010].

[Total liberation] takes the struggle for rights, equality, and nonviolence to the next level, beyond the artificial moral and legal boundaries of humanism, in order to challenge all prejudices and hierarchies, including speciesism [ibid.].

It should be noted in this regard that Dominick does, despite himself, perform something of a reduction in arguing via what could be seen as an appeal to the Marxist notions of subsumption and primitive communism. Dominick argues in this regard that the domestication of other animals has been responsible for, and continues to underpin, the "emergence of patriarchy, state power, slavery, hierarchy and domination of all kinds." This is to some extent echoed in *Beasts of Burden* (Antagonism 1999), another zine released at around the same time that applies a more detailed Marxist analysis.

While the case he makes for animal exploitation as the root form of domination is problematic—and to some extent arbitrary—his essay does provide a strong critique of depoliticized vegan consumerism and liberal single-issue animal rights. Dominick keenly interrogates the myopia of consumer activism and asks how vegans can justify the consumption of corporate products when the human labor embedded in them is so closely analogous to non-human suffering (an analogy that vegans themselves often draw, albeit in the other direction). In place of what he argues—using the vivid example of a coercive, government-supported "War on Meat"—are pointless and easily recuperated liberal reforms, Dominick proposes the practice of veganarchism as an explicitly politicized radical philosophy of animal liberation that retains just as much focus on the subjugation of human beings via capitalism, the state, white supremacy, patriarchy and so on as it does on our relations to other animals. In this regard, the essay supports direct action, endorsing affinity groups ranging from the anti-consumerist vegan propaganda of Food Not Bombs through to the midnight capers of the Animal Liberation and Earth Liberation Fronts.

Dominick's views are echoed in several other pieces produced around this time, and in many of the explicitly radical/anarchist periodicals, news websites, press offices, and so on that have since emerged (the online Talon Conspiracy archive of animal liberation publications is a phenomenal repository of these).

These radical perspectives are also deeply cynical about the identity politics of what they sometimes, perhaps unfairly, term the 'animal whites movement', seeing the endless vegan puritanism and one-upmanship of otherwise completely apolitical middle class consumers as little more than a particularly egregious instance of subjectivities wrought by capitalist social relations attempting to change their lot through what Foucault called the entrepreneurship of the self (Foucault 2008, 226). As insurrectionary anarchist Wolfi Landstreicher notes, "by accepting the idea (promoted heavily by progressive education and publicity) that the structures of oppression are essentially mindsets inside of ourselves, we become focused on our own presumed weakness, on how crippled we supposedly are. Our time is eaten up by attempts at self-healing that never come to an end, because we become so focused on ourselves and our inability to walk that we fail to notice the chain on our leg" (Landstreicher 2005).

The growth of veganarchism and total liberation perspectives within contemporary anarchist circles has also led to the unfolding of a lively debate about the relation between radical (anti-)politics and other animals. Notable essays like *Devastate to Liberate or Devastating Liberal* (Anonymous 2009), the insurrectionary anarchist critique *A Harvest of Dead Elephants* (Anonymous 2007) and disparaging commentary by everyone from far-leftist group Troploin (Troploin) to French post-structuralist and anarcho-syndicalist Daniel Colson (Colson 2001) and arch-anti-vegan and authoritarian Lierre Keith, author of the astonishingly poorly-argued *The Vegetarian Myth* (Keith 2009) have sought to disentangle animal liberation from human liberation struggles, arguing that radicals have fallen prey to sentimentalism, liberalism and distraction. For the most part, however, these critiques operate with a completely false sense of what animal liberation argues for, conflating it with liberal animal rights, philosophical idealism, proscriptive morality and various other positions anarchists rightly find untenable. The level of intellectual dishonesty and the manipulative argumentation of some of these pieces is telling, and echoes the typical defensive postures of meat-eaters within mainstream society. Even here, however, the critique of consumer activism and reform remains unequivocal.

While a full constructive engagement with these critiques will have to wait for a future essay, it is worth considering how strikingly at odds their assumptions are not only with radical animal liberation discourses and practices (including that of the Institute for Critical Animal Studies) but even with most of the contemporary theoretical engagements of the relatively apolitical, liberal animal rights thinkers they disparage.

From Animal Rights to the Abstract Machine of Hierarchy and Domination

It is true that, for the most part, the traditional scope of what we can term 'liberal animal rights' has been single issue focused and operates within the ambit of normative moral discourse. Philosophers like Singer, Francione, Regan and so on tend to argue, however powerful their descriptive registers, from the analytic paradigm of abstract moral cases, endorsing, whether explicitly or not, a set of universally binding proscriptions that rely on a series of un-interrogated assumptions around subjectivity, agency, rationality and the status of moral claims. To unpack this a little, liberal animal rightists assume that there is a general discursive moral framework within which we can argue for the rights of other animals; that through this framework we can make successful moral appeals on behalf of other animals based on observations of familiarity or overlap in traits or capacities with what we understand as morally salient human characteristics; that we can enshrine the rights we win for other animals within a state legal apparatus and that these rights will, by virtue of this apparatus, be successfully defended.

At the same time, liberal animal rights does, it must be noted, invoke other oppressive social relations in order to draw analogies, but it tends to do so in a much more limited manner than advocates of total liberation do. For instance, while liberal animal rightists are quick to argue by analogy that contemporary animal exploitation is equivalent to the Holocaust, or that the institutions of animal exploitation are all too similar to those of slavery and patriarchy, this is seen as merely a means to an end: a strong analogy invokes sufficient moral sentiment to bolster a position that doesn't so much seek to widen the moral circle as to shift it.

This is perhaps also due to what Manuel DeLanda, a contemporary complex systems theorist who in his *Assemblage Theory and Social Complexity* (DeLanda 2006) applies the philosophical concepts of Gilles Deleuze to social organization, sees as the micro-reductionism of liberal political philosophy, wherein the sole socially relevant force is the interaction of rational individual agents. DeLanda contrasts this with the macro-reductionism of vulgar (if slightly caricatured) base-superstructure Marxism, which reduces the explanation of social dynamics to a kind of social constructionism where exploitative economic arrangements wholly structure society and define the trajectories of the individuals embedded within it. In other words, because liberal animal rights so often operates with that same set of assumptions evident in everything from Cartesianism and Enlightenment humanism through to neoliberalism, it lacks the capacity to fully comprehend the partly systemic and highly imbricated nature of various oppressive social relations.

Deleuze and co-author Félix Guattari, along with Foucault, provide a much more useful set of tools with which to explore the contemporary socio-political terrain, something that has been increasingly picked up on by animal rights/liberation theorists working within Critical Animal Studies and (post-) continental schools of thought. Deleuze and Guattari propose that in place of fully bounded discrete entities interacting in linear fashion on a single ontological level in order to produce all the complex dynamisms of contemporary society, we would do better to regard the world as comprised of vast networks of interconnected components, each of which can span several domains (material, linguistic, social, abstract and so on). They refer to these as *assemblages* or *arrangements* (from the French *agencement*, and similar to what Foucault refers to as a *dispositif*, i.e., an arrangement of the visible and the sayable) and see them as allowing for complex flows and processes of feedback and adaptation between different scales or levels of organizational complexity.

> On a first, horizontal, axis, an assemblage comprises two segments, one of content, the other of expression. On the one hand it is a machinic assemblage of bodies, of actions and passions, an intermingling of bodies reacting to one another; on the other hand it is a collective assemblage of enunciation, of acts and statements, of incorporeal transformations attributed to bodies. Then on a vertical axis, the assemblage has both territorial sides, or reterritorialized sides, which stabilize it, and cutting edges of deterritorialization, which carry it away [Deleuze and Guattari 1987, pp. 97–8].

DeLanda's neo–Deleuzoguattarian assemblage theory allows us, therefore, to interrogate social (and other) phenomena in a way that doesn't lead to arbitrary reductionisms in either direction. It is worth noting that a fair amount of work in intersectionality and queer theories operates with a similar, often also Deleuze-inspired, understanding of the social terrain as complex series of intersecting, heterogeneous components.

Deleuze and Guattari, however, don't simply argue that we should conceive of the world in terms of arrangements; following Deleuze's tripartite ontology of virtual, intensive and actual they also see these arrangements as the actualizations of intensive dynamisms driven by virtual multiplicities, something DeLanda and fellow Deleuzian John Protevi see as near-identical with the phase spaces littered with singularities (bifurcation points) and surrounding basins of attraction that are discussed in complexity theory (DeLanda 2005, Protevi 2013, Bonta and Protevi 2004). In short, Deleuze proposes that the actual world of fully described final forms that comprises our everyday reality is the result of underlying dynamisms that operate within a self-differentiating field of potential he terms the virtual and which contains all the *real possibilities* that are actualized (without exhausting these possibilities) in any actual concrete assemblage. For Deleuze, all there is production; this production, which Deleuze also describes as the solving of virtual problems (DeLanda gives the useful example of the minimization of surface tension as a virtual problem solved in different ways by soap bubbles and salt crystals), takes place through the self-*differentiation* of an *undifferentiated* field of singularities that, via intensive dynamisms, *differenciates* into actual/extensive forms that, crucially for Deleuze, do not resemble the multiplicities that give rise to them.

> [T]he nature of the virtual is such that, for it, to be actualized is to be differenciated. Each differenciation is a local integration or a local solution […]. An organism is nothing if not the solution to a problem, as are each of its differenciated organs, such as the eye which solves a light "problem" [Deleuze 2013, p. 211].

The virtual, also termed *the plane of consistency*, and the intensive, thus allow us a way to think about the structures and processes underlying concrete assemblages via a description of their patterns and thresholds of behavior. There is a lot more subtlety and sophistication to what Deleuze calls his *method of dramatization* (Deleuze 2004, pp. 94–116), something DeLanda unpacks brilliantly in *Intensive Science and Virtual Philosophy* (DeLanda 2005), but for the present purposes what is most important for us to understand is the modal status of the virtual and the multiplicities that comprise it. Deleuze does not argue that the virtual is merely the possible; in fact he explicitly contrasts it with this, arguing that it is real without being actual. Nor is he proposing a neo–Platonic world of ideal forms; Deleuze is an immanentist opposed to the transcendent, perennial categories of Platonism and a fair amount of his early work is dedicated to precisely this. The composition of the virtual is as contingent as that of the actual and there is no world of eternal forms that remains transcendent to the actual.

Although Deleuze's terminology morphs in various ways through his oeuvre, he also uses the terms *abstract machine* and *virtual Idea* in ways largely commensurate with the concept of *multiplicity* (in his later work with Guattari (Deleuze and Guattari 1984, 1987), which arguably completely naturalizes his philosophy, Deleuze refers almost solely to abstract machines) to describe a virtual distribution of tendencies and capacities (unformed matters and non-formal functions) as an interwoven collection of singular and ordinary points that underlies and defines each assemblage. Inspired by what has been termed Guattari's *diagrammatic thought*, Deleuze and Guattari propose a way of modeling the functioning of abstract machines not via rigorous blueprints (what they call "tracings") but rather by way of *diagrams* of relations between "pure functions" (i.e., without any content) and unformed but capability-bearing (i.e., intensive) "pure matter"—or as Deleuze puts it in his book on Foucault, intersecting lines of force relations—that describe multiple potential actual instantiations. Referring to Foucault's work on disciplinary societies, for example, they suggest that the idea of the Panopticon refers precisely to a diagram of this sort:

> The panopticon must not be understood as a dream building, it is the diagram of a mechanism of power reduced to its ideal form as a pure architectural and optical system: it is in fact a figure of political technology ... detached from any specific use [Deleuze 1988, p. 205].

In other words, as opposed to the Panopticon being any specific real-world disciplinary practice it instead provides the abstract set of relations—the capacities to affect and be affected—that underlie discipline as a type of social relation.

Why, however, is this excursis into Deleuze and Guattari of relevance to us here? Just as they propose a diagram of discipline, could we not argue that there is, similarly, an abstract machine of hierarchy and domination that is actualized in various heterogeneous and overlapping domains and which does not necessarily resemble any of these actualizations? For instance, for all their specificities of instantiation, could we not understand sexism, racism, class exploitation (via capital and the State) and speciesism as they exist in the real world as complex assemblages that are in part concrete actualizations of the same abstract machine—that reproduce the same diagram of force relations without exhausting the divergent potential actualizations it describes?

If our speculation here holds, then, to return to our earlier discussion of liberalism, the problem with liberal animal rights is not so much that it doesn't recognize relations of hierarchy and domination as they exist in the world but that it remains mired in the actual, failing to recognize the underlying abstract machine and thus the resonance between heterogeneous cases of exploitative social relations, each of which also in part serves as a reification of the diagram. As Protevi and Bonta argue, if we are to understand the functioning of the everyday world around us then we need to remind ourselves that "actual, stratified, systems hide the intensive nature of the morphogenetic processes that gave rise to them—and therefore, a fortiori, the virtual multiplicities structuring those processes—beneath extensive properties and definite qualities. It is as if the actual were the congealing of the intensive and the burying of the virtual" (Bonta and Protevi 2004, p. 49).

Anarchists, on the other hand, are perhaps the exemplary "diagrammatic thinkers," this being evident in the types of cases they make for the abolition of the state form in general as opposed to specific states for example, or exploitative economic relations in general as opposed to merely one or two problematic instantiations of the market. Following a process Deleuze terms variously *counter-effectuation* and *vice-diction*, anarchist critiques and practices often seek to map the flows and processes underlying actual arrangements of knowledge, power, material and so on back to the virtual multiplicities/abstract machines that produce these (and are, importantly, in turn produced by them via a process of *counter-actualization*—a rearrangement of the singularities and basins of attraction defining a virtual multiplicity), which perhaps also explains the anarchist focus on prefigurative practice as a type of warding off of a diagram of hierarchy and domination as well as the anarchist endorsement not of a proscriptive morality but a general ethos that proposes and seeks to construct (in the spirit of what Deleuze and Guattari refer to as a *minor science* that seeks to establish "the Idea/multiplicity of something—'constructing a concept'—by moving from extensity through intensity to virtuality" (Protevi 2007) an alternate diagram of equal-liberty (Newman 2011).

So how might we apply all this to our relations to other animals? Before we look at some tentative answers, it is worth briefly exploring some other alternatives to liberal animal rights that have emerged in recent years.

Aporias and Subtle Normativities

A significant portion of those working in Critical Animal Studies today appear to have heeded Rosi Braidotti's warning that anthropomorphizing animals by seeking to afford them equal rights results in a "becoming-human" of animals that reproduces all the ills of normativity that led to, and continue to lead to, hierarchies and dominations of all kinds. As Braidotti observes, if we wish to become other than we are then we should constantly remind ourselves that "no qualitative becoming can be generated by or at the centre, or in a dominant position. Man is a dead static core of indexed negativity. To introduce animal and earth others into this category is not exactly doing them a favour" (Braidotti 2006, p. 103).

In lieu of rights and normativity, much contemporary work focuses instead on notions of *zoe* or bare life (Agamben 1998), or on a Butlerian sense of shared precarity (Butler 2006), or a Derridean aporetic engagement with our shared animality. As Matthew Calarco (2012) puts it in a recent interview, "continental philosophy ... would have our thinking about animals begin from a site of aporia, of confusion and tumult, about who humans are and who animals are. This starting point asks us to construct alternative concepts and alternative ways of thinking that no longer trust uncritically the categories and distinctions that have structured the dominant culture's ways of thinking and living up to this point."

Calarco also argues that "viewing humans and animals as indistinct entails seeing all of us as caught up in a shared space of ontological and ethical experimentation," echoing Deleuze and Guattari's valorization of minor science. Such sentiments notwithstanding, for much of this work the focus is on a neo–Levinasian infinite demand of the necessarily othered (transcendent) Other to the (transcendental) self; the register is one of ontological vulnerability, trauma, infinite justice, impossible horizons and melancholia that many anarchists, especially those from Nietzsche-inflected post-left style traditions, would argue separates us from our capacity to act by rendering us *a priori* beholden to a set of abstractions that function as a form of alienation and operate in the reverse direction to the affirmation and experimentation concomitant with the "life without measure" (Landstreicher 2005) that is called for both by anarchists and by Deleuze and Guattari.

Additionally, there is still a subtle normativity at work in the ethics of precarity, aporia, etc., in that it remains predicated upon a dialectics of absolute responsibility. This is far from what I have previously termed, following Braidotti, a Deleuzian "aesthetics of imbrication in movement, a reciprocal feedback loop of affect and expression, exchange and becoming" (Eloff 2013), something that, in my view, sits far more comfortably with anarchism.

The World Is Not Just Made of Words

There is another problem endemic to much contemporary thought and action around the dismantling of oppressive relations: we have yet to fully disentangle ourselves from the discursive reductionism of the linguistic turn. Indeed, a fair amount of work in Critical Animal Studies remains trapped in an endless hermeneutics of discourses and ideologies. While an interrogation of the role of dominant significations in constructing social reality is certainly a necessary component of any liberatory practice, it is by no means sufficient. As many of those aligned with the recent shift in philosophy towards neo-materialisms, object-oriented ontologies and speculative realisms (several of whom, interestingly, have recognized the need to deal explicitly with animal liberation, veganism and so on) have argued, we are enmeshed not just in fields of words but also within what Levi Bryant calls *thermopolitics* (Bryant 2014) and what Maurizio Lazzarato, following Guattari, terms *machinic enslavement* (Guattari 2010). These thinkers argue that part of the reason struggles for freedom and equality fail is that they remain solely discursive, seeking to deconstruct the false ideologies that keep us from recognizing our subjugation without recognizing that in many cases we might be intimately aware of this subjugation but materially constrained by the way in which the social terrain has been constructed by contemporary relations of production, distribution and so on.

As Lazzarato (2014, p. 12) argues, in capitalism subjectivity is produced both by apparatuses of social subjection and by machinic enslavement. While the former assigns us "an identity, a sex, a body, a profession, a nationality, and so on," manufacturing individuated subjects and their behavior in "response to the needs of the social division of labor," machinic enslavement simultaneously de-individuates us into component parts of technical and social machines:

> Now, capitalism reveals a twofold cynicism: the "humanist" cynicism of assigning us individuality and pre-established roles (worker, consumer, unemployed, man/woman, artist, etc.) in which individuals are necessarily alienated; and the "dehumanizing" cynicism of including us in an assemblage that no longer distinguishes between human and non-human, subject and object, or words and things [ibid].

If we are to become more effective then, as anarchists or as animal liberationists, we need to engage not just with the words that intersect with the world in myriad complex ways, but with the world itself in its full materiality; with both words and things, as Foucault once said. We also need to eradicate the residual moral normativities that prevent a full unfolding of the type of immanent, situational ethics that best reflects both anarchy and the implications of recent materialist philosophy.

Anarchist/Nihilist Ethics...

> When we use the term "ethical" we're never referring to a set of precepts capable of formulation, of rules to observe, of codes to establish.... No formal ethics is possible. There is only the interplay of forms-of-life among themselves, and the protocols of experimentation that guide them locally.
> —Tiqqun [2012, p. 144].

In *Its core is the negation* (De Acosta 2014), a response to Duane Rousselle's *After Post-anarchism* (Rousselle 2012), Alejandro De Acosta contrasts morality and ethics, arguing that the former, an example of the type of normativity many of us are rightly critical of, functions as a form of social control. More importantly, he also argues that any ethical universalism that emphasizes homogeneous ways of life in the name of a shared good is similarly problematic in its reification of this good—a rejection of transcendent morality that is reintroduced immanently. De Acosta also echoes Rousselle's skepticism of ethical pluralism as retaining a type of universalism:

> The relativist, when put to the test, must defend a universal dimension *for relativism itself* or else risk relativism's own subsumption under the universalist framework. If, for example, I state that each individual builds his own ethical framework then I must account for the fact that each individual is united with others in his relative autonomy to construct an independent ethical framework. At the normative level, for example, if I claim that each individual ought to be capable of realizing his own ethical maxim then I must as a natural consequence also maintain that each individual ought to be protected against the imposition of another ethical maxim; this latter claim can only be accomplished with recourse to the universal dimension. When taken to its conclusion, then, relativism is always a cunning form of universalism [Rousselle 2013].

In other words, the type of meta-ethical relativism invoked in discussions of multiculturalism and cosmopolitanism is a subtle and insidious form of meta-ethical universalism. As anarchists, this will not suffice and so Rousselle and De Acosta advocate instead a form of ethical nihilism, what Rousselle articulates as a "belief that ethical truths, if they can be said to exist at all, derive from the paradoxical non-place within the heart of any place"

(Rousselle 2012, p. 43). This aligns well with anarchism in that "nihilists seek to discredit and/or interrupt all universalist and relativist responses to the question of place ... nihilists are critics of all that currently exists and they raise this critique against all such one-sided foundations and systems."

This is also strikingly similar to the nomadic ethics proposed by Deleuze and Guattari, which I have explored at length elsewhere (Eloff 2010, 2013). In brief, for Deleuze nomadic ethics requires epistemological humility; it is anti-essentialist and non-normative, situated and contingent and emerges from situations themselves instead of being imposed upon them. It is an immanent ethics of experimentation that appeals to nothing outside of itself, a bio-centered, non-anthropocentric egalitarianism that recognizes our enfolding of and enfoldment within the world around us and a care for the self that is immediately a care for the not-self, for the infinitely complex web of relations within, and which are, our shared habitats. It is a practice of becoming together in constant differenciation, in affirmation of a deeper principle of difference, of differentiation, with an enhanced sense of situated accountability that "enlarges the sense of collectively bound subjectivity to non-human agents, from our genetic neighbours the animals, to the earth as a biosphere as a whole" (Braidotti 2006, p. 136).

This ethics, whether anarchist, nihilist or nomadic in flavor, is, its fluid transversality, automatically inclusive of our ethical relations to others of whatever type or species without having to posit a discrete category of animality. Nor do we necessarily need to invoke a separate domain of animal liberation: nomadic ethics is inherently liberatory, both in principle and in practice. It is already (anti-)politics.

... And an Imbricated Monadological Practice of Collective Liberation

There is so much more to discuss, but we must draw to a close. How do we move forward? What are the implications of all this for our everyday practices as anarchists and/or animal liberationists?

In a sense, what Deleuze and Guattari propose, through their ontology and their ethics, is what they poetically describe as the coming of a new people for a new Earth: the unfolding or becoming of a new set of relations between all of us, mineral, plant, animal and otherwise, that, as Deleuze says, allows us to become worthy of what happens to us. In sum, a new vision of nature, or life, or being more generally, a non-totalizable concatenation, in the words of Timothy Morton, of new arrangements and a counter-actualization of new diagrams. And, in the process, a renewed, non-reductive and immanent collection of analyses, tactics and strategies—including a rigorous practice of vice-diction and what Protevi terms, awkwardly but beautifully, a geo-hydro-solar-bio-techno-politics (Protevi 2013) – that will allow us to dismantle and replace the hierarchy and domination, the oppression and subjugation, both of ourselves and each other, that still sadly typifies the contemporary world and that operates in myriad heterogeneous and irreducible actualizations of the same virtual diagrams. There is no easy, final answer here, just a renewed questioning and inexhaustible process of experimentation with no appeal to anything beyond itself; no transcendent, proscriptive morality, no relativism that conceals a subtle universalism, no perennial good, no ground.

As the nomadic, anarchist subjects who will people this new Earth, we will remain neither self-identical nor homogeneous to ourselves; instead, we will be in constant becoming in relation both to the irreducibly multiple nature of our composition and the myriad ways in which we overlap with, are imbricated with, relate to and compose, arrangements on multiple scales, multiple ecologies. We are *metastable* and can remain faithful both to ourselves and to the construction of an emancipatory movement that can defeat all forms of oppression precisely through our becoming other, together, through what Landstreicher calls a *projectual* life underpinned by what Colson terms an anarchist neo-monadology. As Colson argues, this process of experimentation involves a recognition, inspired by anarchism, of the "capacity of beings to rely on themselves," and of "the singularity of the relationship each has to the world," with each being seen as "unique and irreplaceable ... the bearer of all of the others" (Colson 1996).

There is no map to this new Earth save for the one we are always, and always provisionally, drawing together, whatever our phylum, class or order. In drawing, let us hope we remember, as Alain Beaulieu says, that domination is indeed the lowest degree of affectability (Beaulieu 2011, p. 69–88).

REFERENCES

Agamben, G. (1998), *Homo Sacer: Sovereign Power and Bare Life*. Stanford: Stanford University Press.
Anonymous (2007). "The Harvest of Dead Elephants: The False Opposition of Animal Liberation." *A Murder of Crows #2* (USA).
Anonymous (2009). *Animal Liberation: Devastate to Liberate, or Devastatingly Liberal?* London: Pelagian.
Antagonism (1999). *Beasts of Burden*. London: Antagonism Press.
Beaulieu, A. (2011). "The Status of Animality in Deleuze's Thought." *Journal for Critical Animal Studies* XI, 1/2.
Best, S. (2010). *Total Liberation: Revolution for the 21st Century*. Proceedings of the 2nd International Meeting for Environmental Ethics in Athens, 2010. Retrieved from http://drstevebest.wordpress.com/2010/12/31/total-liberation-revolution-for-the-21st-century-4/.
Bonta M. and J. Protevi (2004). *Deleuze and Geophilosophy: A Critical Introduction and Guide*. Edinburgh: Edinburgh University Press.

Braidotti, R. (2006). *Transpositions*. Cambridge: MA: Polity.
Butler J. (2006). *Precarious Life: The Powers of Mourning and Violence*. London: Verso.
Bryant, L. (2014), *Energy, work and thermopolitics* (retrieved from http://larvalsubjects.wordpress.com/2014/01/17/energy-work-and-thermopolitics/)
Calarco, M. (2012). "We Are Made of Meat: An Interview with Matthew Calarco." Retrieved from http://human-nonhuman.blogspot.com/2012/06/we-are-made-of-meat-interview-with.html.
Colson, D. (1996). "Anarchist Subjectivities and Modern Subjectivity." Retrieved from http://theanarchistlibrary.org/library/daniel-colson-anarchist-subjectivities-and-modern-subjectivity.
Colson, D. (2001). *Petit Lexique Philosophique De L'Anarchisme De Proudhon a Deleuze*. Le Livre de Poche.
De Acosta, A. (2014). *The Impossible, Patience*. Berkeley: Ardent Press.
DeLanda, M. (2005). *Intensive Science and Virtual Philosophy*. London: Bloomsbury Academic.
DeLanda, M. (2006). *A New Philosophy of Society: Assemblage Theory and Social Complexity*. London: Bloomsbury Academic.
Deleuze, G. (1994/2013). *Difference and Repetition*. Trans. Paul Patton. New York: Columbia University Press.
Deleuze, G. (1988). *Foucault*. Minneapolis: University of Minnesota Press.
Deleuze, G. (2004). *The Method of Dramatization in Desert Islands and Other Texts: 1953-1974*. Los Angeles: Semiotext(e).
Deleuze, G. and F. Guattari (1984). *Anti-Oedipus*. Trans. R. Hurley. London: Continuum International.
Deleuze, G. and F. Guattari (1987). *A Thousand Plateaus: Capitalism and Schizophrenia*. Trans. Brian Massumi. Minneapolis: University of Minnesota Press.
Dominick, B. (1997). *Animal Liberation and Social Revolution: A vegan perspective on anarchism or an anarchist perspective on veganism*. Chicago: Firestarter Press.
Eloff, A. (2010). *Rethinking the Politics of Animal Liberation*. bolo'bolo publications.
Eloff, A. (2013). *Rites of the Nomads*. bolo'bolo publications.
Foucault, M. (2008). *The Birth of Biopolitics*. Trans. G. Burchell. Basingstoke: PalgraveMacmillan.
Guattari, F. (2010). *The Machinic Unconscious: Essays in Schizoanalysis*. Los Angeles: Semiotext(e) / Foreign Agents.
Guérin, D. (1970). *Anarchism from theory to practice*. New York: New York University Press.
Keith, L. (2009). *The Vegetarian Myth: Food, Justice, and Sustainability*. Oakland: PM Press.
Knoll, S., and A. Eloff. (2010). "The 2010 Anarchist Survey." Retrieved from http://www.anarchismdocumentary.net/survey.
Landstreicher, W. (2005). *Against the Logic of Submission*. Portland: Baby Elephant Editions.
Lazzarato, M. (2014). *Signs and Machines: Capitalism and the Production of Subjectivity*. Los Angeles: Semiotext(e) / Foreign Agents.
Michel, L. (1981). *The Red Virgin: Memoirs of Louise Michel*. Tuscaloosa: University of Alabama Press.
Newman, S. (2011). *The Politics of Postanarchism*. Edinburgh: Edinburgh University Press.
Parry, R. (1987). *The Bonnot Gang*. London: Rebel Press.
Protevi, J. (2007). "Water" *Rhizomes: Cultural Studies in Emerging Knowledge* 15.

Protevi, J. (2013). *Life, War, Earth: Deleuze and the Sciences.* Minneapolis: University of Minnesota Press.
Reclus, E. (1901). "On Vegetarianism" *Humane Review.* January.
Rousselle, D. (2012). *After Post-anarchism.* Berkeley: Repartee.
Rousselle, D. (2013). *Anarchism as Institution.* Retrieved from http://dingpolitik.wordpress.com/2013/08/06/anarchism-as-institution/.
Tiqqun. (2012). *Theory of Bloom.* LBC Books.
Troploin. (n.d.). "Letter on Animal Liberation." Retrieved from http://troploin0.free.fr/biblio/animal/.

Following in the Footsteps of Élisée Reclus
Disturbing Places of Inter-Species Violence That Are Hidden in Plain Sight

Richard J. White

> We hope to live one day in a city in which we no longer risk seeing butcher shops full of carcasses next to silk and jewelry stores.... We want to be surrounded by an environment that pleases the eye and is an expression of beauty.
> —Élisée Reclus [1901, p. 161].

> ...the only way in which widespread animal liberation, or anything approaching it, can be achieved, is by changing the behaviour of ordinary people toward animals.
> —Ronnie Lee, [2014 p. xiv].

Walking from my home to the local railway station takes no more than fifteen minutes. If someone were to observe this relatively short journey, I would probably be seen as one of several people going about their daily morning commute. Should the observer wish to contextualize this scene further, by reference to the broader urban surroundings for example, they may note that for the majority of this time I walk past a range of shops and businesses (fifty-three on the right hand side of the street, forty-seven on the left, if they were paying great attention). These shops sell a modest range of goods and services that can be found across most small towns in England. If their initial observations ended there: "*Richard's route from home to the station is predictably straightforward passes some shops on the way to the station ... nothing out of the ordinary or remarkable or unusual to note,"* they would be in good company (based on my prediction that most observers in this scenario would not depart significantly from this conclusion). Certainly, assuming that I (a sentient animal) had not been attacked *en route* in some way there would be no reference to any act of violence against a sentient animal. And yet there are *extreme* levels of violence and misery that concern more-than-human sentient beings that are entangled within the urban fabric of this public place. Paradoxically, the very fact that this violence is *so* pervasive and commonplace that it becomes, to all intents and purposes, *hidden in plain sight* within the urban environment. This idiom was popularized in "The Purloined Letter" by Edgar Allen Poe (1902). Here Poe hypothesized that things that are deliberately hidden in plain sight are all the more evasive because they

> escape observation by dint of being excessively obvious; and here the physical oversight is precisely analogous with the moral inapprehension by which the intellect suffers to pass unnoticed those considerations which are too obtrusively and too palpably self-evident [p. 36].

Perhaps, were I to push my observer to move beyond an anthropocentric scripting of this encounter with place, and ask that they critically focus instead on the excessively obvious presence (or indeed absence) of more than human animals, then I would hope (and fear) that their urban narrative would generate observations altogether more dark and *disturbing*.

Acknowledging the centrality and contested nature(s) of place has a great deal to offer any praxis that advocates ethical and social justice. There are many important reasons for this, but perhaps the most significant comes with the recognition, as White and Cudworth (2014, p. 205) argue, that the "real geographies of violence, suffering, trauma, and abuse [are] thoroughly embedded in space and place: [physical] violence is neither disembodied nor abstract; it occurs ... *somewhere to someone*." A more conscious and critical awareness of the possibilities that different approaches readings of, and relationships to place provide, is particularly important for activists working to advance an intersectional politics of Total Liberation (Best, 2014, Colling et al, 2014). As the American social activist, feminist and author bell hooks (1984) observed:

> [a]s a radical standpoint, perspective, position, "the politics of location" necessarily calls those of us who would participate in the formation of counter-hegemonic cultural practice to identify the spaces where we begin the process of re-vision [hooks 1984, p. 153].

Many animal right activists make reference to place, but do so in a way that limits place to that of a setting or generic stage designed to give background context to (more extreme) acts of animal abuse. To take one example, think of the popular saying "If slaughterhouses had glass walls, everyone would be a vegetarian (or vegan)." This argument makes reference to a *spatial* invisibility, highlighting hidden places wherein extreme violence and suffering takes place (see Eisnitz, 2006). Slaughterhouses, at least in contemporary urban western society, are deliberately placed *out of the sight*. As Adams (1990) argues: "Geographically, slaughterhouses are cloistered. We do not see or hear what transpires there" (p. 49). These places of slaughter are private and forbidden. Slaughterhouse workers notwithstanding (themselves often representing a group of human animals who are brutalized and exploited, see Grezo [2012]) the general public would rarely be permitted to enter. Indeed the active exclusion of people is aggressively enforced, in the shape of explicit warning signs, electric fences, barbed wire adorning high walls, patrolled by security guards and/or surveyed by CCTV cameras. Any unauthorized person or group who does manage to gain entry does so at great personal risk. The owner(s) of the slaughter house would no doubt appeal to laws against trespassing, and property damage (breaking fences/windows/ doors/locks). In this way the animal liberators find themselves labeled as criminals or, increasingly, denounced as terrorists (see Potter 2014a,b). The increasing pervasiveness of such harshly punitive domestic laws is testament to the immense threat that acts of transgression pose the profiteers of animal abuse. Revealing the deliberately hidden realities created and contained within these places of violence—is never a small or inconsequential act, but one which carries radical and revolutionary possibilities.

In so many important ways the call for Total Liberation embodies an explicitly spatial praxis: the desire to live without *places* of violence. This brings sharply therefore the question: "to what extent does the success of animal liberation—as part of a total politics of liberation –concern an ability to successfully confront, transgress and liberate these violent places?" With this question in mind, the principal aim of the chapter is to encourage the reader to focus their attention not towards those places where violence is deliberately hidden violence, but to think more critically about the disturbing acts and consequences of violence against sentient beings that are all around us: embedded and normalized within *familiar* urban environments. In doing so it is also important to make connections between these "everyday" and "exceptional" places of violence: neither are fundamentally discrete or different. Rather they are co-dependent and co-constitutive, coming together in both time and space in many complex and sometimes unpredictable ways.

The focus on "disturbing" in this essay is two-fold. Places can be *disturbing* (or contain disturbing things) in the sense that they may provoke anxiety, worry or distress. But they also have the capacity to be *disturbed*. Places are highly open to being dis-ordered, over-turned, distressed, given that they are "socially constructed, the product of a host of human [and more than human] practices" (Ward 2007, p. 269). With reference to the first, the intention of the chapter is to show how acts of violence against more than human animals are captured—that is, rendered commonplace, routine, easy going, unremarkable and ultimately invisible—in the everyday urban environment, and to consider the implications that this heightened consciousness brings with it. This discussion takes place within a contextual framework which explicitly draws on critical (animal) geographies, and anarchist geography in particular. It is my belief that an expanded anarchist geographical praxis that embraces more than human animals when speaking of ethics and social justice, and foregrounds questions of space and place when challenging power, domination and oppression has the potential to inform a deeper awareness of, and understanding toward, intersectional strategies of resistance and liberation. To illustrate this, I focus on *On Vegetarianism* (1901) written by the French anarchist geographer Élisée Reclus (1830 –1905) (for other discussions of the importance of this work see also Colling et al., 2014; White and Cudworth 2014). Taking inspiration from this short pamphlet, this chapter seeks to follow in his footsteps, by re-visiting the commute to work highlighted in the introduction, but this time re-worked from personal observations which are sensitive to the inter-species violence that this place contains.

Addressing the question of how violence in place can be disturbed forms the final third of this chapter. Here, there is a strong recognition of the (aspirational) need for anarchist means and ends to be consistent, which demands that forms of violence, coercion and *arche* are rejected (see Springer 2014). A critique focused on everyday, familiar, and highly transferable acts of urban activism designed to draw attention to urban spaces of violence will be made. This, I hope, will reinforce the open and inclusive nature of the possibilities that can be achieved through individual and small groups taking direct action. This politics of hope cannot be underestimated: we must be recognize that nothing is inevitable, and that we are not condemned to walk amidst such violent places evermore. On the contrary we all have the capacity and capability to find new ways to effectively interrogate, transgress and transform these (our) everyday sites of violence and despair, into places of non-violence and hope.

Regarding structure, first the essay explores the contested geographical definitions of space and place. Second, a more explicit discussion focuses on an emerging critical animal geography, and then anarchism and anarchist geography. This actively acknowledges the presence/ absence of more-than-human violence that are contained and captured (in live and dead bodies) in the places I walk through. Fourth, a brief discussion of forms of street-based activism that aim to unsettle and disturb these speciesist violence will be made.

Space, Place and More-Than-Human Animals

The question "what is *place*?" escapes definitive answers. Typically, geographers have identified place with reference to space (and vice versa) in which the two concepts operate on a relative spectrum of difference. Consider this definition by Gieryn (2000) as illustrative of this approach:

> Space is what place becomes when the unique gathering of things, meanings, and values are sucked out. Put positively, place is space filled up by people, practices, objects, and representations [p. 465].

This immediately suggests that, far from being passive, fixed, or predictable our (human) relationship to place is something altogether more dynamic, fluid, open, active, engaged, and unfolding. This transformation of space to places (of meaning and resonance) operates on both physical and mental registers, insofar as places are also "interpreted, narrated, perceived, felt, understood and imagined" (p. 464). If we extend Gieryn's anthropocentric reading of place to acknowledge the presence and agency of "more than human animals," how might this contribute to the way in which place is constructed? In so many ways, the consequences are both ethically disturbing and troubling. For in opening up the interrogation of place through connection with the lived experiences of more than human animals, it insists that we recognize contemporary places as bearing witness (in shape and form) to a speciesist culture, wherein lies the dominant "belief that nonhuman animals exist to serve the needs of the human species, that animals are in various senses inferior to human beings, and therefore that one can favor human over nonhuman interests according to species status alone" (Best 2008, p. 190). In a great number of (explicit and implicit) ways our urban environments embodies this ugly speciesism. This reinforces, rather than challenges, the animal condition, which, for the majority of more than human animals, speaks of their "actual life situation with its routine repertoire of violence, deprivation, desperations, agony, apathy, suffering, and death" (Pedersen and Stănescu 2012, p. ix).

The distinction between the "ordinary" and "exceptional" acts of violence involving humans and other animals is an important distinction. Violence against non-human animals in a speciesist society is rarefied and attributed to the latter: we can readily emphasize with the victim of an exceptional act of violence, while being unaffected by the daily products of extreme violence that confront us in the everyday. Paradoxically it may be that the very intimate familiarity of a known place (which we are never encouraged to challenge) desensitizes an individual to suffering and violence. In some cases, perversely, the more extreme the violence exacted on more than human animals, wrapped up in religious or cultural traditions, the more likely it will be enjoyed rather than condemned. Johnson (1991) drew attention to this in a graphic way:

> At fiesta time in many a Spanish or Latin American village, a gory spectacle is enacted. Live chickens or geese are tethered to the top of a pole while the local braves take turns at hurling arrows or stones, or try to seize and pull off the

birds' heads from horseback. How the little children clap their hands, and what pious tears of joy their mothers weep, to see the holy festivities [p. 103].

Importantly though, Johnson uses this illustration as a means to a further end: to unsettle his intended Western-based readership. No doubt upset, if not outraged, by the violence that is evident in this "foreign" place, Johnson then makes unsettling and uncomfortable parallels with the (British) slaughterhouse, telling his readers: "In the still hours of darkness, many a sleepy English village is the setting for a pageant no less bloody" (ibid).

Within critical geography circles an interest in the relations between human and non-human animals has gained notable momentum in the last twenty years (see Wolch and Emel 1995; Philo and Wilbert 2000; Emel et al., 2002; Gillespie and Collard 2015). Importantly, within this body of research, a number of geographers have developed important research agendas "in response to our political and ethical responsibilities to the species who share our planet" (Johnston 2008, p. 633). Here, the most critical contributions are those which have responded to Wolch and Emel's (1998) urgent call to recognize the plight of more-than-human animals. They write:

> The plight of animals worldwide has never been more serious than it is today. Each year, by the billions, animals are killed in factory farms; poisoned by toxic pollutants and waste; driven from their homes by logging, mining, agriculture, and urbanization; dissected, re-engineered, and used as spare body-parts; and kept in captivity and servitude to be discarded as soon as their utility to people has waned. The reality is mostly obscured by the progressive elimination of animals from everyday human experience, and by the creation of a thin veneer of civility surrounding human-animal relations, embodied largely by language tricks, isolation of death camps, and food preparation routines that artfully disguise the true origins of flesh-food. Despite the efforts made to minimize human awareness of animal lives and fates, however, the brutality of human domination over the animal world and the catastrophic consequences of such dominionism are everywhere evident [p. xi].

Though perhaps not an obvious connection, anarchism and geography have enjoyed a long, if uneven, common history from the 20th century to the present day. Certainly, at the time of writing, contemporary events (animated by wider economic, political, and environmental crises) have provoked and inspired new and important lines of flight to emerge between anarchist praxis and geography in recent years (see Springer et al., 2012). Writing as a self-identified anarchist geographer, the mutual benefits of such comings together between anarchists and geographers can be captured and understood in many ways. One of these is, as Ince (2010, p. 296) argues, rooted in the fact that anarchism and geography both converge on matters of everyday life: "Anarchism's tendency to foreground the everyday as crucial to the revolutionary project combined with geography's tendency to foreground the everyday and a primary terrain of human [and non-human] (inter)action provide a potent theme of synergy for the two."

Though sadly more often conspicuous by their absence in the broader anarchist canon, meaningful references to the condition of non-human animals can be found. These are certainly present within the writings of two highly influential late 19th- and early 20th-century anarchist geographers, Élisée Reclus and Peter Kropotkin. Encouragingly, aspects of their work and the recognition of inter-species suffering and oppressions are beginning to inspire new critical conversations in the contemporary field of critical animal geographies. When exploring the historical anarchist archive it is striking how appeals to common suffering and struggle that connect both humans and non-human animals have been used to epitomize and embody the very *spirit* of anarchism. As Giovanni Baldelli (1971) writes:

> Anarchism is a purity of rebellion. A pig who struggles wildly and rends the air with his cries while he is held to be slaughtered, and a baby who kicks and screams when, wanting warmth and his mother's breast, he is made to wait in the cold—these are two samples of natural rebellion. Natural rebellion always inspires either deep sympathy and identification with the rebelling creature, or a stiffening of the heart and an activation of aggressive-defensive mechanisms to silence an accusing truth. This truth is that each living being is an end in itself; that nothing gives a being the right to make another a mere instrument of his purposes [p. 17].

In many ways, a commitment to an intersectional politics, advanced by a politics of total liberation—to challenge *all* forms of unjustified hierarchy and dominion and the places in which these occur—has a natural alignment with anarchist praxis (see Dominick 1997 and Dominick's essay in this book). Of all the radical traditions, anarchists have consistently strived to recognize how:

> capitalism, imperialism, colonialism, neoliberalism, militarism, nationalism, classism, racism, ethnocentrism, Orientalism, sexism, genderism, ageism, ableism, speciesism, carnism, homophobia, transphobia, sovereignty and the state as interlocking systems of domination. The mutually reinforcing composition of these various dimensions of "archy" consequently means that to uncritically exempt one from interrogation, is to perpetuate this omnicidal conglomeration as a whole [Springer 2012, p. 1614].

In seeking ways to make visible, and disturb, everyday places of animal violence, the anarchist writings of Élisée Reclus have much to offer. Reclus was noted to be a man driven by "a concern for the self-realization of all beings in their uniqueness and particularity, and a practice of love and care for those beings" (Clark 2013a, p. 6). This led to his integrating a biocentric social and ecological ethic at the heart of his work. As a visionary, Reclus anticipated

> current debate in ecophilosophy and environmental ethics, is his effort to raise both ethical and ecological issues concerning our treatment of other species. His

ideas are important in view of the fact that he was not only a pioneer in ecological philosophy but also an early advocate of the humane treatment of animals and of ethical vegetarianism. Even today, after several decades of discussion of "animal rights" and "ecological thinking," there are few theorists who have attempted to think through the interrelationship between the two concerns [Clark 2013b p. 31].

One of the most striking arguments for respecting the lives of non-human animals can be found in the short pamphlet "On Vegetarianism" (1901). Here Reclus, draws on his own experiences and memories concerning the violence against animals in the familiar places he grew up with. Importantly, Reclus builds his argument to transgress normalized (violent) relations toward other animals not by appealing to rights-based argument, but by appealing to strong emotional and effectual registers of the reader through citing the disturbing, ugliness of violence in place. In highlighting some key passages to illustrate this, I will then attempt to re-visit this by focusing on the daily commute outlined in the beginning of the essay.

On Vegetarianism begins with a disturbing recollection, recalled through Reclus's childhood eyes, which focuses on his visit to the village butcher:

> One of the family had sent me, plate in hand, to the village butcher, with the injunction to bring back some gory fragment or other. In all innocence I set out cheerfully to do as I was bid, and entered the yard where the slaughter men were. I still remember this gloomy yard where terrifying men went to and fro with great knives, which they wiped on blood-besprinkled smocks. Hanging from a porch an enormous carcass seemed to me to occupy an extraordinary amount of space; from its white flesh a reddish liquid was trickling into the gutters. Trembling and silent I stood in this blood-stained yard incapable of going forward and too much terrified to run away. I do not know what happened to me; it has passed from my memory. I seem to have heard that I fainted, and that the kind-hearted butcher carried into his own house; I did not weigh more than one of those lambs he slaughtered every morning" [1901 p. 2].

Place is absolutely central to the terror and tenderness in this memory. For the former, the gloomy, blood-stained yard, and the (occupied space) of the carcass makes Reclus a prisoner of place: as somewhere so deep and terrifying that it is impossible to escape. Indeed, as a relevant observation, we can note though Reclus is *physically* no longer in that place, psychologically and this place still exerts a horrifyingly real and bloody grip within his (childhood) imaginary. Elsewhere, the memory also highlights how place forms a strong contrast: the bloodied slaughter-in-the-yard, is the same kind-hearted man who, in taking pity on the young Reclus, carries him away to recover in the comparative safety of that warm, peaceful place known as "his own house."

Later, Reclus draws attentions to the manner in which, removed from the slaughterhouse to the street, people are (deliberately) distracted from such thinking literally about the ugliness of animal flesh:

Butchers display dismembered carcasses and bloody pieces of meat before the eyes of the public, even along the busiest streets, next to perfumed shops decked with flowers. They even have the audacity to decorate the hanging hunks of flesh with rose garlands to make them aesthetically pleasing [1901 p. 158].

With these powerful thoughts in mind, the next section re-visits the opening discussion concerning my daily commute. Here, unlike the imagined observer, I want to emphasize how a seemingly unremarkable engagement through the urban places of my home town, actively captures and presents a range of complex, and contradictory encounters that concern humans and more-than human animals: from care and compassion on the one hand, to violence, abuse, neglect and death on the other.

Re-Visiting the Urban Commute in Reclus's Footsteps: Disturbing Geographies of Place

Two minutes after leaving my front door, till the railway station itself, I walk past the windows of shops. Some of these windows contain living more-than-human animals in small cages that would make "ideal pets" (goldfish, hamsters, guinea pigs, gerbils); another shop window advertises a range of weapons (with which to fish, hunt, shoot, deceive, catch and kill "wild" animals and birds); elsewhere I pass a veterinary surgery (there to heal and help [all] animals. However, again, the complex—indeed ambivalent—reality of these places challenges such overtly positive interpretations. Think, for example, of how veterinary drugs are tested on other animals; or how vets training routinely involves practicing vivisecting on the species that they will be expected to heal). At frequent intervals I walk in front of the windows of fast-food restaurants (selling roasted fragments of animal bodies to "eat in or takeaway"), or local businesses advertising a range of fried fish (and chips) to buy. Two local butchers, both claiming to stock the finest quality "meat" (animal corpses) in the area. While never the same, I would be bold to say that a similar urban story composed by reference to the complex presence(s) and absence(s) of other-than-human animals would be repeated, more often than not in most other towns and cities throughout western society.

What do these observations have to contribute to our understanding of the complex ways in which we (ab)use more than human animals in society? In its best light it creates an impression of both respect and care: providing more than human animals with medical facilities for example, and food and shelter for companion animals (pets). At its worst the streets and shop windows bear silent witness to cruelty that is as immense as it is incomprehensible. There are far more numerous examples of shops which reflect the reality that we kill and exploit (many) more animals for trivial purposes: to eat their body parts or for so-called "sport" and recreation pursuits (to hunt).

Raising consciousness about the ways in which urban places display and hold up non-human animals (literally in the shop window) is so important, because these places form such powerful sites of education about the role of more than human animals, sites which are particularly influential upon the minds of children. We only have to recall how (most) children delight in seeing (and perhaps "interacting"—touching the glass, tapping on the wires of the cage) with the animals and fish imprisoned within the pet shop. Cajoled by their parents to move on, they may then wait outside the butchers as their parents seek to purchase a selection of fleshy, dead lumps of "farmed" animals. These encounters presented—and vigorously enforced—as "natural" and "normal" and "healthy" inter-species relations, powerfully and openly legitimized by an urban space which provokes neither ethical questions, nor questions of social justice. For the first eighteen years of my life I internalized all of these messages, never thinking to question or challenge them. Yet in the subsequent eighteen years, being increasingly influenced by anarchist praxis and a Critical Animal Studies approach, the urban windows of my home town slowly revealed their dark reality. They are silent witnesses to the ongoing story of human domination, unrestrained exploitation and gratuitous violence characteristic of a speciesist society (see Weitzenfeld and Joy 2014) which guides us toward love and compassion for some animals, indifference toward the fate of many others, and indeed (beyond the shop windows) encourages abuse and hostility toward the presence of other urban animal dwellers (for example, rats, mice and pigeons, and urban foxes as "vermin"). Needless to say, over time my appreciation of these places—which collectively form the "place" of my home town—have changed markedly. My emotions are one of repulsion, hostility, resentment, anger, sadness, exclusion, and alienation. At times, surrounded by these windows it feels best, perhaps, not to think too much. Yet such dis-engagement is in many ways self-defeating. Without challenge and confrontation this normalized violence-in-place will forever remain undisturbed and untroubled. In this direct—immersed—silence of my daily commute, the conscious appraisal of the violence that is embedded all around me speaks of the silence of the omnipresent animal referent, is an accusing one: "You, who see us but no longer see, who hear us but no longer hear, how can you carry on as you do, so wilfully blind, wilfully deaf, wilfully silent."

Unfortunately, the violence in place is far from unique. Indeed, it relates to many places that we all encounter: the seemingly mundane, ordinary, everyday, routine, familiar. These are places which capture and reflect highly speciesist geographies: in both structure and form they exist as testament to the geographies of violence and death that are visited upon many non-human animals in contemporary society. How to respond?

Disturbing Violence in Everyday Places: The Importance of Non-Violent Activism on the Street

As mentioned in the opening to this chapter, the focus on disturbing violence pays particular attention to (a small number) of wonderful everyday forms of activism that focus on "the street" level. Certainly, the visibility and centrality of street-based activism has long been seen as an important site for direct action, both symbolically and strategically for (animal) liberation movements (see White and Cudworth 2014). This type of activism, is fundamentally concerned with education, raising conscious in a way that encourages (rather than forces) individuals—and groups—to *see the same things differently*. Anarchists and critical animal scholars alike have long emphasized the importance of education in maintaining, or disturbing, broader social norms and the importance of changing hearts and minds at the individual and societal level to make for truly progressive and lasting change (see Socha and Mitchell 2014). Thus, while street-based activism and protest can assume many forms, and take on different shades of legality, thinking carefully about how violent spaces can be meaningfully and effectively disturbed and transformed is important (see Rowlands, 2002). In this context I would identify strongly with Springer's (2012, p. 1606) conviction that "anarchism should embrace an ethic of non-violence precisely because violence is recognized as both an act and process of domination." Anarchist praxis, wherever possible, must be prepared to demonstrate an admirable commitment toward consistency between the means and ends. The Italian anarchist theorist Giovanni Baldelli (1972, pp. 19–20) eloquently points out the logics of this argument:

> The tree is known by its fruit but the so-called ends of political organizations and movements seem never to manage to ripen. Let the tree be judged then, by what it feeds upon, the so-called means. To say that the end justifies the means is to acknowledge that the means, judged separately, are unjust. If they are unjust, it is because there are concepts of justice prior to, and independent of, the ends to be realized. What will not be permissible tomorrow is permitted today in order that it is not permissible tomorrow. This is to declare today's humanity in some way inferior to tomorrow's, and to burden the latter with a debt of gratitude unasked for and more likely to be cursed than blessed.

In the context of activism and non-human animals, Rowlands (2002) suggests that "acts of rescue" are distinguished from "attempts to change society." While recognizing this to be an overly simplistic duality, this section is very much concerned with animal activism in the context of attempting to change society. For acts of rescue, many key strategies of resistance to confront and transgress places of animal abuse have justifiably and necessarily included acts that many people instinctively consider violent. These would include breaking and entering (into factory farms or vivisection laboratories), and destroying private property as a form of economic sabotage (see Mann 2007). However, in their attempts to change society, indisputably non-violent forms of direct action continue to inform the vast majority of tactics foregrounded by animal activists. These include, but are not limited to, leafleting, fundraising, demonstrations and marches, undercover surveillance, candle-lit vigils (a powerful form of night-based street activism), and other covert forms of animal rescue. Amidst this diversity of non-violent tactics, there are important common aims to be found. Principal among these is the way in which they are intentionally employed to draw attention to violence through education, and hoping to make visible the violence and suffering of non-human animals that most people choose to overlook and ignore. Herzog (1993, p. 112) for example, when writing about the psychology of animal rights activists, noted that many activists are driven by the common assumption that "the major cause of the abuse of animals was public ignorance rather than indifference. In this context, it is timely to re-emphasize the importance of the often taken-for-granted role of two popular forms of activism: campaign stalls and the act of leafleting."

Campaign Stalls and Leafleting

Whether they are strategically positioned (for example, targeting particular shops that more obviously benefit from the violence and oppression of other animals: butchers shops, sea-food shops, fur-selling shops) or aim to occupy space on the street more generally, information stalls and leafleting perform very powerful acts that serve to disrupt (both mentally and physically) the normal—unconscious—flows of urban space. Obviously they invite active conversation and dialogue between people, or some form of contact by process of giving/receiving printed materials. A local activist group, Sheffield Animal Friends (SAF), have consistently acknowledged the importance of these forms of direct, human contact and interaction, through which they can meaningfully draw attention to the cruelty of fur, vivisection, meat, animal entertainment industries. Importantly, they have successfully combined a general message for respect and non-violence against all animals, through focusing on particular businesses and shops who have vested interests in selling, or supporting, systems of exploitation and animal abuse (including banks and charities that directly fund vivisection). Moreover the stall could also be used to appeal to other senses of information—of taste, of smell, of sight, by cooking and freely distributing vegan food. Again this was seen as incredibly successful in constructively addressing and overcoming many deep seated prejudices about the type of food (and people) involved when eschewing animal based products.

Even if passers-by do not actively take a leaflet, or approach a demonstration stall, they are forced to engage with its presence. Such a deliberate act of avoidance interrupts regular flow and momentum. Physically they have to adjust their steps to move beyond the stall and the activists. Mentally, they have to avoid seeing the information that the stall is conveying. But, at some cognitive level they will have had to have seen that this is an animal rights stall: they cannot un-see what they have seen.

As a testament to the power of street-based activism, regrettably, it should also be recognized that non-violent forms of activism act often generate violent responses in others. This can be seen in the physical and psychologically abuse from both members of the public or (and speaking volumes about the erosion of personal rights, and freedom of expression) the police. *Red Pepper* (Bowman, 2009) magazine, for example reported on the illegal removal of information stalls from ten different political organizations (including animal rights groups) that were set up in Church Street, Liverpool:

> Merseyside Police arrived rapidly and asked them to move on, later claiming to be acting upon retailers' complaints about "obstruction of the highway" [a difficult task to accomplish with a few pasting tables, given the street's breadth]. Assured of the legality of their actions, the campaigners refused.
> Without explaining what powers they were acting under, police officers began seizing campaign literature and tables. They also demanded participants' names and addresses. Five people who complied with this demand were later issued with court summons. Those who refused to give their details were threatened with immediate arrest. Two quickly found themselves joining the tables and literature in the back of a police van, arrested for "willful obstruction of the highway" and public order offences.

As a scholar-activist, I've witnessed individuals hurl abuse, insults and threats at campaigners. In conversation with other animal rights activists, and through personal experience, I'm aware of many instances where—with alarming regularity—animal activists have been threatened, and subjected to actual bodily violence, with stalls upturned and destroyed. How ironic given the fact this activism—rooted in an ethics of care, education, compassion and love—can, through disturbing violence in place, be themselves the cause of further acts of violence and intimidation. At the same time, this speaks volumes of the omnipresent threat that disturbing place—by revealing new unsettling truths—has for those who are interested in maintaining a (speciesist) status quo, and the lengths they will go to preserve it.

This violence against humans who are seeking to challenge the violence meted out to other animals also focuses on the need for activists to critically reflect on the intersectional natures of violence. As Fitzgerald and Pellow (2014, p. 31) argue: "Intersectionality reminds us that we cannot understand one form of oppression without understanding others and that various forms of inequality interrelate and work together to produce advantages and disadvantages for individuals and groups." Commonalities between interlocking forms of oppression, violence toward other animals and humans have been made elsewhere (for example, Kemmerer 2011 and Glasser and Roy 2014), and not least in Reclus's work. Here, for example, he draws parallels between the slaughtering of animals and the murder of people:

> But is there not some direct relation of cause and effect between the food of these executioners, who call themselves "agents of civilisation," and their ferocious deeds? They, too, are in the habit of praising the bleeding flesh as a generator of health, strength, and intelligence. They, too, enter without repugnance the slaughter house, where the pavement is red and slippery, and where one breathes the sickly sweet odour of blood. Is there then so much difference between the dead body of a bullock and that of a man? The dissevered limbs, the entrails mingling one with the other, are very much alike: the slaughter of the first makes easy the murder of the second, especially when a leader's order rings out, or from afar comes the word of the crowned master, "Be pitiless" [1901, p. 159].

Recognizing the interconnected and overlapping nature of oppression between humans and non-humans, and promoting this activism demands a more nuanced and critical approach (one that is sensitive to class, race, gender, sexuality, ethnicity, etc.). Campaigns must be constantly critical and reflective on their structure and approach. At the very least, this means avoiding fighting on behalf of one form of oppression, while advocating strategies that play upon and reinforce another (for example, the sexist advertising used by in the campaigns by the People for Ethical Treatment of Animals [see Pennington 2013]). Similarly, internal structures in terms of organization and representation must be constantly critiqued and open to criticism should they privilege certain individuals and groups, or conversely discriminate, suppress, censor and marginalize "other" particular sub-groups within the total liberation movement.

Some Final Thoughts

The chapter has sought to impress upon the reader the importance of taking seriously place when understanding how violence toward non-human animals is normalized, and made invisible in society. Importantly, this chapter has not focused attention on those marginal or "exceptional" places of violence, such as the slaughterhouse, but on those deceptively "civilized" public places that we regularly encounter, but rarely interrogate. Recognizing place as being "not just a thing in the world but a way of understanding the world" (Cresswell 2004, p. 11) becomes important because it allows us all to be potential agents of change: nothing about space or place is inevitable, everything is possible. What would an urban place look like which emphasized liberty, freedom, ethics, justice, love toward all (sentient) beings: human and non-human? In *On Vegetarianism* Reclus articulates (his/our) vision:

> We look forward to the day when we will no longer have to rush quickly past hideous sites of killing to see as little as possible of the rivulets of blood, the rows of cadavers hanging from sharp hooks, and the blood-stained workers armed with gruesome knives. We hope to live one day in a city in which we no longer risk seeing butcher shops full of carcasses next to silk and jewellery stores, or across from a pharmacy, a stand with fragrant fruit, or a fine bookstore full of engravings, statuettes and works of art. We want to be surrounded by an environment that pleases the eye and is an expression of beauty [1901, p. 601].

Strategies focused on total liberation, which are sensitive to the tangled and interconnected nature of oppression and violence between human and more than human animals, should also pay great attention to the ways in which this involves liberating "the spatial" landscapes, by disturbing and displacing the normalized nature of violence toward non-human animals. Place is *never neutral* or simply *in-the-background*. As Best (p. 198) argued,

> the fight for animal liberation demands radical transformations in the habits, practices, values, and mindset of all human beings as it also entails a fundamental restructuring of social institutions and economic systems and economic systems predicated on exploitative practices [2008].

To be successful, a radical praxis will duly inspire, indeed demand, transformative changes that impact upon everyday *spaces* that humans engage, and give meaning to. In this context, I hope that the principal themes, arguments and conclusions made here, and which have all drawn inspiration from anarchist praxis are of relevance and merit. At the very least I hope that they will in turn inspire greater reflections concerning (a) the complex natures of place—of meaning and experience—that the reader has a relationship with, and (b) suggest ways in which the they (and others) can engage in a meaningful way to co-create places that embody ethics, justice and non-violence towards all animals, human and non-human. The brave new world that we strive for through prefigurative praxis and critical education on the streets and elsewhere, will be embedded in the spaces and places that will emerge and prosper. These will reflect and represent positive, life-affirming relationships with all animals: one that speaks openly of love, freedom, hope, peace, care, justice and—in the *Reclusian* sense—beauty.

Acknowledgments

I would like to thank Erika Cudworth and Michael White for their ever helpful, insightful and supportive comments which have helped greatly sharpen my thoughts on the structure and content of this essay.

References

Adams, C.J. (1990). *The sexual politics of meat: a feminist-vegetarian critical theory*. New York: Continuum.
Baldelli, G. (1971). *Social anarchism*. Harmondsworth: Penguin.
Best, S. (2008). "Rethinking revolution." In R. Amster, A. DeLeon, L.A. Fernandez, A.J., Nocella II, and D. Shannon, eds., *Contemporary anarchist studies: an introductory anthology of anarchy in the academy*. London: Routledge.
Best, S. (2014). "Total liberation: revolution for the 21st Century." Retrieved from http://drstevebest.wordpress.com/category/total-liberation-2/.
Bowman, A. (2009). "Taking back the streets." *Red Pepper*. Retrieved from http://www.redpepper.org.uk/Taking-back-the-streets/.
Colling, S., Parson, S., and Arrigoni, A. (2014). "Until all are free: total liberation through revolutionary decolonization, groundless solidarity, and a relationship framework." In A.J. Nocella II, J. Sorenson, K. Socha, A. Matsuika, eds., *Critical Animal Studies Reader: An Introduction to an Intersectional Social Justice Approach to Animal Liberation*. New York: Peter Lang.
Clark, J.P. (2013a). "The Earth Story, the human story." In J.P. Clark and C. Martin, eds., *Anarchy, geography, modernity: The radical social thought of Elisée Reclus*. Lanham, MD: Lexington.
Clark, J.P. (2013b). "The Dialectic of Nature and Culture." In J.P Clark and C. Martin, eds., *Anarchy, geography, modernity: The radical social thought of Elisée Reclus*. Lanham, MD: Lexington.
Creswell, T. (2004). *Place: A Short Introduction*. Oxford: Wiley-Blackwell.
Cudworth, E. (2015). "Intersectionality, Species and Social Domination." In A.J. Nocella II, R.J. White and E. Cudworth, eds, *"Anarchism and Animal Liberation: Essays on Complementary Elements of Total Liberation*. Jefferson, NC: McFarland.
Dominick, B.A. (1997). *Animal liberation and social revolution: A vegan perspective on anarchism or an anarchist perspective on veganism*. Chicago: Firestarter Press. (pp. 1–18). Retrieved from http://zinelibrary.info/files/animalandrevolution.pdf.
Dominick, B.A. (2015). "Anarcho-veganism revisited." In A.J. Nocella II, R.J. White and E. Cudworth, eds., *"Anarchism and animal liberation: Critical Animal Studies, intersectionality and total liberation*.
Eisnitz, G. A (2006). *Slaughterhouse: The Shocking Story of Greed, Neglect, and Inhumane Treatment Inside the U.S. Meat Industry*. New York: Prometheus.
Emel, J., Wilbert, C., and Wolch, J. (2002). "Animal geographies." *Society and Animals* 10(4), 407–12.
Fitzgerald, A.J., and Pellow, D. (2014). "Ecological Defense for Animal Liberation: A holistic understanding of the world." In A.J. Nocella, J. Sorenson, K. Socha, and A. Matsuika, eds., *Critical Animal Studies Reader: An Introduction to an Intersectional Social Justice Approach to Animal Liberation*. New York: Peter Lang.
Gieryn T.F. (2000). "A space for place in sociology." *Annual Review of Sociology* 26: 463–496.
Gillespie, K., and Collard, R-C. (eds.) (2015). *Critical Animal Geographies: politics, intersections, and hierarchies in a multispecies world*. New York: Routledge.
Glasser, C.L., and Roy, J.A. (2014). "The ivory trap: bridging the gap between activism and the academy." In A.J. Nocella II, J. Sorenson, K. Socha, and A. Matsuika, eds., *Critical Animal Studies Reader: An Introduction to an Intersectional Social Justice Approach to Animal Liberation*. New York: Peter Lang.

Grezo, C. (2012). "Animal abuse leads to human abuse." *New Internationalist* blog. Retrieved from: http://newint.org/blog/2012/11/29/animal-abuse-leads-to-human-abuse/.
Herzog, H.A. (1993). "'The movement is my life': the psychology of animal rights activism." *Journal of Social Issues* 49 (1): 103–119.
hooks, b. (1984). *Feminist theory from margin to center*. Boston: South End Press.
Johnson, A. (1991). *Factory farming*. Oxford: Basil Blackwell.
Johnston, C. (2008). "Beyond the clearing: toward a dwelt animal geography." *Progress in Human Geography* 32 (5): 633–649.
Ince, A. (2010). "Whither anarchist geography." In N. J. Jun and S. Wahl, eds., *New Perspectives on Anarchism*. Lanham, MD: Lexington.
Kemmerer, L., ed. (2011). *Sister Species: women, animals, and social justice*. Urbana: University of Illinois Press.
Kropotkin, P. (1978 [1885]). "What geography ought to be." *Antipode* 10: 6–15.
Lee, R. (2014). Preface. *Critical Animal Studies reader: An introduction to an intersectional social justice approach to animal liberation*. New York: Peter Lang.
Mann, K. (2007). *From dusk 'till dawn: an insider's view of the growth of the animal liberation movement*. London: Puppy Pincher Press.
Pedersen, H. & Stănescu, V. (2011). "Series editor's introduction: What is 'critical' about animal studies? From the animal 'question' to the animal 'condition.'" In K. Socha, ed., *Women, destruction, and the avant-garde: a paradigm for animal liberation*. Amsterdam: Rodopi Press.
Pennington, L. (2013). "Has PETA Gone Too Far? Sexism, Pornography and Advertising." *Huffington Post*. Retrieved from http://www.huffingtonpost.co.uk/louise-pennington/peta-has-it-gone-too-far-sex_b_2425174.html
Philo, C., and Wilbert, C. (2000). "Animal spaces, beastly places: an introduction." In Philo, C., and Wilbert, C., eds., *Animal spaces, beastly place*. London: Routledge, 1–34.
Poe, E.A. (1902). "The purloined letter." In J. A. Harrison, ed., *The complete works of Edgar Allan Poe*, Vol. VI. New York: Thomas Y. Crowell. Retrieved from http://www.eapoe.org/works/harrison/jah06t03.htm.
Potter, W. (2014a). "The FBI Considers These Animal Rights Activists Terrorists." Retrieved from http://www.greenisthenewred.com/blog/huffpost-live-fur-farm-terrorism-case/7942/#more-7942.
Potter, W. (2014b). "2 Animal Activists Indicted as Terrorists for Freeing Mink." Retrieved from http://www.greenisthenewred.com/blog/aeta-olliff-lang/7900/.
Reclus, E. (1901 [2013]). "On Vegetarianism." In J.P. Clark and C. Martin, eds., *Anarchy, geography, modernity: The radical social thought of Elisée Reclus*. Oxford: Lexington pp 156–162.
Rowlands, M. (2002). *Animal Like Us*. Verso: London.
Socha, K., and Mitchell, L. (2014). "Critical animal studies as an interdisciplinary field: a holistic approach to confronting oppression." In A.J. Nocella II, J. Sorenson, K. Socham, and A. Matsuika, eds., *Critical animal studies reader: an introduction to an intersectional social justice approach to animal liberation*. New York: Peter Lang.
Springer, S. (2012). "Anarchism! What geography still ought to be." *Antipode* 44: 1605–1624.
Springer, S. (2014). "War and pieces." *Space and Polity* 18(1): 85–96.
Springer, S., Ince, A., Pickerill, J., Brown, G., and Barker, A. J. (2012). "Reanimating anarchist geographies: a new burst of colour." *Antipode* 44: 1591–1604.

Ward, K. (2007). "Thinking geographically about work, employment and society." *Work, Employment and Society* 21(2): 265–276.

Weitzenfeld, A., and Joy, M. (2014). "An overview of anthropocentrism, humanism, and speciesism in Critical Animal Studies." In A.J. Nocella II, J. Sorenson, K. Socha., and A. Matsuika, eds., *Critical animal studies reader: An introduction to an intersectional social justice approach to animal liberation.* New York: Peter Langp.

White, R.J., and Cudworth, E. (2014). "Challenging Systems of Domination from Below." In A.J. Nocella II, J. Sorenson, K. Socha., and A. Matsuika, eds., *Critical animal studies reader: an introduction to an intersectional social justice approach to animal liberation.* New York: Peter Lang.

Wolch, J., and Emel, J. (1995). "Bringing the animals back in." *Environment and Planning D: Society and Space* 13(6): 632–6.

About the Contributors

Nekeisha Alayna **Alexis** is a writer and speaker with wide-ranging interests related to human and other animal liberation and intersecting oppressions. She is the intercultural competence and undoing racism coordinator at Anabaptist Mennonite Biblical Seminary.

Will **Boisseau** is a Ph.D. student at Loughborough University. His research focuses on the place of animal advocacy within the British left, particularly within anarchism and parliamentary socialism. Through his research he addresses a wide range of questions including the marginalization of animal rights in mainstream labor politics and the class and gender issues which influence these relationships.

Erika **Cudworth** is a reader in international politics and sociology at the University of East London and is co-chair of the Feminist Research Group. She is the author of *Environment and Society* (Routledge, 2003), *Developing Ecofeminist Theory* (Palgrave, 2005), *The Modern State* (with Tim Hall and John McGovern, Edinburgh University Press, 2007), *Posthuman International Relations* (with Steve Hobden, Zed, 2011) and *Social Lives with Other Animals* (Palgrave, 2011).

Brian **Dominick** is a radical social theorist interested in holistic solutions to systemic problems. He primarily writes economic vision, social change strategy, and news analysis. He was co-founder of the nonprofit hard news outlet NewStandard News and has been involved in many aspects of media production and journalism for more than 20 years.

Jim **Donaghey** is pursuing a Ph.D. on the relationships between anarchism and punk in contemporary international contexts at Loughborough University. He has been active in the Irish, UK, and European punk and anarchist scenes for more than a decade and was exposed to animal liberation and veganism through these networks.

Lara **Drew** is a Ph.D. candidate at the University of Canberra. Her research examines the animal liberation movement and seeks to show through narrative stories how activists learn as they engage in activism. Her other research and writing activities include radical education, feminism and the body, and anarchist and anti-capitalist positions.

Aragorn **Eloff** is an anarchist, animal liberationist and radical environmentalist. He is part of the bolo'bolo collective, a Cape Town–based anarchist group that runs the bolo'bolo infoshop and vegan coffee house (www.bolobolo.co.za). An independent researcher, his interests lie in the application of poststructuralist, neo-materialist and anarchist ethical and political philosophy as it relates to oppressive social and ecological practices of hierarchy, exploitation and domination.

John **Lupinacci** is an assistant professor at Washington State University. He teaches in the Cultural Studies and Social Thought in Education program using an approach that advocates for the development of activist-scholar educators. His experiences teaching as a high school teacher, an outdoor environmental educator, and a community activist contribute to examining the relationships between schools and the cultural roots of social suffering and environmental degradation.

Anthony J. **Nocella** II, professor, author and community organizer, is a senior fellow of the Dispute Resolution Institute at the Hamline School of Law, editor of the *Peace Studies Journal*, and co-founder and executive director of the Institute for Critical Animal Studies and Save the Kids. He has published more than 55 scholarly articles and chapters and twenty books including *Contemporary Anarchist Studies: An Introductory Anthology of Anarchy in the Academy* (Routledge, 2009). He lives in Brooklyn.

Sean **Parson** is an assistant professor in the departments of Politics and International Affairs and Sustainable Communities at Northern Arizona University. He is academically interested in environmental activism, Critical Animal Studies, and exploring our culture's obsession with superheroes. He has been involved in Food Not Bombs, climate justice activism, and the Northwest forest defense movement.

Mara J. **Pfeffer** is an instructor in the First Year Seminar Program at Northern Arizona University where she teaches courses on animal liberation, holistic justice and youth empowerment. Her research topics include ecofeminist and queer activisms; art as resistance; the intersections of earth, human and nonhuman animal liberation; and food justice, specifically decorporatizing campus foods and decolonizing veganism.

Kim **Socha** is the author of *Women, Destruction, and the Avant-Garde* (Rodopi, 2012) and *Animal Liberation and Atheism* (Freethought House, 2014). She is also a contributing editor to *Confronting Animal Exploitation* (McFarland, 2013) and *Defining Critical Animal Studies* (Peter Lang, 2014). She works as an English professor and social justice activist.

Richard J. **White** is a senior lecturer in economic geography at Sheffield Hallam University, specializing in anarchist geographies. His two longstanding research interests focus on developing a post-capitalist economic imaginary and problematizing human-animal relationships in society. He has published his research in key international interdisciplinary journals and in scholarly texts.

Drew Robert **Winter** is a scholar, writer and activist focused on Critical Animal Studies and intersectional approaches to social justice. Named one of the top 20 animal activists under 30 by *VegNews* magazine, he mentored more than 100 student animal rights groups and was director of publications at the Institute for Critical Animal Studies. He is a Ph.D. student in the Department of Anthropology at Rice University.

Index

ableism 2, 7, 11, 13, 40, 41, 44, 49, 52, 168, 181, 186, 218
aboriginal 56
Africa 101, 127
ageism 2, 7, 11, 44, 168, 218
Alessio, John 4
Alexis, Nekeisha Alayna 5, 15, 16, 51, 100, 108
Alston, Ashanti 1
Animal Enterprise Terrorism Act (AETA) 50
animal industrial complex 153
Animal Liberation Front (ALF) 13, 14, 17, 24, 41, 45, 74, 76, 84, 141, 144, 156, 179
Asia 101
Australia 166, 170, 172, 175

Bakunin, Mikhail 41, 44, 183, 184
Berkman, Alexander 42
Best, Steve 9, 13, 45, 46, 47, 135, 136, 141, 143, 144, 146, 153, 165, 174, 186, 198, 213, 216, 226
Black Liberation Army 1
Black Panther Party 1
Boisseau, Will 4, 14, 16, 71, 141
Bookchin, Murray 15, 94, 95, 96, 97, 102, 103, 104, 150, 183

Canada 56, 110, 130
Chomsky, Noam 40, 42, 183
Churchill, Ward 149
class 2, 10, 11, 15, 16, 17, 34, 42, 54, 63, 76, 86, 87, 93, 96, 99, 102, 103, 112, 132, 136, 142, 143, 145, 147, 152, 153, 155, 156, 181, 184, 186, 187, 198, 199, 204, 209, 218, 225
coalition 3, 10, 13, 65, 69
Colling, Sarat 13, 48, 51, 135, 144, 156, 186, 213, 215
colonialism 7, 10, 15, 16, 93, 99, 100, 101, 132, 133, 136, 137, 164, 218

critical education 56, 180, 226
critical pedagogy 169, 180
critical theory 165
Cudworth, Erika 7, 15, 93, 98, 100, 101, 169, 170, 175, 176, 213, 215

Davis, Angela 49, 52, 133
De Cleyre, Voltairine 175
diet-industrial complex 166
direct action 8, 14, 17, 35, 36, 45, 61, 74, 77, 143, 144, 145, 146, 148, 149, 150, 152, 155, 173, 174, 175, 179, 180, 181, 183, 184, 185, 186, 189, 198, 199, 215, 222, 223
direct democracy 7, 42, 44, 47, 56
disability 11, 43, 48, 49, 53, 179
domination 2, 7, 8, 9, 10, 11, 12, 13, 14, 15, 18, 24, 25, 33, 40, 42, 44, 46, 48, 51, 54, 55, 56, 59, 85, 87, 93, 94, 96, 97, 98, 99, 101, 102, 103, 104, 105, 109, 116, 120, 136, 145, 148, 149, 165, 169, 170, 175, 176, 183, 186, 187, 190, 191, 195, 196, 199, 200, 204, 205, 209, 215, 217, 218, 221, 222
Dominick, Brian 5, 13, 23, 25, 143, 166, 198, 199
Donaghey, Jim 4, 14, 71
Drew, Lara 5, 17, 163, 173, 174

Earth Liberation 13, 17, 136, 143, 179, 199
ecofeminism 98
ecopedagogy 179, 180, 190
ecosystem 2, 3, 16, 168
Eloff, Aragorn 18, 194, 206, 208
England 127, 212

Federal Bureau of Investigation (FBI) 45, 47, 55
feminism 11, 73, 93, 94, 98
Food Not Bombs 14, 59, 60, 61, 62, 63, 64, 65, 66, 67, 68, 69, 73, 75, 85, 145, 199
Freire, Paulo 164, 170, 176, 180

233

gender 5, 10, 11, 15, 16, 93, 97, 98, 99, 100, 103, 109, 117, 122, 142, 143, 153, 155, 184, 187, 195, 218, 225
genocide 45, 126, 127, 188
geography 8, 18, 95, 109, 129, 143, 171, 197, 213, 214, 215, 217, 218, 220, 221
Goldman, Emma 41, 170, 171, 172, 184
green anarchism 16, 93, 126, 135

hooks, bell 10, 117, 213

Iceland 67
imperialism 7, 15, 93, 218
indigenous 2, 43, 65, 127, 131, 188
intersection 3, 5, 7, 10, 11, 12, 14, 15, 17, 18, 19, 41, 49, 51, 56, 72, 73, 86, 87, 92, 94, 96, 98, 99, 100, 101, 102, 103, 105, 112, 118, 132, 153, 155, 164, 165, 183, 195, 198, 202, 203, 206, 213, 215, 218, 224

Jensen, Derrick 135, 149, 184

Kahn, Richard 45, 47, 155, 164, 180
Kropotkin, Peter 5, 15, 41, 42, 43, 44, 94, 95, 96, 97, 102, 104, 143, 172, 183, 184, 218

Lupinacci, John 5, 6, 17, 179, 184, 189

Malcolm X 55
Marcuse, Herbert 11
Marx, Karl 5, 127
Marxism 27, 44, 198, 199, 201

Native American 45, 50, 188
Nazi 48, 67
Nocella, Anthony J., II 4, 7, 8, 9, 11, 12, 13, 14, 40, 43, 45, 46, 47, 50, 54, 72, 141, 142, 143, 144, 145, 146, 153, 154, 155, 156, 165, 167, 174, 183, 186, 190, 191
non-profit industrial complex 175

Parson, Sean 4, 16, 126, 135
patriarchy 2, 5, 11, 15, 16, 24, 39, 99, 101, 108, 109, 117, 118, 122, 132, 186, 195, 198, 199, 201
Pellow, David 1, 7, 8, 51, 224
Pfeffer, Mara J. 4, 16, 126, 132, 135
pornography 164
posthumanism 96, 104
praxis 8, 10, 14, 17, 40, 60, 72, 78, 101, 163, 169, 176, 213, 214, 215, 217, 218, 221, 222, 226
prison 1, 16, 19, 41, 43, 49, 50, 51, 52, 53, 55, 56, 61, 66, 74, 136, 142, 155, 156, 188, 219, 221
Proudhon, Pierre-Joseph 41, 43, 102, 183

Quaker 56
queer 2, 93, 179, 195, 202

racism 2, 7, 11, 13, 16, 33, 39, 40, 41, 44, 49, 50, 51, 55, 68, 99, 112, 132, 136, 151, 154, 168, 181, 184, 186, 188, 197, 198, 204, 218
repression 9, 42, 43, 45, 49, 50, 51, 52, 53, 55, 65, 66, 72, 109, 146, 148
Russia 119

sexism 2, 7, 11, 16, 33, 44, 68, 112, 132, 136, 137, 155, 181, 198, 204, 218
Sharp, Gene 46
Singer, Peter 98, 99, 116, 200
Socha, Kim 5, 7, 8, 17, 142, 163, 165, 166, 167, 222
solidarity 2, 3, 10, 12, 13, 16, 18, 60, 64, 69, 96, 132, 135, 137, 147, 153, 155, 156, 167, 180, 181, 182, 183, 185, 187, 188, 189, 190, 195
South America 47, 100, 129, 195
speciesism 2, 5, 7, 32, 33, 39, 44, 48, 68, 98, 99, 132, 146, 151, 181, 195, 197, 198, 199, 204, 216, 218
Stop Huntingdon Animal Cruelty (SHAC) 61, 74, 141, 143, 148, 149

terror 9, 14, 45, 46, 50, 108, 114, 117, 141, 152, 214, 219
Torres, Bob 32, 33, 40, 46, 101, 102, 103, 105, 143, 167, 168, 170
total liberation 1, 2, 3, 7, 8, 9, 11, 12, 13, 16, 18, 72, 122, 126, 135, 136, 183, 184, 195, 198, 199, 200, 201, 213, 214, 218, 225, 226
transformative 3, 7, 9, 12, 53, 54, 55, 56, 60, 153, 190

violence 4, 8, 16, 17, 18, 26, 39, 42, 46, 48, 53, 54, 61, 68, 82, 100, 103, 104, 108, 109, 111, 112, 113, 115, 117, 119, 120, 122, 126, 127, 134, 142, 144, 146, 147, 148, 149, 150, 152, 155, 166, 180, 183, 184, 188, 199, 212, 213, 214, 215, 216, 217, 218, 219, 220, 221, 222, 223, 224, 225, 226

White, Richard J. 7, 18, 169, 170, 175, 176, 212, 213, 215, 222
Winter, Drew Robert 14, 59
World Bank 101

Zerzan, John 127

www.ingramcontent.com/pod-product-compliance
Ingram Content Group UK Ltd.
Pitfield, Milton Keynes, MK11 3LW, UK
UKHW041942140426
5217IPUK00014B/622